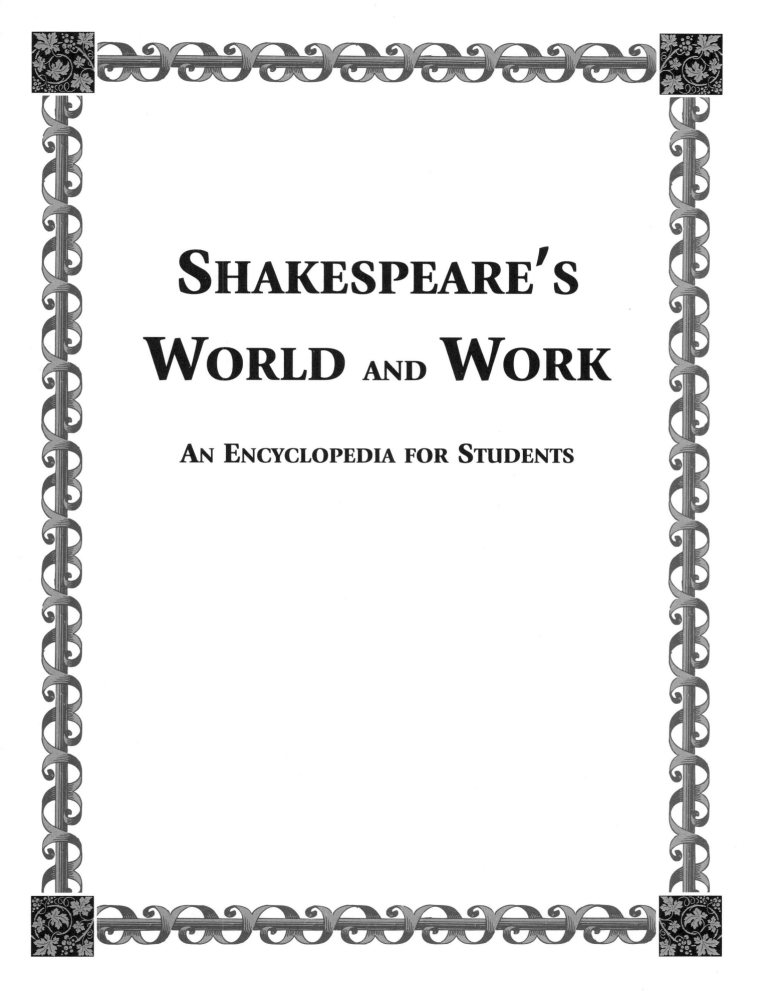

SHAKESPEARE'S WORLD AND WORK

AN ENCYCLOPEDIA FOR STUDENTS

JOHN F. ANDREWS
The Shakespeare Guild
Editor in Chief

WILLIAM M. HILL
The Peddie School
Associate Editor

SHAKESPEARE'S
WORLD AND WORK

AN ENCYCLOPEDIA FOR STUDENTS

John F. Andrews, *Editor in Chief*

Volume 3

Charles Scribner's Sons
an imprint of the Gale Group
New York • Detroit • San Francisco • London • Boston • Woodbridge, CT

Developed for Charles Scribner's Sons by Visual Education Corporation, Princeton, N.J.

For Scribners
PUBLISHER: Karen Day
EDITOR: John Fitzpatrick
COVER DESIGN: Jennifer Wahi

For Visual Education Corporation
PROJECT DIRECTOR: Jewel G. Moulthrop
WRITERS: Guy Austrian, Jean Brainard, John Haley, Mark Mussari, Rebecca Stefoff
EDITORS: Amy Livingston, Joseph Ziegler
COPYEDITING SUPERVISOR: Helen Castro
COPY EDITORS: Marie Enders, Eleanor Hero
INDEXER: Sallie Steele
PHOTO RESEARCH: Martin A. Levick
PRODUCTION SUPERVISOR: Paula Deverell
PRODUCTION ASSISTANTS: Susan Buschhorn, Brian Suskin
INTERIOR DESIGN: Maxson Crandall
ELECTRONIC PREPARATION: Fiona Torphy, Christine Osborne
ELECTRONIC PRODUCTION: Rob Ehlers, Lisa Evans-Skopas, Holly Morgan

Library of Congress Cataloging-in-Publication Data

Shakespeare's world and work : an encyclopedia for students / John F. Andrews.
    p. cm.
    Includes bibliographical references and index.
    ISBN 0-684-80629-0 (set) — ISBN 0-684-80626-6 (v.1) —
ISBN 0-684-80627-4 (v.2) — ISBN 0-684-80628-2 (v. 3)
    1. Shakespeare, William, 1564–1616—Encyclopedias. 2. Dramatists, English—
Early modern, 1500–1700—Biography—Encyclopedias. I. Andrews, John F.
(John Frank), 1942–

PR2892 .S56 2001
822.3'3—dc21
[B]

00-068743

SHAKESPEAREAN CHRONOLOGY

Note: The dating of Shakespeare's plays is often uncertain. For simplicity, we have listed the *earliest* dates accepted by *The Riverside Shakespeare,* 2nd ed., 1997.

YEAR	EVENTS
1532	King Henry VIII breaks with the Catholic Church to marry Anne Boleyn.
1533	The future Queen Elizabeth I is born to King Henry VIII and Anne Boleyn.
1534	King Henry VIII becomes head of the Anglican Church.
1536	Anne Boleyn is executed.
1547	King Henry VIII dies. Edward VI is crowned.
1553	King Edward VI dies. Mary I assumes the throne and begins to reestablish Catholicism.
1555	Roman Catholicism is officially reestablished. Persecution of Protestants begins.
1558	Queen Mary I dies. Elizabeth I is crowned.
1559	Elizabethan Settlement reforms the Anglican Church. Strict sumptuary laws prohibit Elizabethans from wearing clothing above their station.
1564	William Shakespeare is born to John and Mary Shakespeare. Christopher Marlowe is born.
1566	John Shakespeare is appointed an alderman of Stratford-upon-Avon. King James VI of Scotland is born. Edward Alleyn is born.
1567	Richard Burbage is born. Thomas Nash is born.
1568	John Shakespeare is elected mayor of Stratford-upon-Avon. Mary, Queen of Scots, takes refuge in England.
1570	Pope Pius V excommunicates Queen Elizabeth I.
1571	John Shakespeare is elected chief alderman.
1572	Ben Jonson is born.
1573	Henry Wriothesley, 3rd earl of Southampton, is born.
1576	The Theater playhouse opens.
1577	The Curtain opens. Raphael Holinshed's *Chronicles* is published.
1579	John Fletcher is born.
1580	Sir Francis Drake completes circumnavigation of the world.
1582	William Shakespeare marries Anne Hathaway.
1583	A daughter (Susanna) is born to William Shakespeare and Anne Hathaway. The Queen's Men acting company is formed.
1585	Anne Hathaway gives birth to twins, Judith and Hamnet. First English colony is established in North America.
1586	Queen Elizabeth I outlaws printing presses outside of London, Cambridge, and Oxford. Philip Sidney dies.
1587	The Rose opens. Mary, Queen of Scots, is executed.
1588	Spanish Armada is defeated. Richard Tarlton dies.
1589	Shakespeare writes *Henry VI, Part 1.* Thomas Kyd writes *The Spanish Tragedy.* King James VI of Scotland marries Princess Anne of Denmark.

1590 Shakespeare writes *Henry VI, Part 2* and *Part 3*. Edmund Spenser's *The Faerie Queene* is published. Thomas Lodge's *Rosalynde* is published.

1591 Shakespeare writes *Richard III*. Philip Sidney's *Astrophel and Stella* is published.

1592 Shakespeare writes *The Comedy of Errors*. Robert Greene's *Groatsworth of Wit* is published. Philip Henslowe begins his *Diary*.

1593 Shakespeare's *Venus and Adonis* is published. Shakespeare writes *Titus Andronicus* and *The Taming of the Shrew*. Christopher Marlowe is killed in a tavern brawl. Theaters are closed throughout the year due to plague.

1594 Shakespeare's *The Rape of Lucrece* is published. Shakespeare writes *The Two Gentlemen of Verona, Love's Labor's Lost,* and *King John*. The Chamberlain's Men acting company is formed. Thomas Kyd dies.

1595 Shakespeare writes *Richard II, Romeo and Juliet,* and *A Midsummer Night's Dream*. William Shakespeare is named as one of the players paid for performing for Queen Elizabeth I. The Swan opens.

1596 Hamnet Shakespeare dies. John Shakespeare is granted a coat of arms. William Shakespeare writes *Henry IV, Part 1; Henry IV, Part 2;* and *The Merchant of Venice*.

1597 William Shakespeare purchases New Place in Stratford-upon-Avon. Shakespeare writes *The Merry Wives of Windsor*. Performance of *The Isle of Dogs* at the Swan theater results in the imprisonment of the playwrights and the temporary closing of all theaters. The Poor Law is passed.

1598 Shakespeare writes *Much Ado About Nothing*. War of the Theaters begins. Shakespeare acts in Ben Jonson's *Every Man in His Humour*. The Theater is dismantled.

1599 Shakespeare writes *Henry V, Julius Caesar,* and *As You Like It*. Robert Devereux, Earl of Essex, fails to quell rebellion in Ireland. The Globe opens. Edmund Spenser dies.

1600 Shakespeare writes *Hamlet*. The Fortune opens.

1601 John Shakespeare dies. Shakespeare's *The Phoenix and Turtle* is published. Shakespeare writes *Twelfth Night* and *Troilus and Cressida*. The Chamberlain's Men are hired to perform *Richard II*. Robert Devereux, Earl of Essex, is executed for revolting against Queen Elizabeth I.

1602 William Shakespeare purchases land in Old Stratford. Shakespeare writes *All's Well That Ends Well*. War of the Theaters ends.

1603 Queen Elizabeth I dies. King James VI of Scotland is crowned King James I of England. The Chamberlain's Men become the King's Men. Theaters are closed due to plague.

1604 The King's Men participate in King James I's coronation procession. King James ends war with Spain. Shakespeare writes *Measure for Measure* and *Othello*. Theaters reopen.

1605 William Shakespeare buys an interest in Stratford-upon-Avon tithes and writes *King Lear*. Gunpowder Plot is discovered. The Red Bull opens.

1606 Shakespeare writes *Macbeth, Antony and Cleopatra,* and *Pericles*. John Lyly dies.

1607 Susanna Shakespeare marries John Hall. Shakespeare writes *Coriolanus* and *Timon of Athens*. Jamestown, Virginia, is settled. Theaters are closed for three months due to plague.

1608 Mary Shakespeare dies. The King's Men lease Blackfriars.

1609 Shakespeare's *Sonnets* and *A Lover's Complaint* are published. Shakespeare writes *Cymbeline*. Theaters temporarily close due to plague.

1610 Shakespeare writes *The Tempest*. Ben Jonson writes *The Alchemist*.

1611 Shakespeare writes *The Winter's Tale*. The King James Bible is published.

1613 William Shakespeare buys Blackfriars Gatehouse and writes *Henry VIII* and *The Two Noble Kinsmen*. The Globe burns down. The Hope opens.

1616 Judith Shakespeare marries Thomas Quiney. William Shakespeare revises his will and dies.

1623 John Heminges and Henry Condell produce the First Folio. Anne Shakespeare dies. Sometime prior to this date a monument to William Shakespeare is placed in the Holy Trinity Church of Stratford-upon-Avon.

1625 King James I dies. Charles I is crowned.

1642 English Civil Wars begin. Puritans seize control of government. London theaters are closed.

1660 Ban on theaters is lifted. Women appear in plays on the English stage. Samuel Pepys begins his *Diary.*

1674 William Davenant produces a musical adaptation of *Macbeth.*

1709 Nicholas Rowe's edition of Shakespeare's works is published.

1725 Alexander Pope's edition of Shakespeare's works is published.

1729 Voltaire translates Shakespeare's works into French.

1730s Drury Lane and Covent Garden acting companies are granted theater monopolies in London.

1741 David Garrick debuts as Richard III.

1765 Samuel Johnson's edition of Shakespeare's works is published.

1769 Shakespeare Jubilee is held in Stratford-upon-Avon.

1803 First Variorum edition is published.

1807 Thomas Bowdler's *The Family Shakespeare* is published.

1823 Charles Kemble stages *King John* at Covent Garden.

1826 Ira Aldridge debuts as Othello.

1838 William Charles Macready restores the original text of *King Lear* to the stage.

1843 Monopolies on London theaters end.

1849 Astor Place Riot erupts in New York.

1883 Samuel Taylor Coleridge's *Lectures and Notes on Shakespeare and Other English Poets* is published.

1895 Elizabethan Stage Society is founded.

1899 A scene from a Shakespeare play is captured on film for the first time.

1910 Herbert Beerbohm Tree stages an elaborate *Midsummer Night's Dream.*

1912 Harley Granville-Barker produces the first authentic Shakespearean production of modern times.

1920s Barry Jackson introduces 20th-century costuming in Shakespeare's plays.

1930s Theodore Komisarjevsky introduces mixed-period costuming.

1937 First production of a Shakespeare play is made for television.

1944 Laurence Olivier produces a film version of *Henry V.*

1948 Olivier's *Hamlet* is released, the first foreign film to win the Academy Award for best picture.

1957 Performances of Shakespeare's works begin in New York City's Central Park.

1961 Royal Shakespeare Company is founded.

1965 Peter Hall directs his influential production of *Hamlet.*

1970 Peter Brook directs a film version of *King Lear.*

1985 Akira Kurosawa directs *Ran,* a film based on *King Lear.*

1989 Kenneth Branagh directs and stars in a film version of *Henry V.*

1996 Baz Luhrmann directs *Shakespeare's Romeo + Juliet.*

1999 BBC audience survey names Shakespeare as Britain's "Man of the Millennium."

CHRONOLOGY OF SHAKESPEARE'S WORKS

Note: All dates are based on *The Riverside Shakespeare,* 2nd ed., 1997.

1 Henry VI	1589–92
2 Henry VI	1590–91
3 Henry VI	1590–92
Richard III	1591–93
Venus and Adonis	1592–93
The Comedy of Errors	1592–94
Sonnets	1592–1609
Titus Andronicus	1593–94
The Rape of Lucrece	1593–94
The Taming of the Shrew	1593–94
The Two Gentlemen of Verona	1594
Love's Labor's Lost	1594
King John	1594–96
Richard II	1595
Romeo and Juliet	1595
A Midsummer Night's Dream	1595–96
Henry IV, Part 1	1596
The Merchant of Venice	1596–97
Henry IV, Part 2	1596–97
The Merry Wives of Windsor	1597
Much Ado About Nothing	1598–99
Henry V	1599
Julius Caesar	1599
As You Like It	1599–1600
Hamlet	1600–01
The Phoenix and Turtle	1601
Twelfth Night	1601–02
Troilus and Cressida	1601–02
All's Well That Ends Well	1602–03
A Lover's Complaint	1602–08
Measure for Measure	1604
Othello	1604
King Lear	1605
Macbeth	1606
Antony and Cleopatra	1606–07
Pericles	1606–08
Coriolanus	1607–08
Timon of Athens	1607–08
Cymbeline	1609–10
The Tempest	1610–11
The Winter's Tale	1611
Henry VIII	1613
The Two Noble Kinsmen	1613

PROSPERO

* **protagonist** central character in a dramatic or literary work

* **usurper** one who seizes power from a rightful ruler

* **allegory** literary device in which characters, events, and settings represent abstract qualities and in which the author intends a different meaning to be read beneath the surface

Prospero is a magician and the ruler of the island that serves as the setting for Shakespeare's *The Tempest*. Once the duke of Milan in what is now Italy, Prospero neglected his governing duties in order to study the "liberal arts." As a result he was deposed by his brother, Antonio, who was aided in his revolt by King Alonso of Naples. After being set adrift in a small boat, Prospero and his two-year-old daughter, Miranda, eventually found themselves on an island inhabited by Ariel (the sprite who serves Prospero) and Caliban (the half-human monster whom Prospero enslaves).

Prospero is unique among Shakespeare's creations. The protagonists* in other plays struggle with forces that are frequently beyond their control. Prospero, on the other hand, manipulates events by commanding the elements of nature. At the beginning of the play, for example, he conjures up a storm in order to bring a ship carrying Antonio, Alonso, and other members of Alonso's court ashore. He then uses his magic to lead the other characters about, punishing those who deposed him. In Act III he lets the hungry castaways sit down to a magical feast, which disappears as they attempt to eat. He further torments Alonso by having Ariel tell him that his son, Ferdinand, is dead.

Prospero also uses his powers to shape a reconciliation between himself and his enemies. He ensures that Ferdinand and Miranda will fall in love and bring about a new dynastic union. By the end of the play, Prospero forgives his usurpers*, renounces magic, and announces that he will return to Milan to resume his former duties as ruler.

Despite the magician's decision to pursue "virtue" rather than "vengeance" (V.i.27–28), many critics see him as an unappealing character. They point out his harsh treatment of Ferdinand, Ariel, and especially Caliban. Some have even interpreted *The Tempest* as an allegory* on colonialism and regarded Prospero as an oppressor of the island's inhabitants. Most observers agree, however, that Prospero's magic powers are used for good, citing his liberation of Ariel from a witch's spell and his attempts to civilize Caliban.

Prospero has sometimes been seen as a self-portrait of Shakespeare. Like his creator, Prospero controls the events of the play and the destinies of its characters. Because *The Tempest* is one of Shakespeare's last plays, some viewers have interpreted Prospero's speech following the betrothal MASQUE as the playwright's farewell to his career in the theater:

> Our revels now are ended. These our actors
> (As I foretold you) were all spirits, and
> Are melted into air, into thin air,
> And like the baseless fabric of this vision,
> . . . .
> Yea, all which it inherit, shall dissolve,
> And like this insubstantial pageant faded
> Leave not a rack [cloud] behind. We are such stuff
> As dreams are made on; and our little life
> Is rounded with a sleep.
>
> (IV.i.148–58)

PSYCHOLOGY

Psychology is a branch of science that seeks to explain why people think and behave as they do. Elizabethan ideas about how the mind works help account for some of the motivations behind the actions of Shakespeare's characters. But modern psychology has also provided insights into these characters' thoughts and behavior.

SHAKESPEARE AND ELIZABETHAN PSYCHOLOGY. Most Elizabethans, including Shakespeare, believed that human emotions and actions were governed by four basic fluids, or "humors": blood, phlegm, yellow bile, and black bile. If the humors were in balance, a person would behave with reason. An excess of one humor, however, would cause a person to behave irrationally. An individual with an excess of yellow bile, for example, tended to be angry and hateful, whereas one with an excess of black bile was characterized by a gloomy, or melancholy, personality.

Some of Shakespeare's characters exhibit the traits and behaviors that typify someone with an overabundance of one of the four humors. Perhaps the best example is Hamlet. The prince's personality is consistent with the Elizabethan idea of a melancholy person. He broods instead of acts and often has suicidal thoughts. SHYLOCK, the moneylender in *The Merchant of Venice*, probably has too much yellow bile. He is filled with murderous hatred, a symptom of this condition. When asked why his anger is so great, he answers simply that it is his "humor." Explanations based on humors appear in more than 150 passages in Shakespeare's plays.

SHAKESPEARE AND MODERN PSYCHOLOGY. Shakespeare's characters have also been analyzed in terms of other behavioral theories, including those of Sigmund Freud. Freudian psychology, which was developed in the early 1900s, asserts that human thought and behavior can be explained in part by childhood conflicts. According to Freud's theory, children pass through an Oedipal phase, during which they experience sexual feelings toward the parent of the opposite sex and feelings of jealousy toward the parent of the same sex. In most people these feelings are resolved and forgotten. In some, however, they remain unresolved and lead to personality and behavioral problems later in life. Some critics regard Hamlet as a textbook case of Oedipal problems. They point out that he seems preoccupied with his mother's sexual behavior and that, later in the play, he kills his stepfather.

Many critics have also noted that several of Shakespeare's male characters have contradictory feelings toward women. Although they love and desire women, they also fear and distrust them. Such contradictory feelings, some Freudian psychologists believe, stem from experiences in which young children long for the security of their mother's affection while at the same time desiring independence from her. Such contradictory feelings toward women are especially evident in Benedick, a protagonist* in *Much Ado About Nothing*. He praises women as mothers but says he distrusts them as wives: "That a woman conceiv'd me, I thank her; that she brought me up, I likewise give her most humble thanks . . . Because I will not do them the wrong to mistrust any, I will do myself the right to trust none; and the [conclusion] is . . . I will live a bachelor" (I.i.238–46).

* *protagonist* central character in a dramatic or literary work

(*See also* **Characters in Shakespeare's Plays; Feminist Interpretations; Madness; Shakespeare's Works, Changing Views.**)

PUCK

In creating the mischievous Puck, Shakespeare drew on Robin Goodfellow, a traditional figure in English folklore who enjoyed mocking human foolishness.

Puck is the mischievous fairy who is responsible for many of the hilarious mishaps that occur in *A Midsummer Night's Dream.* In Act II, OBERON, the spirit king, orders Puck to place a love potion on the eyelids of Demetrius. The magic substance is intended to cause Demetrius to fall out of love with Hermia and in love with Helena. When Puck mistakenly gives it to Lysander, who also loves Hermia, he delights in the chaos that ensues. Observing Hermia's two former admirers pledging their eternal love to Helena, Puck says "Lord, what fools these mortals be!" (III.ii.115).

In addition to causing trouble for the lovers, Puck ridicules human folly. As if to show his disdain for human beings, he places the head of an ass on the shoulders of the simpleminded weaver Nick Bottom. Puck performs the role usually played by fools and jesters in Shakespeare's other plays.

Puck uses his trickery to help humans as well as to ridicule them. When Demetrius and Lysander resolve to duel for Helena's love, Puck uses his supernatural powers to summon a dense fog. He then impersonates each man's voice to the other in order to lure the combatants in opposite directions, thereby avoiding harm to either man.

Puck is variously referred to as a fairy, a sprite, and a goblin. This variety reflects Puck's origins. In creating the playful fairy Shakespeare combined two supernatural creatures: Robin Goodfellow and Puck. According to English folklore Robin Goodfellow was a good-natured spirit who enjoyed playing tricks but also helped perform household chores for those who honored him. Puck, on the other hand, was a devilish spirit who misled travelers at night. Shakespeare hints at Puck's darker side when the fairy reminds Oberon that they must hide from the approaching dawn like "ghosts, wand'ring here and there" and other "damned spirits" (III.ii.381–82). The modern word *puckish,* meaning "whimsical," derives from this impish creature. (*See also* **Fairies; Fools, Clowns, and Jesters; Magic and Folklore.**)

QUARTOS AND FOLIOS

The terms *quarto* and *folio* are used to refer to the formats of books. To make a quarto, each sheet of paper is folded in half twice, producing a gathering of four leaves or eight pages. To make a folio, each sheet of paper is folded in half just once, forming a gathering of two leaves or four pages. Of Shakespeare's 38 plays, at least 22 were initially published as quartos. The first edition of Shakespeare's collected plays, however, was published in folio format and is known as the FIRST FOLIO.

Early scholars used the First Folio as their main source for the plays, but modern scholars rely heavily on the quartos to help reconstruct

Shakespeare's original text. Quartos have long been categorized as "good" and "bad." Good quartos are based on sources that appear to reflect Shakespeare's authentic work, such as his handwritten manuscripts, which are called foul papers. Bad quartos are unauthorized and flawed reconstructions of plays, noted for such errors as peculiar repetitions of words or phrases, the addition of material from other plays, and inaccurate speeches. For example, Hamlet's famous line "To be, or not to be, that is the question" (III.i.55) is reproduced in a bad quarto as "To be, or not to be, I there's the point." Many scholars believe that these bad quartos were memorial reconstructions, written down from the recollections of actors who had performed the plays. As evidence, those who support this theory point out that the lines of certain characters are recorded with greater accuracy than those of other characters. (*See also* **Printing and Publishing.**)

RACE AND ETHNICITY

See
color plate 6,
vol. 2.

Elizabethan England was neither a racially nor an ethnically diverse society. Compared with the rest of Europe, Britain was isolated from foreign peoples and outside influences. Its isolation was a product of both history and geography. Britain was first invaded by the Romans, under Julius Caesar, around 55 B.C. Northern European tribes, known as Saxons, had settled the island around A.D. 400. Over time other peoples, such as the Scandinavians, came to England and married into Saxon families. Then came the Normans, invaders from France who conquered the Saxons in 1066. By 1500 the vast majority of the English were descended from a mixed group of northern European ancestors.

Because England was cut off from the European mainland, few immigrants made their way to its shores. Other countries that bordered on the easily navigable Mediterranean Sea were much more accessible to merchants and invaders from the Middle East and Africa. While many residents of Spain, Portugal, and Italy encountered Arabs, JEWS, Africans, and other "exotic" peoples, an average English person might spend a lifetime without ever seeing a foreigner. Africans and American Indians occasionally appeared in LONDON, but this was unusual. A law passed in 1290 had banished all Jews from the country; the law was unevenly enforced, however, so a small Jewish community had managed to survive in London.

England's cultural isolation produced strong suspicion and distrust of other races and cultures. Portrayals of foreigners in Elizabethan literature were generally based on stereotypes. For example, the English considered all Frenchmen to be overly emotional and excitable characters who boasted exaggeratedly about their skill as lovers. Jews were typically portrayed as greedy and villainous, like the moneylender SHYLOCK in *The Merchant of Venice*. Africans tended to be cast as villains in popular literature, such as Aaron the Moor in *Titus Andronicus*. The term *Moor* referred to dark-skinned people from North Africa. Moors were doubly feared in England, because of their skin color and because many were Muslims and thus assumed to be the enemies of Christianity.

Shakespeare probably shared some of the common prejudices against foreigners and people of other races. His portrayals of characters from different ethnicities often reflect popular stereotypes. But he always goes beyond them to make his characters truly human. Complex characters such as Shylock and Othello undoubtedly provoked mixed reactions from Elizabethan audiences, responses that ranged from fear and disgust to sympathy and on occasion respect. Shakespeare's portrayals of ethnically diverse personalities may even have helped increase tolerance for cultural differences in his native land. (*See also* **Foreigners; Religion.**)

RAPE OF LUCRECE, THE

* *stanza* section of a poem; specifically, a grouping of lines into a recurring pattern determined by meter or rhyme scheme

An early poem by Shakespeare, *The Rape of Lucrece* is based on a well-known story from ancient Rome about the wife of a Roman general who is raped by the king's son. The lengthy narrative is written in a verse form called rhyme royal, which consists of seven-line stanzas*.

Lucrece (or Lucretia in Latin), the wife of Collatine (Collatinus), is widely admired among her husband's fellow officers for her beauty and virtue. Sextus Tarquinius (known as Tarquin), the son of King Lucius Tarquinius, is so taken with Lucrece's beauty that he decides he must have her. After her husband has returned to camp, he creeps into Lucrece's chamber and rapes her, despite her pleas. A lengthy section of the poem is devoted to Lucrece's laments over her fate. Eventually she sends a messenger to fetch her father and husband. They arrive, accompanied by two other officers, and she tells them what Tarquin has done. After making them swear to avenge her, Lucrece stabs herself to end her dishonor. The men then inform the Roman citizens of Tarquin's villainy, causing an uprising that forces Sextus Tarquinius and his father to leave Rome and results in the establishment of a republic in place of the monarchy.

* *patron* supporter or financial sponsor of an artist or writer

Versions of this story appeared in many sources, from the works of the Roman poet OVID to William Painter's *Palace of Pleasure* (1566). Scholars generally agree that Shakespeare chose this tragic subject to offset criticism of his first published poem, *Venus and Adonis,* a frequently comic treatment of sexual desire. In his introduction to *Venus and Adonis,* which he dedicated to his patron* the earl of Southampton, Shakespeare promised a "graver labor" to come. *The Rape of Lucrece* is generally assumed to be that promised work. Its praise for Lucrece's virtue and condemnation of Tarquin's lust make it a more serious poem than *Venus and Adonis.* (*See also* **Morality and Ethics; Poetry of Shakespeare.**)

RELIGION

Religion in Elizabethan England was not only a question of personal faith but also a matter of national politics. Divisions between Catholics and Protestants went much deeper than disagreements about different forms of worship and church organization.

England was a Protestant nation whose chief political rivals, Spain and France, were Catholic countries. Religious affiliation thus touched on issues of loyalty to the English crown. Moreover, religious disputes were not limited to disagreements between Protestants and Catholics. Various Protestant groups held conflicting opinions on the proper relationship between God and humanity, as well as on the ideal relationship between the church and state.

RELIGION AND POLITICS

Most Englishmen in Shakespeare's day were members of the Church of England, known at the time as the new religion or the established church. Created by King Henry VIII, who broke from the Roman Catholic Church in 1534, the Church of England retained many basic Catholic beliefs. At the same time it rejected many of the specific doctrines and rituals of Catholicism.

THE REFORMATION. Until the early 1500s all European countries had accepted the Catholic Church as the representative of God's will on earth. This changed when a German priest named Martin Luther rebelled against what he saw as the corruption of the Catholic Church. He rejected the authority of the pope and of certain major Catholic doctrines and practices. Luther's attacks sparked a movement known as the Protestant Reformation, which led many northern European countries to abandon Catholicism.

During the early years of the Reformation, England remained loyal to the Catholic Church. It might have stayed so indefinitely if not for the politics of royal birthright. Frustrated by his wife's failure to produce a male heir, Henry VIII sought an annulment* so that he could remarry in the hope of fathering a son. When the pope refused to grant the annulment, King Henry responded by establishing the Church of England and declaring himself its leader. Henry closed monasteries and convents throughout England and seized their lands, which became a rich source of income for his court. However, he took few other actions against the Catholic Church and its followers. Although he rejected the authority of the pope, his bishops and priests retained their former positions, and he ensured that religious practices were altered little during his reign.

This state of affairs remained unchanged until Henry's daughter Mary became queen in 1553. "Bloody Mary" reestablished Catholicism as the country's official religion, and under her rule some 300 Protestants were put to death. After Mary died in 1558 ELIZABETH I became the new monarch and set about returning her nation to the Church of England.

ELIZABETHAN PROTESTANTISM. One of Elizabeth's first actions as queen was to craft the Elizabethan Settlement, which attempted to make the Church of England acceptable to Catholics and Protestants alike. She rejected the authority of the pope but retained many Catholic rituals and practices. Some criticized this compromise as too harsh, while others saw it as too lax; but most people were able to live with it. Like her father,

* *annulment* formal declaration that a marriage is legally invalid

See color plate 1, vol. 3.

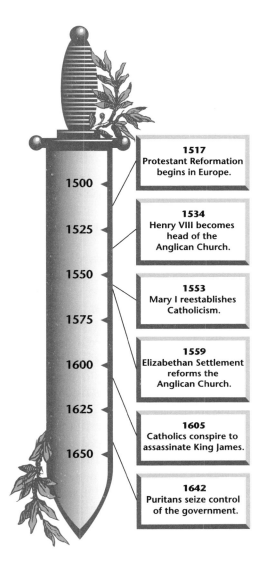

1517
Protestant Reformation begins in Europe.

1500

1534
Henry VIII becomes head of the Anglican Church.

1525

1553
Mary I reestablishes Catholicism.

1550

1575

1559
Elizabethan Settlement reforms the Anglican Church.

1600

1625

1605
Catholics conspire to assassinate King James.

1650

1642
Puritans seize control of the government.

* *hierarchy* ordered structure based on rank

Elizabeth took few drastic anti-Catholic measures early in her reign. Believing in Catholicism was not a criminal offense, but failure to attend Protestant services was punishable by a fine and occasionally imprisonment.

In 1570 the pope declared that English Catholics did not owe loyalty to Elizabeth because she rejected the Catholic faith. He also stated that the Catholic Church would not consider anyone who assassinated the queen to be guilty of murder. A person who killed Elizabeth would automatically be forgiven. Elizabeth was greatly agitated by the pope's actions, which she considered equivalent to a declaration of war. Her fears were compounded in the late 1570s when Jesuit colleges in France began sending Catholic priests to England to convert Protestants and stir up anti-Protestant feelings.

Hovering above these developments was the constant threat of invasion by Catholic Spain. The English feared not only the presence of Spanish warships and troops but also the possibility of an uprising of English Catholics in support of an invasion. Loyal Protestants viewed Catholics as potential traitors and agents of the kings of Spain and France. These fears led to increased persecution of English Catholics after 1570. Fines for failure to attend Protestant services increased dramatically, and large numbers of Catholics were arrested. Over the course of Elizabeth's 45-year reign, some 250 Catholics were executed or died in prison.

RELIGIOUS DIVERSITY IN ENGLAND

The Church of England faced criticism not only from Catholics but also from anti-Catholics, who believed that the established church was still too close to Catholic practice. In England those who held such beliefs were known as Puritans because they wanted to purify the new religion of all traces of Catholicism. They were sometimes also called Precisionists. Puritanism was not a distinct religion but a movement within the Church of England.

COMMON RELIGIOUS BELIEFS. Although Catholics tended to focus on their differences with the Church of England, there were many similarities in their religious doctrines. Both churches taught that every being on earth had a proper place, or *degree,* in a universal hierarchy* known as the Great Chain of Being. God sat at the top of this divine order, followed by angels, humans, animals, plants, and inanimate objects such as rocks. Individuals within each category were also arranged according to rank. Kings, viewed as God's representatives on earth, occupied the highest level among humans. Below them were nobles and other humans in descending order, down to the lowest beggars and criminals. Harmony ruled as long as every being knew and respected its place in this order. Writers including Shakespeare played on this theme frequently. A famous speech in *Troilus and Cressida* (I.iii.75–137) describes the importance of "degree, priority, and place" and goes on to depict the chaos that results when this principle is violated. Examples of such disruption appear in *King Lear* and *Richard II.*

Protestants and Catholics also shared other basic religious beliefs. Both groups claimed that faith in God was necessary for salvation and

that God's word was revealed through the BIBLE, or holy scriptures. They also taught the importance of attending church regularly.

DOCTRINAL DIFFERENCES. Despite their agreement on a number of basic doctrines, Protestants and Catholics clashed over others. Many of these controversies centered on Protestants' attitude toward the pope, bishops, and priests, who claimed to be God's representatives. The pope claimed that his authority descended directly from St. Peter, whom Jesus had named as the head of his church on earth. Therefore, the pope's views on faith and morality were considered infallible*. Bishops were the pope's local representatives, responsible for ordaining priests and overseeing the church's affairs away from Rome. The church argued that only members of the clergy could interpret the scriptures and thus the average person could not hope to understand God's word without the direction of the church. Protestants believed that any faithful Christian who read the Bible could understand the will of God without the help of a priest.

Protestants severely objected to two practices that reflected the power of the Catholic Church and its representatives. One was the mass, which could only be performed by an ordained priest. Masses were elaborate church services conducted in Latin in a chapel decked out with gold and silver cups, candleholders, bells, and other ornaments. Many Protestants saw this as a vulgar display intended to separate worshipers from God and continue the power of the church. They favored simpler ceremonies, performed in the native language of the congregation. The other objectionable practice was the granting of indulgences, which allowed a person to buy grace or forgiveness from sin by making a contribution to the church. The practice of selling indulgences was widespread and generated substantial revenue for the Catholic Church. To Protestants it was one more example of Catholic corruption that had no basis in scripture.

PURITANS AND JEWS. Puritans, as well as Catholics, posed challenges to established authority. The Puritans were an offshoot of the Calvinists, a Protestant sect that followed the teachings of the French theologian John Calvin. They believed in predestination, or the idea that people were selected at birth to be bound for heaven or hell and that nothing they did in life could alter their fate. Puritans denied the authority of bishops and other appointed church officials. Each Puritan congregation was independent of all others and answered only to its own elected leaders. Puritans were opposed to luxuries of any sort and were particularly critical of the theater. At times Puritans held enough sway with the government to limit the activities of the dramatic profession.

For the most part, however, Puritans were outsiders in the area of government because they rejected the idea of degree, claiming that monarch and commoner alike were equal in the eyes of God. Such thinking flew in the face of accepted doctrine and posed an unacceptable challenge to the nobles who controlled the state and the Church of England. Puritans were often persecuted as vigorously as Catholics, and they were included in the lists of recusants, people who refused to accept the authority of the

* *infallible* incapable of error

PROTESTANT OR PAPIST?

Shakespeare's personal religious beliefs are a matter of debate among scholars. His father and his daughter Susanna appeared on lists of Catholic recusants, and the master of his grammar school was a Catholic who later became a Jesuit priest. In 1611 an English historian referred to the Jesuit priest Robert Parsons and Shakespeare as "this Papist and his Poet." Other contemporary writers also refer to Shakespeare as a Papist, and his financial sponsor, the earl of Southampton, was from a leading Catholic family. Shakespeare himself, however, was never arrested for recusancy, and there is no known reason to think he was not a loyal member of the Church of England.

Church of England. Many Puritans fled England for Holland, which was much more tolerant and allowed them to practice their faith openly.

Protestants and Catholics were united in their fear and hatred of JEWS. They considered Jews responsible for the death of Jesus and suspected them of such atrocities as kidnapping and sacrificing Christian children. Jews were also criticized for practicing usury—the practice of charging interest on loans—something Christians were forbidden to do. The average Englishman, however, had little or no contact with Jews. Laws dating from the 1200s banned Jews from living in England, but these laws were irregularly enforced, allowing a small Jewish community to exist in London. (*See also* **Astronomy and Cosmology; Church, The; Fate and Fortune; Morality and Ethics; Philosophy.**)

RENAISSANCE, INFLUENCE OF THE

* *medieval* referring to the Middle Ages, a period roughly between A.D. 500 and 1500

The Renaissance was a period of tremendous intellectual and artistic activity in western Europe, one that lasted from the mid-1300s to the early 1600s. During the Renaissance thinkers focused primarily on human achievements in this world rather than on questions about the afterlife, which had occupied the attention of most medieval* scholars. This emphasis on man's potential, known as humanism, significantly influenced Shakespeare's works. In *Hamlet,* for example, the young prince expresses the humanistic view of man: "What a piece of work is a man, how noble in reason, how infinite in faculties, in form and moving, how express and admirable in action, how like an angel in apprehension, how like a god! the beauty of the world; the paragon of animals" (II.ii.303–7). The value placed on everyday experience inspired Shakespeare to explore human nature and the depth and complexity of people's emotions.

The Renaissance also brought a revival of interest in ancient Greek and Roman culture. Humanists studied the history of the ancient world in part to learn how best to govern. Historians, such as Raphael Holinshed, wrote about England's past, which in turn inspired Shakespeare to pen the history plays in which he chronicled the power struggles of English kings. Shakespeare's histories explore the qualities that make an effective ruler, and in the process they question any belief in the divine right of kings. In *Richard II,* for example, a monarch is deposed by Henry Bolingbroke, who is a much more capable leader than the presumed legitimate ruler.

The Renaissance value that seems to have influenced Shakespeare the most was its emphasis on the importance of language. According to humanist beliefs God placed humans above animals when he endowed them with reason, which can be expressed only through language. For this reason the ability to communicate effectively and persuasively was a basic requirement for any civilized activity and was especially important for governing. In 1564 Queen ELIZABETH I spoke before a group of scholars at Cambridge University: "I would have all of you bear this one thing in mind, that no road is straighter, none shorter, none more adapted to win the good things of fortune or the good-will of your Prince, than the

Revenge and Forgiveness

* *rhetoric* art of speaking or writing effectively

pursuit of Good Letters." The queen's respect for rhetoric* was shared by many of those who lived during England's renaissance. The richness, complexity, and inventiveness of Shakespeare's writings show that he catered to an audience that valued and appreciated the power of words. (*See also* **Education and Literacy; Language; Schools and Universities.**)

REVENGE AND FORGIVENESS

lizabethan attitudes toward revenge and forgiveness were complex. The Christian moral code promoted love and forgiveness as the highest of virtues, yet many Elizabethans considered it a matter of honor to seek personal revenge for injuries. The government strongly discouraged this practice, fearing that it would lead to blood feuds and widespread violence. The proper way to settle injuries was through the law, and rulers saw personal revenge as a threat to the authority of the state. Those who took the law into their own hands were subject to severe punishment. Nevertheless, there were many types of injuries the courts could not address, particularly insults and attacks on a person's honor. Elizabethans placed such a high value on honor that they believed they could not allow such attacks to go unpunished.

Many Elizabethan dramas focused on the theme of revenge. These revenge tragedies were influenced by the works of the ancient playwright Seneca and by stories, or novelle, from Renaissance Italy. Revenge plots tended to be exceedingly violent and sensationalistic. The first Elizabethan tragedy in this genre* appears to have been Thomas Kyd's *The Spanish Tragedy* (1587). Many of its plot devices became conventions*, including a scheming villain, real or pretended madness, the use of trickery to achieve vengeance, and the appearance of a ghost who gives a supernatural justification for the act. The avenger typically hesitates to do the deed because of moral reservations and often turns into a bloody villain himself in the process of carrying out his revenge.

* *genre* literary form
* *convention* established practice

Shakespeare wrote two plays of this type. The first, *Titus Andronicus*, is a straightforward revenge play patterned after Seneca's works. One of Shakespeare's earliest plays, it follows many of Kyd's conventions and is regarded as a crude but powerful first attempt at tragedy. The themes explored in this play were developed much more fully in later works, especially *Hamlet*, which also centers on the idea of revenge. Hamlet is a far more complex character than Titus and devotes much more thought to the task of revenge. Another difference is that *Titus Andronicus* is set in a pre-Christian world, while Hamlet is a distinctly Christian character troubled by the spiritual implications of his situation. Both of these plays, but especially *Hamlet*, illustrate the complexity of Elizabethan views toward revenge. They suggest that vengeance is sometimes morally necessary, and they illustrate the tragic consequences that can result when this course of action is carried too far. Eight people die in *Hamlet* for a murder that only one has committed.

See color plate 6, vol. 2.

In some of Shakespeare's later plays, the idea of revenge is contrasted with that of forgiveness. In *The Merchant of Venice,* for example, SHYLOCK

seeks the life of the merchant Antonio as punishment for the insults and injuries he has inflicted on the Jewish community. When a skilled lawyer saves Antonio's life, the merchant has the chance to exact revenge from Shylock, but instead he chooses forgiveness. Antonio allows Shylock to keep half his property on the condition that he convert to Christianity and leave his remaining property to Lorenzo when he dies. The importance of reconciliation is also illustrated in *The Tempest*, where PROSPERO pardons the brother who usurped* his title and tried to kill him. Prospero explains his actions with a reflection that "the rarer action is in virtue than in vengeance" (V.i.27–28). (*See also* **Duels and Feuds; Morality and Ethics.**)

*** usurp** to seize power from a rightful ruler

REVISION IN SHAKESPEARE'S SCRIPTS

See *Printing and Publishing; Quartos and Folios; Shakespeare's Works, Adaptations of; Shakespeare's Works, Influential Editions.*

RHETORIC

R hetoric is the study of language—particularly its form, content, and structure—and its use as a tool for persuading and entertaining an audience. It was the core of the Elizabethan educational system, which treated the mastery of language as essential preparation for any kind of civilized activity. All students at Elizabethan grammar schools (so named because they focused on teaching Latin grammar) received thorough training in rhetoric. Students read, memorized, and recited passages in Latin and were expected to be able to translate them into English. These Latin sources provided models of rhetorical techniques: choosing the proper words, arranging them effectively, and using linguistic devices, such as puns and metaphors, to express ideas. Students were also expected to demonstrate their mastery of these rules by creating their own Latin compositions using the same techniques. For example, a student might be presented with a situation from classical* literature and asked to create original dialogue or poetry to fit the material.

*** classical** in the tradition of ancient Greece and Rome

The best Elizabethan writers, including Shakespeare, drew on this training to craft elaborate passages of rich and expressive language. Shakespeare's rhetorical skill is revealed in his clever wordplay, his references to mythological or biblical figures, and his use of devices such as repetition and words with multiple meanings. The complexity of his language, which confounds many modern readers, was undoubtedly a source of delight to audiences of his time. Trained in the same rhetorical techniques, they could recognize Shakespeare's skillful use of those techniques in a way that is difficult for modern audiences to appreciate. (*See also* **Education and Literacy; Language; Poetic Technique; Prose Technique; Renaissance, Influence of the; Schools and Universities; Shakespeare's Sources; Soliloquy.**)

Richard II

RICHARD II

** **tetralogy** four-part series of literary or dramatic works*

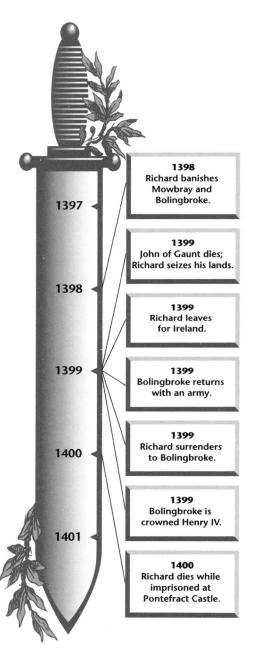

1398
Richard banishes Mowbray and Bolingbroke.

1397

1399
John of Gaunt dies; Richard seizes his lands.

1398

1399
Richard leaves for Ireland.

1399

1399
Bolingbroke returns with an army.

1399
Richard surrenders to Bolingbroke.

1400

1399
Bolingbroke is crowned Henry IV.

1401

1400
Richard dies while imprisoned at Pontefract Castle.

** **depose** to remove from high office, often by force*

Shakespeare's *Richard II* is the first play in a tetralogy* that explores the events that led to the WARS OF THE ROSES, the dynastic conflict that dominated the second half of the 1400s. The other plays in the series are *Henry IV, Part 1; Henry IV, Part 2;* and *Henry V.* In *Richard II,* Shakespeare asked questions of profound importance to a monarchy such as England's. What happens when the rightful ruler is not the best person for the job? What are the consequences of removing a ruler from the throne?

Shakespeare also painted a masterful portrait of a tragic character, a weak, self-centered king who loses his throne to a more practical and decisive man but who nevertheless evokes sympathy for the suffering he endures. As Richard's emblems of kingship are stripped away, he is forced to recognize that he is no longer a "native king" but merely a flawed human being.

PLOT SUMMARY. The action begins at Windsor Castle, the royal residence. The kingdom of Richard II is in complete disarray. Henry Bolingbroke (the king's cousin) accuses Thomas Mowbray (the duke of Norfolk) of stealing royal funds and of murdering the duke of Gloucester. Richard agrees that the two should settle their dispute with a trial by combat. He later changes his mind, however, and banishes them from the kingdom—Mowbray for life and Bolingbroke for six years.

Gloucester's widow urges John of Gaunt (Bolingbroke's father) to punish her husband's murderer, but Gaunt reveals that the king ordered the killing. He reminds her that the monarch is "God's substitute" and that only God can punish him. Gaunt declares that as a loyal Englishman he "may never lift / An angry arm against His [God's] minister" (I.ii.40–41). Meanwhile, as Richard prepares to leave for Ireland to crush a rebellion, he reveals his alarm at Bolingbroke's popularity with the people.

In Act II, Gaunt delivers a much-quoted speech (II.i.40–68) from his deathbed, praising England as "this sceptred isle" and "this precious stone set in the silver sea." Then after warning Richard that his participation in the murder of Gloucester, his excessive taxation, and his misrule will cause his downfall, Gaunt dies. Furious with Gaunt and in need of funds, Richard seizes the dead man's property, which rightfully belongs to Bolingbroke. Several noblemen protest, alarmed at Richard's blatant disregard for the law. The illegal confiscation prompts Bolingbroke to return from exile with an army to reclaim his inheritance.

In Act III, Richard returns from Ireland to find that the kingdom's leading nobles have allied themselves with Bolingbroke. After the king takes refuge in Flint Castle, Bolingbroke arrives and tells him that he will end his rebellion if Richard will return the duke's inheritance and allow him to stay in England. Richard admits his cousin to the castle, knowing that he lacks the power to resist. A short time later the queen learns that Bolingbroke has taken the king, in effect a prisoner, to London.

Act IV is set in Westminster Hall, site of the English Parliament. Bolingbroke, the nobles, and several churchmen debate whether it is permissible to depose* God's chosen deputy. The bishop of Carlisle asks, "What

In *Richard II* the king orders a trial by combat to settle a dispute between Henry Bolingbroke and Thomas Mowbray. This photograph from the 1973 Royal Shakespeare Company production of the play shows Richard (played by Richard Paxo) observing the two combatants from his seat on the throne.

subject can give sentence on his king?" (IV.i.121), and he warns that deposing Richard will lead to "disorder, horror, fear, and mutiny" (IV.i.142). After speaking movingly of his sorrows and misfortunes, Richard hands over his crown and scepter, the symbols of his kingship, to Bolingbroke, whom he calls King Harry.

In Act V, Richard is imprisoned in Pomfret Castle. Bolingbroke, now King Henry IV, learns of a plot against him by Richard's few remaining supporters. Sir Pierce of Exton, one of King Henry's men, arrives and kills Richard in his cell, believing that Henry has hinted that he wants the deposed king dead. The play ends with Henry secure in the knowledge that all those who had opposed him have been removed from the scene. When he learns of Richard's death, however, Henry regrets that his rise to power is now tainted with Richard's murder, saying, "Lords, I protest my soul is full of woe / That blood should sprinkle me to make me grow" (V.vi.45–46). He vows to make a pilgrimage to the Holy Land "to wash this blood off from my guilty hand" (V.vi.50).

SOURCES AND HISTORY. In 1597 *Richard II* was entered in the Stationer's Register, a record kept by English printers and publishers of works they intended to publish. Similarities between *Richard II* and Samuel Daniel's poem "The Civil Wars between the two Houses of York and Lancaster," however, suggest that Shakespeare may have written the play as early as 1595, the year that Daniel's poem was published.

Shakespeare's main source for *Richard II* was the 1587 edition of HOLINSHED'S CHRONICLES, a work completed by the English historian in 1577. The playwright also drew on *A Mirror for Magistrates* (1559), a collection of biographical poems about well-known leaders, including King Richard II. *Thomas of Woodstock*, a tragedy written in the early 1590s by an

* **metaphor** figure of speech in which one object or idea is directly identified with a different object or idea

* **usurpation** seizing of power from a rightful ruler

REHEARSAL FOR A REBELLION

The first known performance of *Richard II* occurred in 1601—and may have been intended to incite the overthrow of Queen Elizabeth I. Supporters of the earl of Essex arranged for the play to be performed on February 7 at the Globe. The following day Essex led a brief and unsuccessful rebellion against the queen. Some historians think that Essex's coconspirators believed that Shakespeare's play, which portrays the removal of a weak king from the throne, would encourage the population of London to support the removal of their own ruler. Government authorities later investigated the matter but found the theater company blameless.

unknown author, was probably the source of several elements in Shakespeare's drama, including the character of John of Gaunt. Shakespeare may have modeled his depiction of Richard—a likable but ineffective ruler whose weaknesses cause his downfall—on Christopher Marlowe's portrait of the title character in *Edward II*, written around 1592.

COMMENTARY. *Richard II* is written entirely in verse, and it has a deliberately theatrical quality. Using metaphors* and other figures of speech, Richard displays an indulgent series of images of himself as king rather than seeing himself and his circumstances as they really are. When he returns from Ireland, for example, he says he is reunited with his kingdom "as a long-parted mother with her child" (III.ii.8). Yet it is Richard's own neglect and misrule that have brought disorder to his realm. Only after his downfall does the king attain real insight and acknowledge his mistakes: "I wasted time, and now doth time waste me" (V.v.49).

The British poet Samuel Taylor Coleridge wrote that the language in which Richard reveals the workings of his mind reflects the "utmost richness" of thought. He argued that if an actor could properly represent the king, the role would delight audiences more than any of Shakespeare's other creations, except perhaps King Lear. As Coleridge recognized, Richard's lush poetic language is one of the play's most striking features. The king's expressive speeches reflect the strength and depth of his thoughts and feelings, yet he cannot act decisively. Bolingbroke, on the other hand, has comparatively little to say and does not reveal his inner self, yet he takes control of events. In setting up the contrast between the thoughtful man and the man of action, Shakespeare poses questions about the qualities a good ruler should possess.

The structure and theme of *Richard II* are rooted in an ironic political problem. Bolingbroke sees that Richard's incompetence is hurting England. To rid the kingdom of a ineffectual monarch, however, he must do further damage by overturning the law and claiming a throne to which he has no clear right, acts that will eventually lead to decades of turmoil. Yet Richard has paved the way for his own usurpation* by unlawfully seizing Bolingbroke's inheritance. In a further irony the play ends as it began, with a king whose hands are stained with royal blood and who is in debt to his nobles.

PERFORMANCE HISTORY. As far as is known, *Richard II* was staged only twice during Shakespeare's lifetime, once in London in 1601 and again in 1607 aboard an English ship off the African coast. *The Sicilian Usurper*, a version of the play produced in London in 1681, changed the setting to Italy because dramatizing the overthrow of an English monarch on the stage was considered politically reckless. Despite the change, the government closed down the play after two days.

Richard II enjoyed some popularity in England in the early 1700s and again a century later, when the famed actors Edmund Kean and Charles Macready played Richard. Charles Kean's highly acclaimed 1857 production featured an elaborate scene with 500 actors depicting Bolingbroke's triumphant entry into London. The 1900s brought new interest in the play and numerous productions, with notable performances in the role of Richard by John Gielgud, Maurice Evans, Alec Guinness, John Neville, and David Warner. Several renderings have also been filmed for television, including a 1970 British production with Ian McKellen as Richard and a 1979 BBC drama with Derek Jacobi as Richard and John Gielgud as John of Gaunt. (*See also* **Henry IV, Part 1; Henry IV, Part 2; Henry V; History in Shakespeare's Plays: England; Plays: The Histories.**)

RICHARD III

* *soliloquy* monologue in which a character reveals his or her private thoughts

THE MONSTER AND THE MAN

Shakespeare followed his sources in portraying Richard III as a "hunchback" whose physical deformity is matched by his warped inner character. Richard's enemies make much of his ugliness, referring to him as an animal or a monster. The idea that physical disfiguration was an outward sign of inner hideousness, a notion common to Europeans of the Middle Ages and Renaissance, persisted for centuries. Ironically, historians believe that the real Richard III had little or no deformity.

Shakespeare's *Richard III* is a history play that portrays the final events of the WARS OF THE ROSES. It is the last in a series of four plays that also includes *Henry VI, Parts 1, 2, and 3*. Probably written between 1591 and 1593, *Richard III* is among the greatest of Shakespeare's early plays. Its title character is a fascinating villain who swaggers across the stage, manipulating the other characters with casual violence and vicious humor. The play tracks his ascent from the court of his brother King Edward IV to his own bloody reign as Richard III. His quick rise to power is matched by an equally sudden fall that marks the ultimate defeat of the house of York and the beginning of the Tudor dynasty (1485–1603).

SUMMARY. In a long and famous opening soliloquy*, Richard reveals that the crowning of his brother King Edward IV has brought about peace between his family, the house of York, and the house of Lancaster, family of the late King Henry VI. Because he is deformed, however, Richard is unsuited for the romantic pastimes of a court at peace, and therefore he is "determined to prove a villain" (I.i.29). He has convinced the king that their brother George, the duke of Clarence, is plotting to take the throne. Clarence is arrested, and Richard pretends to sympathize with him, accusing the queen and her relatives of framing him. When Richard hears that King Edward is seriously ill, he reflects that he must have Clarence killed before Edward dies in order to inherit the crown.

To strengthen his claim to the throne, Richard plans to marry Lady Anne, widow of the late Prince Edward, son of King Henry VI. He finds Anne attending the funeral of her father-in-law, and she rails at Richard for murdering Henry and her husband. Outrageously, Richard insists that he has done so only out of love for her. At first she scorns him, but gradually he persuades her of his sincerity. After she leaves, Richard mocks her for yielding to him: "Was ever woman in this humor woo'd? / Was ever woman in this humor won?" (I.ii.227–28). Richard then proceeds to the court, where he quarrels with the queen and her relatives. Margaret, widow of Henry VI, heaps curses on all those present.

Two murderers, hired by Richard, slip into Clarence's cell and kill him. King Edward, meanwhile, tries to restore peace at the court between the queen's family and the powerful nobles Hastings and Buckingham. Richard ruins the new mood of joy and friendship by announcing Clarence's death, which he attempts to blame on the king's orders and the queen's plotting. Soon after, the king dies, and the queen's allies go to

Laurence Olivier's portrayal of Richard III influenced many subsequent performances. The British actor is shown here playing Richard in the 1955 film version of the play.

See color plate 12, vol. 2.

Wales to fetch his heir, young Prince Edward. Richard and Buckingham quickly send ambassadors of their own to join this escort and to control the prince's arrival. The prince and his younger brother, the duke of York, are taken to be housed in the TOWER OF LONDON.

Richard moves rapidly to assure himself of the crown. He sends a knight named Catesby to obtain Hastings's reaction to a proposal that Richard be king, but Hastings rejects the idea. Meanwhile Richard sends the queen's allies to their deaths. At a council meeting later Richard accuses Hastings of plots against his life and has him arrested and executed. After calming the doubts of the mayor of London, Richard plots to eliminate his other rivals, sending Buckingham to spread a rumor that the two young princes are not legitimate sons of King Edward. Finally, the mayor arrives with a group of citizens and asks Richard to take the crown. After pretending to reject the offer, Richard accepts. Once he is crowned, Richard suggests to Buckingham that the two princes must be killed. Buckingham hesitates to act on the new king's implied command, so Richard sends a man named Tyrell to do the deed. He also breaks his former promise to grant a new title to Buckingham, who then resolves to desert the king.

His evil intentions deepening, Richard decides that he must marry the late king's daughter, Princess Elizabeth, to secure his power. He starts a rumor that Lady Anne, who is now his queen, has fallen ill. She dies soon after, and Richard promptly meets with Edward's former queen to seek the hand of her daughter. She pretends to accept. Messengers arrive with news of an invasion led by the earl of Richmond, heir to the house of Lancaster, which Buckingham is supporting. In his first sign of weakness, Richard panics. He sends Richmond's stepfather, Lord Stanley, to negotiate with the rebels but insists that he leave his son behind as a prisoner to ensure that he will not join the revolt. Richard regains his confidence on learning that a storm has hit the fleet and that Buckingham has been taken prisoner. He orders Buckingham's execution and takes command of his army.

The opposing forces meet in the final act. Richard and Richmond set up their tents at opposite sides of the stage. That night, as they sleep, the ghosts of Richard's victims appear to both men, haunting Richard's dreams while assuring Richmond of victory. Richard wakes in a panic, stricken by guilt and despair, but recovers his composure as he thinks of the coming battle. News arrives that Stanley has refused to march to Richard's aid. In a fury Richard orders the execution of Stanley's son and rushes into battle. He continues to fight after his horse is slain, madly shouting "A horse, a horse! my kingdom for a horse!" (V.iv.13). Richmond kills Richard in single combat, declares victory, and receives the title of King Henry VII. He promises to marry Princess Elizabeth, thereby joining the warring families of York and Lancaster and ushering in a new era of peace.

SOURCES. Shakespeare's main sources for *Richard III* were the same two books he used to write the *Henry VI* plays: HOLINSHED'S CHRONICLES (1587) and Edward Halle's *Union of the Two Noble and Illustre Famelies of*

classical in the tradition of ancient Greece and Rome

Lancastre and York (1548). Halle, in turn, drew much of his material from earlier works by Sir Thomas More and Polydore Vergil.

The style of the play also reveals the influence of several other sources, both classical* and contemporary. Shakespeare borrowed themes and character traits from the tragedies of the ancient Roman playwright Seneca and from his own colleague Christopher MARLOWE, who had scored a success in 1587 with *Tamburlaine the Great,* another portrait of a charismatic villain. The playwright also modeled Richard after the VICE in the morality plays* of the Middle Ages. The Vice was a character whose evil was matched by the carefree pleasure he took in it. The political works of Italian author Niccolò Machiavelli—especially *The Prince* (1509), which explains how rulers can remain in power by ruthlessly eliminating their opponents—may also have influenced Shakespeare's idea of Richard.

morality play religious dramatic work that teaches a moral lesson through the use of symbolic characters

COMMENTARY. The most striking aspect of *Richard III* is the title character. Critics have long regarded King Richard as Shakespeare's first great invention, a complex character, larger than life, who dominates the stage. He is both a calculating conspirator who ruthlessly maneuvers his way toward the throne and a brash jester who takes obvious pleasure in his own evil intelligence. Moreover, the charisma that helps him deceive the other characters works equally well to charm the audience. From the opening lines of the play, Richard addresses the audience in numerous soliloquies and asides*, drawing in all of his observers as co-conspirators in his wicked plans.

aside remark made by a character onstage to the audience or to another character, unheard by other characters present in the same scene

In his evil magnificence King Richard can be seen as the Vice, who is not so much a realistic character as the embodiment of all human evils. Completely without morals, he is also humorous and clever, laughing at his own mischief and at the weaknesses of others as he tempts ordinary people to sinful deeds. Yet Richard is not a pure Vice; he turns out to be a human being whose frailty is revealed in later scenes. Unlike the Vice, who never shows any remorse for his deeds, Richard suffers pangs of guilt and laments the fact that no one will mourn his death. A newer tradition that probably influenced Shakespeare's portrayal of this character was the practice of centering plays on villainous protagonists*, a point that may be illustrated by Marlowe's Tamburlaine, who towers over the other characters. Richard is Shakespeare's first great villain, the forerunner of such complex characters as IAGO (in *Othello*) and Edmund (in *King Lear*).

protagonist central character in a dramatic or literary work

Various themes in the play reflect the influence of Seneca's tragedies. One is the idea of hubris, the kind of excessive pride that is displayed by such characters as Buckingham, who refuses to believe that Richard will betray him. A more prominent Senecan theme is that of revenge, seen most clearly in the minor but powerful character of Margaret. She resembles the Furies of ancient Greek and Roman drama, shrieking tormentors who came from the underworld to demand justice for unpunished crimes. Margaret has no real function in the plot of *Richard III*, but she appears several times to deliver venomous curses and to cry for heavenly justice. Most of the characters in *Richard III* suffer the fate she wishes on them, and her words take on the air of prophecy.

Richard III

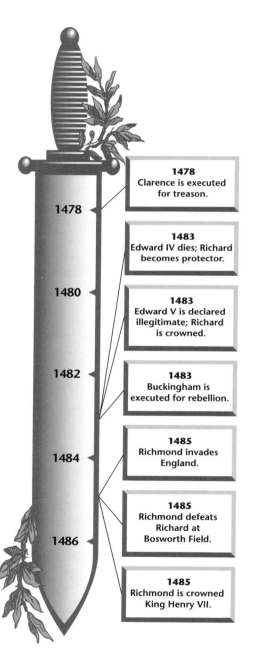

1478
Clarence is executed for treason.

1478

1483
Edward IV dies; Richard becomes protector.

1480

1483
Edward V is declared illegitimate; Richard is crowned.

1482

1483
Buckingham is executed for rebellion.

1484

1485
Richmond invades England.

1485
Richmond defeats Richard at Bosworth Field.

1486

1485
Richmond is crowned King Henry VII.

Margaret's "predictions" are just one example of the role of FATE in *Richard III*. Richard dominates the stage so thoroughly that it is easy to overlook the larger significance of the play as a social allegory*, exemplifying the restoration of order in a country shattered by war and treachery. Richard is not simply a charismatic villain but an instrument of God's will, bringing death to the bickering, disloyal nobles who have plunged the country into civil war. Richmond, who defeats Richard, is likewise a tool of divine justice. In fact he shows no significant character traits of his own; he comes across as the pure embodiment of virtue and the restorer of peace, law, and social order. Shakespeare may have had a political interest in making Richmond appear holy and righteous because Queen ELIZABETH I was the granddaughter of Henry VII.

To create his allegory and make his drama more gripping, Shakespeare freely altered the historical record, which was already biased because it had been written by historians friendly to the Tudor dynasty. The playwright compressed the events of years into weeks and blamed Richard for many deaths, including some for which there is little evidence of his guilt. Most modern historians believe, for example, that Richard served loyally under Edward IV and did not plot to take the throne until events made it necessary. They also argue that Lady Anne died of natural causes and that the deaths of duke of Clarence and Edward's sons were probably ordered by others. But Shakespeare was an artist, not a historian, and he placed drama and character ahead of historical accuracy.

PERFORMANCE HISTORY The character of Richard has been a prized role for many great actors, beginning with Shakespeare's own leading man, Richard Burbage. Burbage was a great success in the role, and the play remained popular through the early 1600s.

In 1700 the actor Colley Cibber produced a drastically altered version of the play. He cut much of Shakespeare's text and added fragments from other Shakespearean history plays, as well as many lines that he wrote himself. Cibber's version remained more popular than Shakespeare's for decades, with such acclaimed actors as David Garrick and John Philip Kemble in the title role. In 1751 Cibber's version of *Richard III* was the first Shakespearean play presented in the United States.

William Charles Macready attempted to present Shakespeare's original version of *Richard III* in 1821, but audiences were displeased and he was forced to switch back to Cibber's version. Shakespeare's full text was finally restored to the English stage in 1845 and to the American stage in 1877. Extravagant productions of the play with large casts were favored throughout the 1800s. The most noteworthy modern performance of *Richard III* was that of Laurence Olivier, who played the role on stage in the 1940s and directed and starred in a film version in 1954. Olivier's Richard is vibrant and powerful, controlling the actions of the other characters like a master puppeteer. In addition to Olivier's, there have been seven other film interpretations of the play to date, including a notable one with Ian McKellen in the title role in 1995, plus three television productions. (*See also* **History in Shakespeare's Plays: England; Plays: The Histories; Shakespeare's Sources.**)

ROMANCES, THE

See *Plays: The Romances.*

ROMEO
AND JULIET

* *pathos* emotion of pity or sympathy

* *bawdy* indecent; lewd

See color plate 2, vol. 2.

Written around 1595, *Romeo and Juliet* is the tragic story of two young people whose love is forbidden because of a feud between their families. It is one of Shakespeare's earliest tragedies and is among his best-known plays. To judge from the well-thumbed pages of *Romeo and Juliet* in the Bodleian Library's copy of the FIRST FOLIO, this drama was as popular among Oxford undergraduates in the 1600s as it is among young people today. The reasons are plain to see. Apart from the exquisite pathos* of the tragedy, the beautiful love poetry Shakespeare wrote for his "star-crossed lovers" remains among the best ever written, in English or any other language.

PLOT SUMMARY. The play is set in the Italian city of Verona, where two noble families, the Montagues and the Capulets, are engaged in a feud. The action begins with some bawdy* wordplay that leads to a brawl between the servants of these two families but soon passes into the realm of romantic comedy. Romeo, a member of the Montague family, enters as a lovesick young man sighing over the lady Rosaline, who refuses to return his love. His friend Benvolio persuades him to go to a masked ball the Capulets are giving and see the other beauties there. As they approach the party, they meet another friend, Mercutio, who engages Romeo in a witty dialogue about love. Mercutio teases Romeo about his passion for Rosaline, accusing him of falling under the influence of Queen Mab, the fairy who brings dreams into lovers' brains.

Romeo enters the Capulets' house in disguise and meets Juliet, their daughter. The two immediately fall in love, but both recognize the dangers that face them as members of opposing families. When Juliet's cousin Tybalt sees Romeo at the ball, he becomes furious at this intrusion and must be restrained by his uncle from attacking Romeo. After the party ends, Romeo, who cannot bear to leave his love, sneaks into the Capulets' garden and stands outside her window. Hidden in the garden he overhears Juliet, standing on her balcony, sighing over her love for him. In one of Shakespeare's most famous scenes, they swear their eternal love to each other. The following day, Friar Lawrence marries them in secret, believing that their marriage may succeed in reconciling the two feuding families.

Soon afterward Tybalt finds Romeo in the town square and challenges him to fight. Romeo refuses to duel with a man who is now related to him by marriage, claiming that he has better reason than Tybalt knows to wish him well. Mercutio, outraged at Romeo's behavior, fights Tybalt instead. When Romeo tries to break up the duel, Mercutio is fatally wounded. Feeling that he must now avenge his friend's death, Romeo kills Tybalt. When the prince of Verona learns what has happened, he banishes Romeo from the city forever.

Romeo and Juliet

In this scene from Franco Zeffirelli's 1968 film *Romeo and Juliet,* Juliet (played by Olivia Hussey), thinking her beloved Romeo has died, prepares to end her own life.

Mercutio's death marks the point at which the play turns from comedy to tragedy. Romeo returns secretly to Juliet, but they have only one night together before he is forced to leave the city. Unaware that their daughter is already married, Juliet's parents order her to wed her suitor, Paris. Juliet turns for advice to her old Nurse, who urges her to marry Paris because Romeo is banished. At this moment Juliet matures from a girl into a woman. Quietly rejecting the Nurse's advice, she seeks help from Friar Lawrence. He gives her a potion that will make her seem dead, though she will really be in a temporary deep sleep. Her family, believing she has died, will place her body in the family's tomb. Friar Lawrence plans to send word to Romeo to return to Verona, find Juliet in the tomb, and carry her away from the city.

By an unfortunate mischance, however, Romeo does not receive Friar Lawrence's letter explaining the plan. Hearing only that Juliet has died, he buys a vial of poison from a down-on-his-luck apothecary* and returns to Verona. He finds Paris in the Capulets' tomb, mourning his intended bride, and kills him in an unfortunate skirmish. Romeo then takes the poison and dies beside Juliet just before she awakens. Friar Lawrence, hurrying to the tomb, tries to spirit Juliet away, but she refuses to leave. Instead, she chooses to die with her beloved Romeo, stabbing herself with his dagger. The death of the two lovers ends the feud between their families. The heads of the Capulet and Montague households recognize their foolishness at last and clasp hands, pledging to build golden statues of their children as a memorial. But this reconciliation comes at a terrible price: the sacrifice of their two children, cut off in their youth before they had a chance to live out their lives in love and happiness.

SOURCES AND COMMENTARY. Shakespeare wrote *Romeo and Juliet* around 1595 or 1596, at roughly the same time that he was writing *A*

* *apothecary* pharmacist

Midsummer Night's Dream and *Richard II*. These three plays are known as Shakespeare's lyric group because they contain an abundance of rhyming and songlike verse. With them he began to master the skills with which he would soon create some of the greatest works in the tragic form, including *Julius Caesar, Hamlet, Othello, King Lear,* and *Macbeth*.

Shakespeare's main source for his tragedy was Arthur Brooke's narrative poem *The Tragicall Historye of Romeus and Juliet*, written in 1562, but as usual the playwright altered his source considerably. He greatly enlarged the role of Mercutio, barely mentioned in Brooke's poem, and essentially redefined the character of the Nurse, making her warmer and more comical. He also drew on other sources, such as handbooks on dueling that were popular at the time, despite the fact that dueling had been outlawed in England during the reign of King Henry VII. Mercutio's wonderful Queen Mab speech may have been inspired by parts of Edmund Spenser's *The Faerie Queene* (1590–1596) or Thomas Nash's *The Terrors of the Night* (1594).

The Italian tradition of love poetry, particularly the SONNET form, also shows a clear influence in the play. Romeo and Juliet's first lines of dialogue take the form of a sonnet, as does the play's Prologue. Much of the IMAGERY and many other poetic devices in the play also borrow from this tradition, which originated with the Italian poet Petrarch and was popularized by Shakespeare's contemporaries.

In Brooke's poem FATE AND FORTUNE play a large part in determining the outcome of the story, and Shakespeare's text largely reflects this influence. At several places the characters in Shakespeare's play see themselves as victims of a cruel destiny. After killing Tybalt, Romeo cries, "O, I am fortune's fool!" However, critics do not universally regard these characters as the victims of fate. On one hand it is pure chance that Romeo fails to receive Friar Lawrence's message informing him of the scheme to prevent Juliet's wedding with Paris. On the other hand the young couple's own actions have much to do with their tragedy. Their love is, as Juliet says, "too rash, too unadvised, too sudden," driving them into a hasty marriage without their parents' permission, which was expected, if not required, for young couples in Shakespeare's time. One critic, Franklin M. Dickey, has argued that fortune operates in the drama as the servant of a higher power, the tool that punishes the young lovers for their uncontrolled passions. As Friar Lawrence warns Romeo before his marriage, "These violent delights have violent ends."

The lovers' ultimate destiny is the result of their own choices. Born into a society in which they cannot control their own lives, they feel that the only way they can fulfill their desires is to seek a better world elsewhere.

PERFORMANCE HISTORY. *Romeo and Juliet* seems to have been popular on the stage from the very beginning, when it was performed by Shakespeare's company, the Chamberlain's Men (later called the KING'S MEN when JAMES I became their patron*). Richard Burbage, the leading actor of the company, probably created the role of Romeo; Master Robert Goffe played Juliet in the first performances, as women did not perform on the

SHAKESPEAREAN LOVE

The motion picture *Shakespeare in Love* is a fictional account of the composition and first performance of *Romeo and Juliet*. In the screenplay, written by Tom Stoppard and Marc Norman, a stagestruck young noblewoman disguised as a boy plays the part of Romeo and falls in love with Shakespeare. However witty and entertaining, this story is pure fiction. Nonetheless, the film does offer the viewer an enlightening glimpse of the atmosphere of Elizabethan London and its theater.

* *patron* supporter or financial sponsor of an artist or writer

Romeo and Juliet

* Puritan English Protestant who advocated strict moral discipline and a simplification of the ceremonies and beliefs of the Anglican Church

public stage at that time. The title pages of the play's earliest QUARTOS indicate that it was frequently staged, but there is no actual record of a performance before 1642, when all the ELIZABETHAN THEATERS were shut down by the Puritans*.

In 1662 after the theaters were allowed to reopen, William Davenant staged a revival of *Romeo and Juliet* in London, with Henry Harris as Romeo, Thomas Betterton as Mercutio, and Mary Saunderson—probably the first woman to enact the role on the professional stage—as Juliet. Samuel PEPYS saw a performance and hated it. In the 1700s David Garrick rewrote the play so that Juliet awakens before Romeo dies, and in a moving dialogue they profess their eternal love before both expire. Garrick also introduced an elaborate funeral procession after Juliet's pretended death in Act IV. Not until the next century was Shakespeare's original ending restored.

Perhaps the most fascinating and successful production of *Romeo and Juliet* in the 1800s was staged by Charlotte Cushman, the noted American actress, who herself took the role of Romeo playing opposite her sister Susan as Juliet. It was Cushman who restored much of the original text and rid the play of what she regarded as Garrick's "flummery." Other famous productions included those by Samuel Phelps (who played Mercutio) and by another American, Mary Anderson, who played Juliet. Johnston Forbes-Robertson was also highly praised for his role as Romeo.

In the 1920s and 1930s John Gielgud became justly famous for his portrayal of Romeo very early in his career. In later productions Gielgud and Laurence Olivier traded the roles of Romeo and Mercutio on alternating nights. In a 1960 production at London's Old Vic theater, the Italian director Franco Zeffirelli broke new ground by casting two very young actors (Judi Dench and John Stride) in the leading roles. He also rejected the romanticism of previous productions and designed Verona as a real Italian city inhabited by real Italian families.

In Zeffirelli's 1968 film version, he again cast young actors in the leads, but while they looked the parts very well, they were not so well equipped as Dench and Stride to handle Shakespeare's rich verse. Zeffirelli's screenplay cut about 60 percent of Shakespeare's text, perhaps because he preferred to show through scenic display what Shakespeare had conveyed through verse imagery. The film was immensely popular, not least because of the musical score composed especially for the film by Nino Rota.

See color plate 3, vol. 2.

A later film version of *Romeo and Juliet,* directed by Baz Lurhmann in 1996, also cut the text heavily. In addition it moved the play's setting from Verona, Italy, to present-day Verona Beach, Florida. Guns replaced swords, the Capulets and Montagues looked more like Mafia families than Renaissance aristocrats, and the prince of Verona became Captain Prince, chief of police in Verona Beach. Drugs and alcohol are ever-present in Lurhman's film and the Capulets' ball resembles a disco, complete with rock music and a swimming pool in which Romeo and Juliet frolic after their first meeting. Obviously intended for the MTV generation of the 1990s, the film was commercially successful and especially popular with young people. (*See also* **Actors, Shakespearean; Dreams;**

Duels and Feuds; Literature and Drama; Love; Plays: The Tragedies; Shakespeare on Screen; Shakespeare's Sources; Shakespeare's Works, Adaptations of.)

ROSALIND

* *usurp* to seize power from a rightful ruler

Rosalind, the central character in the comedy *As You Like It*, is one of Shakespeare's strongest and most popular heroines. Her uncle, Duke Frederick, has usurped* her father's title and banished him to the Forest of Arden, while allowing her to remain at his court as a companion for his daughter Celia. While there, Rosalind meets and falls in love with ORLANDO, a young nobleman whose brother has cheated him out of his inheritance.

Later both Rosalind and Orlando are forced to flee the court, and Rosalind disguises herself as a shepherd boy named Ganymede in order to travel safely. Both of them find their way to the Forest of Arden, where Orlando meets the disguised Rosalind without recognizing her. Hearing him express his deep love for her, she decides to test the strength of Orlando's feelings by telling him that she can "cure" him of his lovesickness. She then engages him in a mock courtship in which, while remaining disguised as Ganymede, she assumes the role of Rosalind. These multiple levels of role-playing must have been particularly complicated in Shakespeare's time, with a young male actor playing the part of Rosalind.

As a woman playing the role of a man, Rosalind is able to take liberties in her "courtship" that would not otherwise be possible for a female. Throughout the play she controls the action, testing Orlando's feelings for her and occasionally intervening on behalf of other young lovers. She explores her own emotions at the same time, and her satirical claims that "love is merely a madness" (III.ii.400) are designed to examine the basis of her affection for Orlando as well as his devotion to her. As Orlando continues to declare his love, Rosalind comes to recognize the soundness of its foundation. By the time she reveals her true identity, both Rosalind and Orlando have grown emotionally, and the childish game playing of the young lovers has been replaced by a mature understanding. Their marriage in the last act of the play is a union of two people who are truly in love but now free of romantic illusions. (*See also* **Love; Pastoralism; Plays: The Comedies.**)

ROSENCRANTZ AND GUILDENSTERN

In *Hamlet*, Rosencrantz and Guildenstern are two of the prince's former schoolmates, who are employed to find out the cause of his depression. They are summoned to court by Hamlet's uncle Claudius, who has become king by murdering Hamlet's father and marrying Gertrude, his queen. Gertrude is sure that her son will confide his problems to his old friends, but Hamlet does not trust them because he

quickly figures out that they are acting on behalf of Claudius. Critics disagree as to whether Rosencrantz and Guildenstern should be seen as agents of evil who serve the king for personal gain or as innocent victims unaware of Claudius's wicked plots.

When the prince first encounters Rosencrantz and Guildenstern in Act II, they claim that the reason for their presence in Denmark is to visit him. When pressed, however, they admit that the king and queen have sent for them. Hamlet correctly guesses the reason for the summons, admitting that his personality has undergone a serious change and that he has lost all enthusiasm for life. They suggest that his depression must be due to frustrated political ambition, but he denies that explanation and keeps them guessing as to whether he is truly insane. Later, in Act III, Hamlet turns on his former friends, insulting them and accusing them of attempting to "play" him like a musical instrument. For their part, Rosencrantz and Guildenstern are baffled by Hamlet's reaction to their efforts. Unaware of how Claudius became king, they do not realize that Hamlet sees them as enemies. They plead with Hamlet to confide in them, but he rejects them.

Hamlet's final break with his friends comes near the end of the play. Claudius asks them to escort Hamlet to England and gives them a letter to present to the English king when they arrive. Unknown to Rosencrantz and Guildenstern, the letter contains an order that the king of England kill Hamlet. The prince discovers the plot, however, and substitutes a letter that instructs the king to execute Rosencrantz and Guildenstern instead. Their ship is then attacked by pirates who take Hamlet prisoner, while Rosencrantz and Guildenstern continue on toward the death that now awaits them. Hamlet justifies his actions by claiming that his former friends "did make love to this employment" (V.ii.57) and therefore deserved their fate. At the end of the play, after all the main characters have died, a messenger arrives with the blunt announcement that "Rosencrantz and Guildenstern are dead" (V.ii.371).

British playwright Tom Stoppard used that line as the title for a dark comedy that explores the concepts of free will and fate. *Rosencrantz and Guildenstern Are Dead* is a "worm's-eye view of *Hamlet,*" presented from the perspectives of these two minor characters. When the play begins the two men have little memory of anything in their past except that they have been summoned for some reason, which they do not understand. They are not only unable to find out the source of Hamlet's troubles but are also totally confused by the actions of the other characters. They are even unsure of their own identities, as other characters frequently refer to one of them by the other's name. Pulled along by circumstances beyond their control, they finally disappear without ever understanding the reason for their existence. Stoppard suggests that, like all people, Rosencrantz and Guildenstern have lived with only the illusion of freedom, their actions constantly directed by the pen of an author whose existence they do not recognize. The meaning of their lives, as characters in a drama whose full script they cannot read, is completely beyond their ability to perceive. (*See also* **Friendship; Literature Inspired by Shakespeare; Loyalty.**)

ROWE, NICHOLAS

1674–1718
Editor and biographer of Shakespeare

Nicholas Rowe was a poet and playwright who compiled the first critical editions of Shakespeare's works and wrote the first formal biography of the dramatist. Rowe began his career as a lawyer and held a few minor political offices, but he left the legal profession to become a successful writer of tragedies. In 1715 he was named poet laureate of England.

In 1709 Rowe published the earliest collection of Shakespeare's plays to include critical notes. Five years later he produced a second edition of Shakespeare's works that included the poems. Rowe based his dramatic texts on the Fourth Folio, which contains many inaccuracies. He made a number of emendations, or changes, in many cases successfully restoring the material to what appears to be its proper condition. But modern critics and scholars object to some of his alterations because they were intended not to undo printing errors but to correct supposed flaws in Shakespeare's writing.

Rowe added several features to his volumes to make the plays more accessible both to audiences and to those who staged the plays. He was the first editor to divide all the plays into separate acts and scenes, note the stage entrances and exits of various characters, and provide a full list of the dramatis personae (characters) in each drama. He also updated Elizabethan spelling, grammar, and punctuation to make Shakespeare's language more understandable to audiences of the 1700s. His 1709 volume included a brief biography of Shakespeare, based on traditional stories and legends collected by actor Thomas Betterton. It remained the accepted version of the playwright's life for many years, even though much of its material is now considered inaccurate or fanciful. (*See also* **Actors, Shakespearean; Quartos and Folios; Shakespeare's Works, Influential Editions.**)

ROYAL SHAKESPEARE COMPANY

* *acoustics* qualities that determine how well an auditorium can reflect sound waves to produce distinct hearing

The Royal Shakespeare Company (RSC) is a modern British acting ensemble that is widely regarded as the world's foremost producer of Shakespeare's plays. The RSC is based in Shakespeare's hometown of STRATFORD-UPON-AVON, but it also operates in London and tours throughout the United Kingdom and the world. Originally called the Shakespeare Memorial Company, it was founded by Charles Edward Flower, a wealthy Stratford brewer. During the 1870s Flower championed the idea of building a memorial theater to Shakespeare, to be located in the playwright's birthplace. Flower contributed about £20,000 toward the construction of the Shakespeare Memorial Theatre, which opened in 1879. Although small and somewhat cramped, its auditorium had excellent acoustics*, which helped carry the actors' voices.

In 1886 actor and director Frank Benson took over as manager of the theater. Under his leadership it attracted both established and developing actors and staged productions almost every year until 1919. In that year W. Bridges-Adams became the theater's director. (Benson had resigned in protest over the board of directors' insistence that he no longer act in the company's productions.) The old theater burned down in 1926, and six

Royalty and Nobility

The Royal Shakespeare Company is generally considered the finest Shakespearean acting troupe in the world because it attracts star talent. In this 1976 production of *Macbeth,* the title character (Ian McKellan) confronts the three witches.

See color plate 6, vol. 3.

years later it was replaced by a larger, more modern structure that unfortunately had several problems, among them a large space between the stage and the audience. Over the next few decades the interior was modified to eliminate many of these difficulties.

Bridges-Adams resigned in 1934, and several directors ran the company until Barry Jackson took over in 1946. Jackson revitalized the theater, attracting some of the most noted Shakespearean actors and directors of the day. He was succeeded by a series of prominent figures, among them Anthony Quayle and Peter Hall. During the 1950s many famous actors, such as John Gielgud, Laurence Olivier, Peggy Ashcroft, and Richard Burton performed there. In 1961 the company adopted its current name, and its Stratford home was renamed the Royal Shakespeare Theatre. By 1964 about 750,000 people were attending productions of the Royal Shakespeare Company annually. Begun as a small group playing a two-week festival in 1879, the Royal Shakespeare Company now produces plays for a season that stretches for nine months or more each year. (*See also* **Acting Companies, Modern; Actors, Shakespearean; Directors and Shakespeare; Shakespeare Festivals.**)

ROYALTY AND NOBILITY

Elizabethan society had a highly rigid class structure in which individuals were ranked according to their status and importance in the social order. At the top of the pyramid were the monarch and the royal family. Below the royals were the nobles, members of highborn and wealthy families who often had much power and exercised significant political influence. The royalty and nobility formed an exclusive

circle that effectively ran the country and controlled most of its wealth and resources.

ROYALTY. The term *royalty* usually refers to the monarch of a country and his or her extended family. European monarchs claimed to rule by divine right, on the assumption that power was granted by God to them and their heirs. Royal succession, the order in which a ruler's heirs were in line for the throne, was based on primogeniture. According to this principle any title of nobility, including that of the ruler, passed to the oldest surviving son. This rule applied only to legitimate* children. A child born outside of marriage, called a bastard, was illegitimate and had no claim to the throne or to any other title. The monarch, however, had the power to declare a bastard (his own or someone else's) legitimate if he so chose.

If the legal heir was too young to assume the crown when the monarch died, an adult caretaker, called a regent, ruled in the child's place until the heir reached the age of 21. If the monarch had no surviving sons, a daughter could ascend the throne. Queen ELIZABETH I was one of two daughters of King Henry VIII to serve as queen of England after the death of his only male heir, who reigned briefly as King Edward VI. Succession became a more difficult matter if a monarch had no children at all. In such cases the ruler's nearest relatives were likely to argue over who should be considered the rightful heir to the throne. Because such disputes often led to bloodshed, it was wise for a childless monarch to name a specific relative as his or her heir. Near the end of her life, Queen Elizabeth declared her heir to be King James of Scotland, the son of her cousin Mary. On Elizabeth's death he peacefully ascended the throne as JAMES I.

THE PEERAGE. The nobles ranking just below the monarch were known as peers, and as a group they were referred to as the peerage. Peers were distinguished from other nobles by their right to serve in the House of Lords, one of the two houses of Parliament. There were five ranks of peers: dukes, marquesses, earls, viscounts, and barons. The titles of earl and baron were actually established earlier than those of dukes and marquesses, who ranked above them. By the 1500s earls and barons formally occupied a lower place in the hierarchy* of English nobility, but they often had more power than higher-ranking peers because their families had held titles longer.

The highest-ranking nobles were dukes, followed by marquesses. Both of these titles were first used in continental Europe and were introduced in England during the 1300s. The title of marquess, sometimes spelled *marquis,* was often granted to an individual as a sign of the monarch's special favor. Other peers, who had held their titles for many generations, sometimes resented newly created marquesses. Earls had existed much longer than dukes and marquesses, occupying the top spot in the peerage until 1337. Below earls were viscounts, another relatively new designation, first created in England in 1440. In France, where this level of peerage originated, a viscount was at one time the assistant to a count. Baron was the title held by the lowest level of peers, but it was also a term

* *legitimate* born to parents who are married to each other

See color plate 1, vol. 3.

* *hierarchy* ordered structure based on rank

used to refer to the nobility in general. The peerage as a whole was sometimes referred to as the barony.

Peers were addressed by their titles, not their family names. For example, Francis Russell, who held the earldom of Bedford, was referred to as Lord Bedford, not Lord Russell. Dukes and their wives (duchesses) were addressed as "Your Grace" and were referred to indirectly as "His Grace the Duke" or "Her Grace the Duchess." The children of peers held so-called courtesy titles. The sons of dukes and marquesses, and the oldest sons of earls, were addressed as Lord. Unmarried daughters of earls were all addressed as Lady, with the title followed by the individual's first name. For instance, Lord Bedford's daughter Margaret was known as Lady Margaret, while her mother was called Lady Bedford.

OTHER NOBLES. The lowest-ranking nobles, knights and baronets, did not have the right to serve in the House of Lords. Knighthoods were granted to those who had performed some great service to the monarch and could not be passed on to their heirs. The most prominent order of knights in Elizabethan England was the Order of the Garter, created by King Edward III in the 1300s.

King James I created the title of baronet in 1611 as a way to raise money for a military campaign in Ireland. Anyone who gave £1,100 to the crown received the title. Charles I, who succeeded James on the throne, sold baronetcies for as little as £300. Unlike knights, baronets could pass their titles to their descendants. (*See also* **Aristocracy; Social Classes.**)

SAILORS

See *Navigation; Ships; Warfare; Work.*

SANITATION

England in Shakespeare's day lacked what are today considered basic sanitary services, such as waste collection and disposal and indoor plumbing. This is not to say, however, that Elizabethans ignored personal and environmental cleanliness. Their solutions to the problems of sanitation reflected both the available technology and the prevailing attitudes concerning pollution and cleanliness.

Most of England's population lived on farms or in small villages. Because of the smaller concentration of people in these areas, rural sanitation was of less concern than urban sanitation. Large towns and cities, such as LONDON, faced serious problems in dealing with refuse. In most places home owners and tenants were responsible for cleaning up the streets that fronted their houses. In some places, however, citizens paid others to perform this service. In rare instances a city or town itself provided street cleaning. Much of the rubbish was deposited in common dumps that were located outside the city walls.

Without indoor plumbing or flush toilets, most households used chamber pots for human waste. These were typically emptied either into common cesspools or into a drainage channel in the street. Public and private latrines were also used widely. Water was used to flush excrement and other garbage from the streets into the rivers, brooks, and streams. Certain sections of the waterways were set aside for this purpose, while other parts were reserved for washing clothes or for use in manufacturing. City officials recognized the need to keep water supplies in usable condition, and government boards often oversaw the maintenance of these supplies.

In addition to the human waste and garbage generated by households, butcheries, tanneries, and other industrial establishments also produced refuse. Such businesses were usually located outside the city walls and were required to separate waste into forms that could be easily disposed of. Refuse that consisted of dung, animal parts, and sawdust were easily broken down by natural processes. These wastes were thus dumped outside the city walls and were later applied to fields as fertilizer.

The smell of garbage was a serious concern to Elizabethans, who believed that foul odors caused illness. Because municipal authorities worried about epidemic diseases, they took care to reduce odors. Ironically, because they lacked knowledge about how diseases actually spread, they did little to destroy the rats and fleas that carried devastating diseases, such as the plague* that killed millions of people in the 1300s. (*See also* **Cities, Towns, and Villages; Personal Hygiene.**)

* *plague* highly contagious and often fatal disease; also called the Black Death

SCHOOLS AND UNIVERSITIES

See color plate 10, vol. 1.

England in Shakespeare's day did not have a formal, national system of education. The state did not require children to attend school, and for many farmers and laborers reading and writing were regarded as unnecessary skills. The 1500s, however, saw many changes that made education more desirable to the average person. When England became a Protestant nation, ordinary people were encouraged to read the Bible for themselves, and advances in printing made books widely available. By the late 1500s most towns had at least one school at which local children could, if their parents wished, obtain a basic education.

BASIC EDUCATION. The most elementary lessons for children, learning the alphabet and gaining some basic proficiency in reading and writing, were ordinarily taught at home. Reading was introduced before writing, because it was considered a more important skill, and many Elizabethans could read but not write. Parents instructed their own children or, in wealthy homes, hired a private tutor. In large households a tutor might have several children to instruct, and it was fairly common for children of one upper-class family to teach those of another. For those who could not supply home instruction, some type of basic educational institution, generally known as a petty school, was usually available for children between the ages of five and seven. Classes might be taught by the local

No College Football

Students at the universities enjoyed more freedom than did grammar school boys, but there were still many rules governing their behavior. Students were forbidden to dress too extravagantly or to let their hair grow too long. Various types of recreation were prohibited. These included frequenting taverns, hawking (hunting with hawks), or attending any play in English, although plays in Latin were often put on by the students themselves. Even football (or soccer, as Americans know it) was banned on the university grounds. The fact that these rules existed suggests that such activities were fairly common; otherwise there would have been no need for regulations against them.

preacher or by a private instructor employed by the town. The cheapest form of elementary education, which later came to be known as a dame school, was provided by a local woman who offered little more than day-care services.

Since most occupations of the day did not require formal education, few children learned anything beyond the most basic level. If their parents wished it, however, they could continue their education in a grammar school. Most grammar schools had endowments—sums of money that had been set aside by wealthy donors for the purpose of maintaining the institutions. These funds paid for most of a school's costs, so that students had to pay only a small fee to attend. The grammar school young Shakespeare probably attended in Stratford-upon-Avon was free, except for the cost of school supplies: paper, ink, quill pens, and knives to sharpen them.

Most grammar schools catered solely to boys, although a few were open to girls under nine years of age. The curriculum was based on the ancient Roman system, which included the trivium (grammar, rhetoric, and logic) and the quadrivium (arithmetic, geometry, astronomy, and music). In practice the emphasis was on mastering Latin grammar, with little attention to other subjects. Latin was the language of the educated, essential for a career in law, government, or the church. Students typically memorized lessons from a grammar book written by scholar William Lily. Once they had mastered its basic lessons, they moved on to ancient writers such as Ovid, Virgil, and Seneca. Eventually they learned to translate material from Latin to English and vice versa. Other subjects, such as Greek, music, and modern languages, were sometimes taught as "extras" for an additional fee. Some subjects now considered essential were hardly taught at all, such as English grammar, which was supposed to be learned through the study of Latin grammar.

Grammar schools contained both "day" students, who lived nearby and traveled to and from school daily, and boarding students, who lived at the school. Vacations were much shorter than in modern schools, consisting of approximately two weeks off at Christmas and two at Easter. The school day was longer as well, beginning around 6 A.M. and continuing until 5 P.M., with a pause for lunch and one or two short breaks called recesses. Students were expected to remain attentive and well behaved throughout a very long day. A whipping with a birch rod awaited those who failed to learn their lessons or who broke the strict rules of behavior. Some educators objected to the methods used in English schools, arguing that learning should be a rewarding experience for students rather than a painful one. Educational reformers such as Roger Ascham, the former tutor of Queen Elizabeth I, believed that students should learn English as well as Latin and that physical punishment should be rare. Such views, however, had little influence at the time.

HIGHER EDUCATION. There were only two universities in Elizabethan England: Oxford and Cambridge, about 50 miles from London in different directions. Each of these universities was organized into separate colleges, which had originally existed to provide housing for faculty. During

See
color plate 1,
vol. 1.

* *gentry* people of high birth or social status

the 1500s it became common for all students to live and study at a particular college, although they still received their degrees from the university. In Shakespeare's day a student at Oxford could rent a good room for about £1 a year and a satisfactory one for about half that price. To save money, students sometimes shared rooms. A month's worth of meals at the college dining hall also cost about £1. Altogether, a student could enjoy a comfortable lifestyle at college for around £20 per year.

Universities were open only to men. Boys generally enrolled around age 15, although one student is known to have started Cambridge at age 9 and another did not enter until he was 38. Perhaps one-third of the students were from the upper classes—the nobility and the gentry*—with most of the rest belonging to what would today be called the middle class. About 10 percent of the students described themselves as poor. Students with little money could pay for their education by earning scholarships—funds awarded to talented students—or by taking jobs at the college. During Queen Elizabeth's reign the total population of both Oxford and Cambridge was about 3,000 students.

The curriculum at the universities was similar to that of the grammar schools, only more advanced and with somewhat more attention to Greek. Older students often taught younger ones, although quite a few students brought their tutors with them to the university. Unlike modern universities, where students earn a number of credits for each course, Elizabethan colleges awarded degrees solely on the basis of a final examination, a written theme and an oral "disputation," both in Latin, which covered all of a student's work. If the student passed, he received his degree. It took four years to earn a bachelor's degree and another three to earn a master's degree. Many students left residential colleges after receiving their bachelor's degrees, returning three years later to present their disputations and try for a master's degree. It was also common for students to leave without earning a degree at all. Few callings required a university education, and there was no shame in attending college for a few years

There were only two universities in Elizabethan England, Oxford and Cambridge. This engraving from 1882 shows the Ashmolean, a famous museum that is part of the University of Oxford.

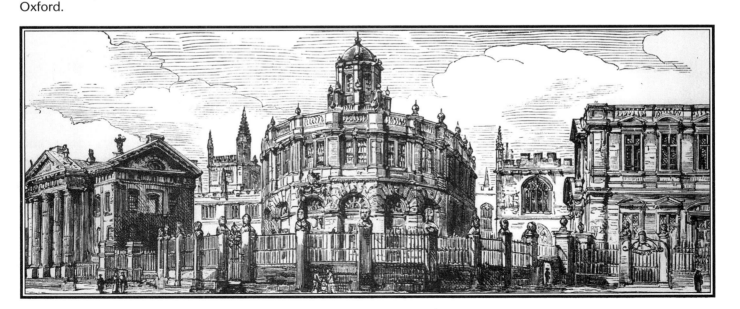

simply for the sake of learning. (*See also* **Education and Literacy; Shakespeare's Sources.**)

SCIENCE AND TECHNOLOGY

* *medieval* referring to the Middle Ages, a period roughly between A.D. 500 and 1500

Shakespeare lived during a time when new scientific ideas were beginning to replace the superstitions and folklore that had shaped European thinking during medieval* times. Discoveries in astronomy challenged the accepted view of the universe, and the invention of the printing press helped spread new scientific theories. This did not mean, however, that people stopped believing in pseudosciences, such as astrology. Science and superstition existed side by side in the minds of many Elizabethans. The same culture that produced great discoveries, such as the circulation of blood, also believed in horoscopes, magical cures, and efforts to transform base metals into silver and gold.

Elizabethan ideas about the natural world were shaped by a combination of ancient Greek philosophy, church teachings, and traditional folk wisdom. The result was a system of beliefs in which the order of the natural world was thought to reflect God's divine plan for creation. By studying the natural world, Elizabethan thinkers hoped to understand the will of its creator.

UNIVERSAL CHAIN OF COMMAND. According to Elizabethan cosmology, a set of beliefs about the origin and structure of the universe, God ordained a fixed and unchanging structure of the universe. This order was sometimes known as the Great Chain of Being. Everything that existed had a place in the hierarchy. Plants were superior to inanimate objects, such as rocks; animals were superior to plants; humans were superior to animals; angels were superior to humans; and God was superior to everything else. This order was supposedly reflected not only in the universe as a whole (the macrocosm) but within every single part of creation (the microcosm). For example, just as God controlled events in the universe from heaven, the human brain was believed to control a person's body and behavior from its position in the head. These beliefs formed the basis of much of Elizabethan science.

THE HEAVENS. In 1543 the Polish monk Nicolaus Copernicus published *On the Revolution of the Heavenly Spheres,* in which he argued that the sun was at the center of the universe and that the earth, moon, and planets revolved around it. Copernicus's theory challenged the accepted view of the cosmos, developed by the Greek philosopher Ptolemy in the A.D. 100s, which maintained that the earth was at the center of creation. In the Ptolemaic system all the heavenly bodies were set in spheres that interlocked with one another and rotated around the earth. The innermost sphere contained the moon, and it was enclosed by spheres holding the sun, planets, and stars. God and the angels occupied the outermost sphere, or primum mobile. When this sphere turned, the others moved with it and produced a sound referred to as the "music of the spheres."

The Catholic Church endorsed the Ptolemaic view of the universe, an unchanging system that was supposedly set in motion at the time of creation and overseen by God. Because Copernicus's theory contradicted this accepted wisdom, the Catholic Church opposed it and threatened to punish those who supported it. Since England no longer recognized the pope's authority, Copernicus's followers in Shakespeare's society had less to worry about than those who lived on the European continent. Indeed some Englishmen were even bolder than Copernicus in challenging Ptolemy's ideas about the universe. In 1576, for example, Thomas Digges published a book in which he rejected the idea that the heavenly realm was separated from the realm of the stars and planets. He argued that there were no heavenly spheres and that the cosmos stretched right out to the spiritual realm inhabited by God. In claiming that the universe was infinite, Digges anticipated modern astronomical thinking by several hundred years.

Although their theories seemed radical, Copernicus and Digges both cited ancient sources as precedents. During the 200s B.C. Aristarchus of Samos, a Greek astronomer, suggested that the earth revolved around the sun. Democritus, an ancient Greek philosopher who lived around the 300s B.C., had previously suggested the notion of an infinite universe. Those who developed new ideas often referred to ancient sources to give their theories legitimacy and shield themselves from the charge of "innovation" (advancing radical ideas that conflicted with church teaching). Copernicus, Digges, and others could claim that they were merely recovering truths that had once been acknowledged but had become lost over time. Elizabethan scientists often invoked religion to support their theories. Digges, for example, claimed that because God's power was infinite, it was fitting that the universe over which he exercised power be infinite as well.

Technological advances during the Elizabethan age made it possible to build machines to help with many tasks. For example, in the 1500s primitive "fire engines" were used to fight blazes in the city.

Science and Technology

* *plague* highly contagious and often fatal disease; also called the Black Death

Regardless of the stir that new theories were causing among scientists, most Elizabethans were unaffected. Although many scholars accepted Copernican ideas, few voiced their support publicly, and most books on astronomy and mathematics did not mention Copernicus at all. It was only in the early 1600s, when the Italian scientist Galileo Galilei made his observations of the heavens with a primitive telescope, that Copernicus's ideas gained wider acceptance.

LEAD INTO GOLD. Alchemy was a field of study aimed at uncovering the secrets of nature through experimentation. Alchemists are perhaps best known for their attempts to turn ordinary metals, such as lead, into precious ones, such as gold. But their efforts, like those of many Elizabethan scientists, were devoted to understanding God's creation, not to achieving wealth. Belief in alchemy was based on the idea that all things in the universe are made of differing combinations of four substances: air, fire, water, and earth. Alchemists believed that they could change one substance into another by altering the balance of the four elements. The process they sought to master was called transmutation.

Many prominent Elizabethans, including Sir Walter Raleigh, dabbled in alchemy, and books on the subject were popular. Queen ELIZABETH I believed that alchemists could help England better utilize the minerals that were being discovered in America. Although it was popular, alchemy was the subject of intense debate between its supporters and critics. To Raleigh it was a type of magic that "containeth the whole philosophy of nature." To detractors such as the playwright Ben Jonson, those who practiced alchemy committed "treason against nature." Jonson wrote a play called *The Alchemist* in which he ridiculed the so-called scientists and their gullible followers.

MEDICAL SCIENCE. Many Elizabethan beliefs about medicine were based on the ideas of ancient Greek physicians. Knowledge of the human body, for example, came largely from the work of Galen, a Greek physician who lived in the A.D. 100s. According to Galen the body was governed by four bodily fluids, or humors: blood, phlegm, yellow bile, and black bile. To maintain good health a person had to keep the humors in balance. Too much black bile, for instance, produced a brooding, depressed state called melancholy. The cures for many diseases involved removing excess humors to restore the body's natural balance. The most common methods of doing this were bleeding the patient (a process that often involved leeches) or purging his or her system with potions that induced vomiting or diarrhea.

With limited knowledge of the human body, Elizabethan doctors had little idea about how to treat most diseases effectively. A licensed physician was as likely as a folk healer to prescribe a potion containing ground up "dragon's eyes." Doctors were powerless in the face of the plague* and other serious epidemics that regularly struck England. Herbal remedies for some ailments had been popular among traditional healers for centuries, but few of them knew why such treatments worked. Some doctors began to experiment with chemical remedies, using mercury, arsenic, and other substances to treat disease. These efforts were few, however, and their results often harmed patients more than they helped them.

Despite these limitations medical advances were made during this time. In 1565 England's College of Physicians was granted the right to dissect human corpses for anatomical study. The bodies of executed criminals were commonly used for this purpose. From his study of the heart and its valves in the early 1600s, the English physician William Harvey discovered the circulation of the blood.

THE SCIENTIFIC METHOD. One factor that prevented more rapid advancement of knowledge was the traditional approach to scientific investigation. The accepted method was to propose a theory and then try to find evidence to support it. Observations that did not fit the theory were often ignored or interpreted in a light favorable to the desired outcome. In the early 1600s the English philosopher and politician Francis Bacon challenged this method. He argued that one should begin by observing nature and then come to conclusions that fit one's observations. He stressed the importance of experimentation to test one's assumptions. Bacon also realized that scientific discoveries were due not to the brilliance of individuals but to the collective efforts of many observers and that one discovery established the basis for further discoveries. Bacon's ideas profoundly influenced the work of Galileo and other scientists later in the 1600s. His concern with empirical* studies and experimentation remains a mainstay of scientific procedure to this day.

* **empirical** based on observation or experimentation

TECHNOLOGY FOR SAILORS. Technology is the application of scientific principles to the solving of practical problems. Many of the scientific breakthroughs of the Elizabethan age aided navigation. The English mathematician and astronomer Thomas Harriot invented new navigational instruments, including one that enabled sailors to determine their position by observing the sun. His work in mathematics led to the development of analytical geometry. In 1600 Sir William Gilbert published his discovery of the earth's magnetic field, which showed why a compass needle pointed north. His work led to improvements in compasses as well as to other navigational tools.

Several Elizabethan navigators published books on the art of navigation. William Bourne's *A Book Called the Treasure for Travelers* (1574) provided readers with the mathematical knowledge needed to undertake voyages. In *The Seaman's Secrets* (1595) English captain John Davys wrote about the uses of the shadow-staff, a tool he invented for the measurement of the sun's altitude. The shadow-staff greatly aided navigators because, unlike the astrolabe, it could accurately measure the sun's altitude from the deck of a ship in rough seas.

See color plate 14, vol. 1.

References to "perspective glasses" in Elizabethan writings suggest that some Englishmen were using primitive telescopes years before Galileo. Even John Dee, England's most famous astrologer, was a scientific innovator who invented new types of compasses. These pioneers helped lay the foundation for an era of discovery in the 1600s that marked the end of the Middle Ages and the beginning of the modern world. (*See also* **Astronomy and Cosmology; Disease; Herbs and Herbal Remedies; Magic and Folklore; Medicine.**)

SET DESIGNS

See *Directors and Shakespeare; Settings; Shakespearean Theater: 17th Century; Shakespearean Theater: 18th Century; Shakespearean Theater: 19th Century; Shakespearean Theater: 20th Century.*

SETTINGS

T he settings of Shakespeare's plays vary widely. In general, they fall into three main groups: English historical locations, classical* historical locations, and locations in Italy and other Mediterranean regions. To complicate matters, however, some of Shakespeare's plays combine real and imaginary settings.

* *classical* in the tradition of ancient Greece and Rome

* *Tudor* referring to the dynasty that ruled England from 1485 to 1603

ENGLISH HISTORICAL SETTINGS. Shakespeare read extensively in English history, using HOLINSHED'S CHRONICLES as his main source but borrowing also from other Tudor* historians, such as Polydore Vergil and Edward Halle. From them he learned where and when major events in English history occurred. Some of these locations were doubtless familiar to him, especially those he would have passed during his travels between STRATFORD-UPON-AVON and LONDON, such as St. Albans, Oxford, and Banbury. Scholars do not know whether Shakespeare ever visited France, the setting for several scenes in *Henry VI, Part 1* and for much of the central action of *Henry V.* He probably knew the cliffs of Dover, which he describes in vivid detail in Act IV of *King Lear.*

Most of the action of the English history plays occurs in and around London, the seat of royal power. In Shakespeare's time, the city was a very different place from the great urban center it is now. Even so, it was probably not so different then from the way it looked in the 1400s, when the action of most Shakespearean history plays occurs. In any case it matters little whether Shakespeare had an accurate image of 15th-century London because his stage lacked the elaborate scenery of a modern theater. Most necessary scenery was supplied by descriptions in the verse—and in the imagination of the audience. In addition Shakespeare sometimes staged elaborate processions in splendid COSTUMES and regalia*, as in the coronation march for Anne Bullen (Boleyn) in *Henry VIII.*

* *regalia* symbols or ornaments of royalty

Some of Shakespeare's greatest tragedies, such as *King Lear,* are also set in parts of Great Britain. When the director Peter Brook filmed this play, he went to Jutland (in present-day Denmark) to capture the primitive landscape he felt was needed. However, the stage play hardly requires that kind of setting. All that is needed is a storm for the scenes in Act III. Actors in Shakespeare's GLOBE Theater could create the effect of thunder by rolling a cannonball on a sheet of metal and could imitate lightning by setting off squibs, or fireworks.

See
color plate 4,
vol. 1.

Macbeth, set in Scotland, also involved a number of stage effects. Witches flew through the air by means of machines that could carry the actors aloft, somewhat like Peter Pan in the modern musical. The cauldron in Act IV, Scene 1, was raised through a trapdoor from beneath the stage and lowered after the scene ended. The moving forest of Birnam wood became soldiers in uniform carrying branches of trees. As in the many other battle scenes in the history plays, only a few soldiers were needed to suggest an army of many men equipped with swords, halberds*, and other weapons for the actual fighting that occurred on stage.

CLASSICAL HISTORICAL SETTINGS. For his plays dealing with classical subjects, such as *Julius Caesar* and *Coriolanus,* Shakespeare borrowed mainly from Sir Thomas North's 1579 translation of PLUTARCH'S LIVES, though he made use of other works as well. Again, the stage settings were not elaborate, nor did they need to be. Actors playing Roman senators could suggest an ancient Roman setting by throwing togas* over their Elizabethan garb. In some modern productions of *Julius Caesar,* the theater audience has been transformed into the Roman mob in the scene following Caesar's assassination, when Mark Antony stirs the crowd to revolt. The audience has served a similar function in stagings of *Coriolanus.*

In *Antony and Cleopatra,* Shakespeare's settings range over the entire known ancient world, from Rome to Athens to the Egyptian city of Alexandria and to parts of Asia Minor (present-day Turkey). In the 1700s neoclassical* critics objected to this violation of the unity of place, the concept that all the action of a play should occur in a single spot. Samuel Johnson addressed this criticism by arguing that a man who can imagine himself in Rome can imagine himself anywhere. The pleasures of Alexandria, where Mark Antony carries on his affair with Cleopatra, are contrasted with the severity of Rome through such devices as the detailed description of Cleopatra's luxurious barge that Enobarbus gives in Act II. The drunken feast aboard Pompey's ship, on the other hand, was dramatized directly on the stage, with drinking, dancing, and singing in which all the actors played their parts with gusto. Modern directors often have trouble with Antony's death scene at the end of Act IV. A literal interpretation would require the dying Antony to be hoisted up to Cleopatra's eager arms in the monument where she is hiding. At the Globe, this action was accomplished simply enough by using ropes to carry Antony into the balcony from the stage below.

Shakespeare used other simple devices to present Greece in *Timon of Athens* and Troy in *Troilus and Cressida.* For the Greek encampments outside the walls of Troy, only the suggestion of a few tents was necessary, and the Trojan council of war required merely a table and some chairs. Warriors were costumed with appropriate armor or weapons. Because plays at the Globe were performed during daylight hours, nighttime scenes were indicated by the dialogue and by the use of a few torches. Today's productions of these plays are often more elaborate, using the full capability of the modern stage and its capacity for sophisticated lighting to create sets well beyond the modest resources of the Globe.

* *halberd* type of ax mounted on a six-foot-long wooden shaft

* *toga* garment of loosely draped fabric worn in ancient Rome
* *neoclassical* referring to a school of thought, prominent in the 1800s, that focused on restoring the traditions of ancient Greece and Rome

YOUR THOUGHTS NOW MUST DECK OUR KINGS

Because Shakespeare's plays were first performed on a bare stage, the playwright relied on his verse and his audience's imagination to set the scene. The Prologue to *Henry V* urges spectators to summon up in their minds the "vasty fields of France" where the play is set and to "Think, when we talk of horses, that you see them / Printing their proud hoofs in the receiving earth" (lines 26 and 27). The audience was also told, "Into a thousand parts divide one man" (line 24), an indication that each of the actors in Shakespeare's small company was playing several roles.

Settings

ITALY AND OTHER COUNTRIES. Italy fascinated Shakespeare and his contemporaries. Travelers sought out Italy, especially Venice. The novels and stories of authors such as Giovanni Boccaccio, Matteo Bandello, and Cinthio (G. B. Giraldi) were translated into English. Many of these stories found their way into English drama and fiction, including the plays of Shakespeare.

Although several of Shakespeare's dramas are set in Italy, scholars do not know whether he ever actually visited that country, or anywhere else outside of England. Two of his earliest comedies, *Two Gentlemen of Verona* and *The Taming of the Shrew*, are set in Italian cities, and one of his most enduring tragedies, *Romeo and Juliet*, is set in Verona. *The Merchant of Venice* and *Othello* are both set in Venice, which was famous throughout the world for its wealth, its system of justice, and its toleration of outsiders, such as Moors*. The exotic qualities of this faraway region, its reputation for hot tempers and cruel behaviors, its love poetry, and its fencing masters, all combined to enchant Elizabethans and other northerners. Even the play *Measure for Measure*, supposedly set in Vienna, has major characters named Angelo, Isabella, Vincentio, and Claudio, giving the characters and the action a very Italian flavor.

*** Moor** native of North Africa; Moorish invaders conquered Spain during the Middle Ages

FICTIONAL SETTINGS. Shakespeare often combined real settings with imaginary ones or gave real places some imaginary characteristics. In *A Midsummer Night's Dream*, set in ancient Athens, the legendary Duke Theseus rules with his queen, Hippolyta. The play's action also moves outside Athens to an enchanted forest controlled by Oberon and Titania, king and queen of the fairies. Yet fairies are not the only creatures found within the borders of this forest: a group of "rude mechanicals" (Athenian craftsmen) meet there to rehearse a play. These workmen are neither products of fantasy nor classical Athenians; rather, there are ordinary men straight out of Shakespeare's Warwickshire (the region surrounding his home village of Stratford). Similarly, the FOREST OF ARDEN, scene of the main action of *As You Like It*, is based on—but significantly different from—a real forest in France known as the Ardennes. Here again, country bumpkins such as William and Audrey live alongside the unrealistically refined shepherds Silvius and Phebe, types drawn from the pastoral* poetry that was popular in England in the late 1500s.

*** pastoral** relating to the countryside; often used to draw a contrast between the innocence and serenity of rural life and the corruption and extravagance of court life

The settings for other plays are sometimes updated in modern productions. In the 1980s the Folger Theatre Group, for example, set the comedy *Much Ado About Nothing* aboard a cruise ship. At the New York Shakespeare Festival in 1972, the same play was set in the United States at the time of the Spanish-American War. In 1993 the ROYAL SHAKESPEARE COMPANY staged *The Merchant of Venice* in contemporary dress, with Shylock's office in the financial district of the City of London. A Young Vic production of *Richard II* presented King Richard looking very much like the Russian czar Nicholas II, and Bolingbroke (who overthrows the king) as Vladimir Lenin. By updating the settings, directors try to bring not only the time of the play but also the action and the themes closer to their audience, as Baz Luhrman did in his film version of *Romeo and Juliet*, set not in Verona, Italy, but in Verona Beach, Florida.

Shakespeare's own use of GEOGRAPHY was far from exact. He gave the landlocked kingdom of Bohemia a seacoast in *The Winter's Tale.* For the setting of *The Tempest*, he invented an isolated island in the Mediterranean Sea that resembled the islands explorers had recently discovered in the Caribbean. None of this is particularly surprising. Most of Shakespeare's settings, after all, are countries of the mind, landscapes of the imagination, peopled by imaginary characters who serve to delight and entertain—even as they reflect the natures, tendencies, and attitudes of an altogether human audience. (*See also* **Arms and Armor; Craftworkers; Dramatic Techniques; Elizabethan Theaters; Exploration; History in Shakespeare's Plays: Ancient Greece and Rome; History in Shakespeare's Plays: England; Italy in Shakespeare's Plays; Shakespeare on Screen; Shakespeare's Sources; Shakespeare's Works, Changing Views.**)

SEVEN AGES OF MAN

One of the most famous speeches in Shakespeare is Jaques' description of the seven ages of man in *As You Like It.* The idea that human life could be divided into seven stages was a familiar one to Renaissance audiences, but Jaques turns the concept into a reflection on the futility of all human striving. His speech, which reflects a pessimistic outlook, is rejected by the other characters, who prefer to take a more positive view of humanity.

Jaques is a member of the court of Duke Senior, who has been banished to the forest of ARDEN after being overthrown by his brother, Frederick. ORLANDO has just stumbled into the duke's camp, seeking food for himself and for his old, faithful servant Adam. Their pitiful situation causes the duke to reflect that "we are not all alone unhappy" in "this wide and universal theater" (II.vii.136–37). Jaques seizes on the duke's metaphor* to remark, "All the world's a stage" (139) on which every person plays different parts. As he describes seven typical roles—infant, schoolboy, lover (adolescent), soldier (young man), justice (middle age), old man, and finally the senile elder near death—Jaques focuses on the weaknesses, follies, and drawbacks of each stage in the normal life span. He concludes his speech with the observation that everyone will end in "second childishness, and mere oblivion, / Sans* teeth, sans eyes, sans taste, sans every thing" (165–66). Immediately after Jaques finishes his speech, Orlando reenters with Adam, and the devotion he shows to the old man contrasts vividly with the gloomy view of old age just expressed.

The idea of the world as a stage appears in several of Shakespeare's other plays as well. Some characters, like Jaques, see the pageant of life as pointless. The title character in *Macbeth*, for example, calls it "a tale told by an idiot" (V.v.25–26). Other characters' observations are not so much bitter as thoughtful. When PROSPERO comments in *The Tempest* that all of life is like an "insubstantial pageant" that will fade away into nothingness (IV.i.155), the idea he expresses is not that life is meaningless but rather that it is fleeting and that its full significance can be understood only in the afterlife if at all.

* *metaphor* figure of speech in which one object or idea is directly identified with a different object or idea

* *sans* without

SEXUALITY

See *Gender and Sexuality; Homosexuality.*

SHAKESPEARE FESTIVALS

Organized by actor David Garrick, the Jubilee of 1769 was the first Shakespeare festival. It ran for three days and included a series of parades and costume balls.

The word *festival* suggests a celebration of some kind, a specific event on a specific date. Many of the organizations that call themselves Shakespeare festivals, however, are actually theater companies that produce the playwright's works on a regular basis. Some of them present other classic works of drama in addition to Shakespeare's. Other festivals are annual events that feature one or more Shakespearean plays. The earliest festivals took place in England, but most of today's important ones are in North America. Canada boasts one of the finest Shakespeare festivals in the world, and more than 30 significant festivals are to be found in locales throughout the United States.

ENGLAND. In September 1769 the world's first Shakespeare festival was held in the playwright's home town of STRATFORD-UPON-AVON. Planned by Stratford's town authorities, the first Stratford Shakespearean festival ran for three days and featured a wide array of ceremonies and events, including parades, masked balls, speeches, and fireworks. The famous actor David Garrick organized and directed these activities, which were collectively known as the Jubilee of 1769. He also provided the highlight of the gathering, an oration titled *Ode upon Dedicating a Building, and Erecting a Statue, to Shakespeare.* The festival was counted a success, even though it

A Shakespearean Setting

Several Shakespeare festivals have attempted to re-create the Elizabethan theaters and stages where Shakespeare's plays were originally performed. The earliest productions of the San Diego Shakespeare Festival were staged in the open-air Old Globe Theater, which was modeled after the Bankside Globe in London. Both the Stratford and Oregon festivals constructed new stages that re-created the look and many of the features of Elizabethan stages.

* **ensemble** referring to a group of actors or musicians working together to produce a single effect

rained heavily and scarcely a line by Shakespeare was spoken or performed during the festivities.

It would be another century before a regular Shakespeare festival was held in England. In 1879 Stratford-upon-Avon again hosted a celebration of Shakespeare's work, this time with actual performances of two Shakespearean plays. The affair began on April 23, Shakespeare's supposed birthday, and lasted for two weeks. This festival became an annual event and eventually gave rise to the Shakespeare Memorial Theater, later renamed the Royal Shakespeare Theatre (home to the ROYAL SHAKESPEARE COMPANY, which continues to perform in Stratford, as well as in London and on tour outside of Great Britain).

CANADA. The Stratford Festival in Ontario, Canada, is the leading Shakespeare festival in North America. The idea of a Canadian festival was first proposed in 1952 by newspaperman Tom Patterson. Stratford's town officials sent him to England to investigate the possibility of arranging such an event. Patterson met with director Tyrone Guthrie and persuaded him to present two plays in Stratford the following year. The world-famous actor Alec Guinness agreed to appear as the lead in *Richard III* and as the king of France in *All's Well That Ends Well*.

Uncertain of the festival's prospects, Stratford officials were reluctant to spend a great deal of money on building a theater. For this reason the initial performances were held in a canvas circus tent. The stage was designed to resemble the open stages of Shakespeare's day, with a large platform projecting out into the audience. At the rear of the main playing area stood a smaller platform raised on columns and accessible by two visible staircases. This structure could be used as an upper level or curtained off to create a hidden inner alcove. This design would eventually become the model for Shakespearean stages in both the United States and England.

The Canadian festival broke ground by hiring local actors and actresses to play most of the roles rather than recruiting star players. This local talent pool formed a powerful ensemble* cast. The festival was a great success and grew tremendously over time, gaining a permanent building in 1957. It has featured the talents of such well-known directors as Peter Hall and John Neville and such performers as Brian Bedford, Zoe Caldwell, Christopher Plummer, Jason Robards, Paul Scofield, and Maggie Smith.

UNITED STATES. The United States plays host to more Shakespeare festivals than any other country in the world. The oldest is the Oregon Shakespeare Festival, which mounted its first production in 1935. It has run continuously from that date, except from 1941 to 1946, during World War II. Most American Shakespeare festivals began after the war. The San Diego National Shakespeare Festival staged some shortened versions of Shakespeare's plays during the 1935–1936 Pacific International Exposition, but it did not become an annual event until 1949, with a performance of *Twelfth Night*. The festival now presents three or more plays each summer, usually chosen from among the playwright's most popular works.

In the early 1950s director Joseph Papp proposed the idea of a free Shakespeare festival to be held in New York City. The first performance took place in 1954 in the Emmanuel Presbyterian Church on East 6th Street. Two years later the city allowed Papp to use the East River Amphitheater for his productions, and in 1957 the festival moved to its current home in Central Park. A permanent theater replaced the temporary stage in 1962. The New York Shakespeare Festival formed a second troupe in 1964 to perform in parks and playgrounds around the city on a specially designed portable stage.

For years Stratford, Connecticut, was home to the American Shakespeare Festival Theater and Academy, which opened in 1955. Some of the world's finest actors have appeared on its stage, among them Hal Holbrook, Raymond Massey, Roddy McDowell, Jack Palance, Katharine Hepburn, and Jessica Tandy. Actor, director, and producer John Houseman served as its artistic director for several years in the late 1950s. Other major festivals in the United States include the Alabama Shakespeare Festival in Montgomery, the Colorado Shakespeare Festival in Boulder, the Utah Shakespearean Festival in Cedar City, and the Shakespeare Theater in Washington, D.C. (*See also* **Acting Companies, Modern.**)

See
color plate 6,
vol. 2.

SHAKESPEARE, LIFE AND CAREER

William Shakespeare lived 52 years, married once, fathered three children, bought a house and lands, and wrote more than a million enduring words of lyric and dramatic literature. For scholars the lack of reliable evidence about the playwright's life is frustrating. Compared with most playwrights of his era, Shakespeare left behind a fair number of documents about his professional, financial, and personal life, but this material provides little sense of what Shakespeare was like as a living, feeling person. Many critics have tried to discover an image of the writer in his works, but this evidence is also subject to scrutiny, since the utterances in his plays reflect the ideas of his characters, not necessarily the playwright's own. Scholars are thus forced to piece together from a limited body of evidence, both literary and biographical, a portrait of the artist.

See
color plate 4,
vol. 3.

A YOUNG MAN IN A SMALL TOWN

Shakespeare was born into a modest but respectable family in a small town in central England. He was probably educated at the local grammar school. He married a woman from a nearby village and might easily have settled into family life and business. Instead he became part of a bustling theater scene in the capital city of LONDON, although no one is sure how and when he ended up there.

FAMILY BACKGROUND. Shakespeare's hometown was STRATFORD-UPON-AVON, about 90 miles northwest of London. The man who was probably Shakespeare's grandfather, Richard Shakespeare, was a farmer in the village of Snitterfield, about three miles north of Stratford. Richard rented land from a man named Robert Arden. Around 1557 Richard's son John married Robert Arden's youngest daughter, Mary. Because the Ardens were landowners with a distinguished history in the area, the marriage boosted the Shakespeares' social status.

John and Mary Shakespeare lived in Stratford, where John went into business treating animal skins and making gloves. They lived in half of a large double house on Henley Street, now known as the Birthplace. The Shakespeares had four daughters and four sons, with William being the third child and the oldest boy. John Shakespeare became a respected citizen, and in 1568 he served a one-year term as bailiff, or mayor. Yet records show that he signed documents with a mark—an X, or perhaps a small symbol representing his trade—which suggests that the father of England's most honored poet could not write his own name.

SHAKESPEARE'S YOUTH. Town records show that William Shakespeare was baptized on April 26, 1564. Since baptism was traditionally performed a few days after birth, Shakespeare's birthday is commonly assumed to have been either April 22 (the date when his granddaughter Elizabeth Hall was later to be married) or April 23 (the date, St. George's Day, when the poet died in 1616). From the age of six or seven, he probably studied at the King's New School in Stratford. Like other grammar schools of the day, this one would have provided a background in Latin, plus a little Greek, and an introduction to classical* works of religion, philosophy, and literature. Shakespeare's first biographer, Nicholas ROWE, reports that William left school in his early teens to help in his father's shop. Records of the time show that John Shakespeare's finances were failing and that he had withdrawn from public life.

See color plate 3, vol. 1.

* *classical* in the tradition of ancient Greece and Rome

Shakespeare grew up in the small market town of Stratford-upon-Avon. This photograph shows his childhood home, which has been preserved by the Shakespeare Birthplace Trust.

SHAKESPEARE IN TROUBLE

Many legends surround the life of Shakespeare, most of them unverified. One story claims that as a teenager he was caught poaching (illegally hunting) deer on land owned by a local gentleman, Sir Thomas Lucy. According to one version, William was whipped and imprisoned for his repeated offenses, and he eventually fled Stratford to escape from Lucy. In revenge Shakespeare supposedly composed vulgar ballads about Sir Thomas. Some see the ridiculous Justice Shallow in *The Merry Wives of Windsor* as a parody of Lucy. In any case Lucy's name now survives thanks to Shakespeare.

* **sonnet** poem of 14 lines with a fixed pattern of meter and rhyme

* **tetralogy** four-part series of literary or dramatic works

* **genre** literary form

In 1582 at the age of 18, William Shakespeare married Anne Hathaway, who lived in the village of Shottery about one mile west of Stratford. Anne was eight years older than William—and she was three months pregnant. To hasten their wedding the local bishop agreed that plans for it could be announced in church on one Sunday only instead of the three Sundays that were normally required. Six months after the ceremony, Anne gave birth to a daughter, Susanna, and two years later came twins, a son named Hamnet and a daughter named Judith.

THE "LOST YEARS." No records related to Shakespeare's life exist for seven years after the birth of the twins. In 1592 the London playwright Robert Greene wrote a pamphlet called A GROATSWORTH OF WIT, in which he criticized Shakespeare as "an upstart crow, beautified with our feathers." Greene's bitterness suggests that Shakespeare had by then become a popular and successful playwright, a young man outshining an older rival.

Historians have no reliable information about these "lost years" between 1585 and 1592. Many theories have been proposed to explain how a young man from Stratford became a skilled dramatist whose plays show extensive knowledge of topics as varied as law, court customs, military life, and Italian cities. Shakespeare may have spent this period engaged in one or more occupations, perhaps as a soldier, a sailor, a law clerk, a schoolteacher, or a traveling actor. The references in his plays suggest that he was familiar with the practices of these and dozens of other occupations.

EARLY LITERARY CAREER

Once he arrived in London, Shakespeare established himself both as an actor and as a playwright. He was as involved in the management of the theater as in its artistic aspects, owning a share in the Chamberlain's Men, a successful acting company. He also won admiration for his lyric and narrative verses, which included two long poems and more than 150 sonnets*.

EARLY PLAYS. Shakespeare probably began as an actor in one of several acting companies. He soon tried his hand at playwriting, and between 1590 and 1593 he scored popular hits with a tetralogy* of history plays about the WARS OF THE ROSES, the English civil wars of the 1400s. *Henry VI*, in three parts, traces the king's development from an innocent youth to a still innocent adult, pleading weakly for peace while his ambitious nobles rebel. The four-play sequence concludes with *Richard III*. Shakespeare's first brilliant villain, Richard manipulates the other nobles to gain the throne, all the while mocking them behind their backs. Taken as a set, the tetralogy emphasizes the idea that God has tested, punished, and purified England through a series of bloody conflicts. Peace is restored when Richard is defeated by Henry VII, the grandfather of Queen ELIZABETH I.

Shakespeare's first play in the genre* of comedy may have been *The Comedy of Errors*, which uses the confusion created when two long-separated twins, with servants who are also twins, arrive in the same city. *The Taming*

See color plate 4, vol. 3.

of the Shrew is a rowdy battle of the sexes in which the sharp-tempered KATHARINA and the fortune-hunting PETRUCHIO come to a mutual understanding. These early comedies combine the classical style, popular in France and Italy, with the vigorous earthy spirit of English comedy. In his other romantic comedies—*The Two Gentlemen of Verona* (believed by some to be his earliest work), *Love's Labor's Lost,* and *A Midsummer Night's Dream*—Shakespeare explored the conventions of PASTORALISM. The lovers in these plays learn about themselves by escaping from society to the green countryside, where they find themselves in unexpected situations. The dialogue in these comedies often suggests that theater is a similar place of escape for the audience.

In the mid-1590s Shakespeare made another venture into English history with *King John,* which dramatizes a power struggle of the 1200s. He also made his second attempt at tragedy with *Romeo and Juliet.* His first tragedy, *Titus Andronicus,* is a grim bloodbath that closely follows the patterns of classical revenge tragedy. *Romeo and Juliet* is much less gory and far more touching. This story of two young people kept apart by their families had as much emotional appeal then as it does today. The characters are sympathetic, and their sad fate comes mainly from bad luck and misunderstanding rather than from the kind of inner flaw or moral failing that plays so important a part in the later tragedies.

LONG POEMS AND SONNETS. In the early 1590s severe outbreaks of the plague* closed the theaters for months at a time. During these lulls Shakespeare seems to have devoted himself to poetry. In 1593 he published *Venus and Adonis,* dedicated to a young nobleman, Henry Wriothesley, the earl of Southampton. Its subject is the goddess Venus and her romantic pursuit of the young hunter Adonis. The poem followed a popular style, with carefully crafted language and witty sexual puns. Of all the Shakespearean works printed during his lifetime, *Venus and Adonis* was the poet's best seller.

A year later Shakespeare published another long poem, *The Rape of Lucrece,* describing a violent incident from Roman history. He dedicated this piece to Southampton, too, describing it as a "graver labor" than *Venus and Adonis.* It seems to have won the praise of critics but was less popular with the public than his earlier poem. In all likelihood Shakespeare carefully supervised the publication of these two poems, something he seems not to have done with his plays, which were considered a lower form of literature at the time.

Shakespeare's SONNETS were not published until 1609, but he probably began writing them during the early 1590s. Some are addressed to a young nobleman whom many scholars identify as Southampton. Handwritten copies of the sonnets were circulated privately among selected acquaintances, whose admiration helped Shakespeare's poetic reputation grow.

RISING FORTUNES. Historical records show that by the time the theaters reopened in 1594, Shakespeare was an established member of the Chamberlain's Men, which like most acting companies was named after its patron*. Shakespeare was one of several "actor-sharers" who managed the

* ***plague*** highly contagious and often fatal disease; also called the Black Death

* ***patron*** supporter or financial sponsor of an artist or writer

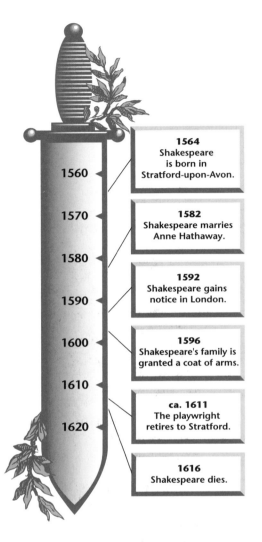

1564
Shakespeare
is born in
Stratford-upon-Avon.

1560

1582
Shakespeare marries
Anne Hathaway.

1570

1580

1592
Shakespeare gains
notice in London.

1590

1596
Shakespeare's family is
granted a coat of arms.

1600

1610

ca. 1611
The playwright
retires to Stratford.

1620

1616
Shakespeare dies.

* *depose* to remove from high office, often
by force

See
color plate 9,
vol. 2.

company and received portions of its profits. He acted in many of the plays the company staged, including his own, often in small but significant roles such as the Ghost in *Hamlet*. But his most significant contribution was scriptwriting, which—along with the talent of Richard Burbage, the era's greatest actor, who usually played the leading male roles—made the Chamberlain's Men the most prominent troupe in England.

Shakespeare lived in various places near the London theaters, but he kept close ties to his family and community in Stratford, probably returning at least once a year. As the Chamberlain's Men prospered, so did its principal dramatist, and he was soon considered a leading citizen of Stratford. His income varied from year to year, but it eventually averaged around £200, an impressive amount in an era when a servant might live on £3 per year. In 1596 the playwright helped his father obtain a coat of arms for the family, improving the family's status in society. That same year his son, Hamnet, died at the age of 11. One year later Shakespeare bought New Place, a three-story mansion in Stratford, and his wife and daughters moved in.

SHAKESPEARE'S ART GROWS. Shakespeare continued to develop his talents during the late 1590s, producing a string of notable successes. The comedies he wrote during this period were darker and more complex than his earlier works. Most of them deal in some way with DISGUISE, which conceals characters' outer identities and frees them to explore their inner selves. In three comedies—*The Merchant of Venice, As You Like It,* and *Twelfth Night*—young women disguise themselves as men, releasing themselves from society's expectations about gender. Another witty and clever woman, Beatrice, steals the show in *Much Ado About Nothing* as she engages in a "merry war" of words with the equally amusing Benedick. These intelligent, unconventional heroines help make Shakespeare's middle comedies some of his most popular and enjoyable works.

While completing these comedies Shakespeare also wrote a masterful new tetralogy of history plays, sometimes called the Henriad because it centers on King Henry IV and his son, Henry V. These plays explore the power struggles behind the civil wars of the previous tetralogy. In *Richard II* the immature and self-indulgent King Richard is deposed* by Henry IV, whose own reign is unstable and troubled as a result. The next two plays—*Henry IV, Part 1* and *Henry IV, Part 2*—focus on the king's son, Prince Hal, whose loyalties are torn between his father and his fun-loving but untrustworthy companion FALSTAFF. Hal eventually accepts his duties and banishes Falstaff, becoming a strong, brave leader in *Henry V,* but he also undertakes a morally questionable war against the French. Shakespeare revived the character of Falstaff in a comedy, *The Merry Wives of Windsor,* in which the old knight tries to woo a married woman and outsmart her jealous husband. The play reflects a style known as the comedy of humors, in which each character is identified by a particular habit or trait.

While writing plays at the rate of about two a year, Shakespeare probably continued to work on his sonnets, and it is conceivable that all 154 poems were completed by 1598. They are Shakespeare's only nondramatic writings in the first person. The sonnets contain many emotions, including devotion, fear, trust, jealousy, and a desire for immortality through art. Many readers have looked for Shakespeare's life and personality in the sonnets, but there is no indisputable way to connect these works with his life. Around 1601 Shakespeare also produced one or two longer poems. In "A Lover's Complaint," a minor poem that some scholars claim is not Shakespeare's work, a shepherdess laments her lover's dishonesty. In "The Phoenix and Turtle" he contemplates the union of two lovers, the embodiments of truth and beauty.

THE MATURE ARTIST

By the early 1600s Shakespeare's career was at its height. He had mastered the romantic comedy and the English history play, and his acting company had just constructed a handsome new theater, the GLOBE. In 1603 Queen Elizabeth died, and the new king, JAMES I, became the company's patron. The leading actors of the group, now known as the King's Men, wore royal colors at James's coronation. Meanwhile in his Stratford life, Shakespeare invested in farmland and other commercial ventures. In 1607 his daughter Susanna married John Hall, a respected doctor.

Shakespeare began to investigate the genre of tragedy. This form enabled him to pursue deep questions about human morality without the need for humor or flashy battle scenes. He also ventured into unusual, mixed forms: the dark, satirical* comedies known as the problem plays and the strange, magical works known as the romances. After writing his last plays, Shakespeare retired to Stratford as a gentleman.

* **satirical** ridiculing human wickedness and foolishness

THE MATURE TRAGEDIES. Shakespeare's major tragedies focus on human madness and weakness. The main character is usually a noble person with some inner flaw that leads to his downfall. In *Julius Caesar,* first performed in 1599, the central character is the Roman statesman BRUTUS. He attempts to save Rome from Caesar's ambitious pride but does not recognize a similar failing in himself. The murder sets off a civil war, causes senseless bloodshed, and eventually leads to Brutus's own death.

Many of the late tragedies focus on the darker side of human nature. Characters are frequently tormented by fear of and disgust for sexuality, especially in women. In *Hamlet,* for example, the hero's dissatisfaction with the world is linked to his inability to accept his mother's second marriage. When he learns that the uncle she has married was responsible for his father's death, Hamlet is torn between his desire for revenge and his fears about the physical and moral consequences of committing suicide or killing a king. The terror of female sexuality is seen most vividly in *Othello.* The interracial marriage between Othello and DESDEMONA appears healthy and strong, but IAGO manipulates Othello's doubts and fears and persuades him that Desdemona is unfaithful. Othello becomes obsessed with images of sex as an act of beasts and, mad with jealousy, strangles his wife.

See color plate 14, vol. 2.

This distrust of women is also a major theme in *King Lear,* where an old king gives up his throne to two ungrateful daughters while mistreating and rejecting his only loyal daughter, CORDELIA. He loses his kingdom, his family, and his sanity, and dies in despair. A similar violation of social

order occurs in *Macbeth.* A fiercely driven Lady Macbeth taunts her husband into murdering King Duncan and taking his crown. Her desire for power is presented as perverse and unnatural, a violation with parallels to Macbeth's own crime.

Antony and Cleopatra is a tragic love story like *Romeo and Juliet,* but the doomed lovers do not evoke the audience's sympathy in the same way. Antony, a Roman general, abandons Rome for a life of pleasure with Cleopatra in Egypt. He knows that his choice is shameful, but he prefers it to the cold politics of Rome. Unlike the strong women in most of Shakespeare's tragedies, Cleopatra is confident in her sexuality without being monstrous or unnatural.

Shakespeare's final tragedies are profoundly pessimistic. *Coriolanus* portrays a fiery Roman warrior whose dependence on his fearsome mother, Volumnia, ends up bewildering him and leads to his downfall. The main character in *Timon of Athens* is a bitter old man who retreats from a society he sees as utterly corrupt. He drives away his loyal friends and servants and resolves to live alone in a cave, cursing all of humanity.

VARIATIONS ON COMEDY. Although many of the plays Shakespeare wrote toward the end of his career have been classified as comedies, they include elements of tragedy that complement and complicate their comical aspects. The three "problem plays," written in the early 1600s, feature an uneasy mixture of humor and bitterness. *All's Well That Ends Well* portrays a young woman's unrequited* love for a nobleman and the trickery she is forced to use to win him as her husband. *Troilus and Cressida* centers on an ill-fated love affair, but unlike Romeo and Juliet or Antony and Cleopatra, the lovers in this play are too limited by time and circumstance to form a meaningful commitment. The characters of *Measure for Measure* struggle with a fear of sexuality that leads them to extremes of self-righteous purity and guilty lust. All these plays combine tragic or near-tragic events with a darkly mocking humor and few, if any, completely admirable characters.

A more optimistic outlook is found in the romances, a new genre that Shakespeare developed around the time he completed his major tragedies in 1608. These plays resemble romantic comedies, but the characters are more anxious and troubled. Events seem destined to lead toward tragedy, but with a sense of magic and wonder, they ultimately end in reunion and renewed hope. Death is a real presence in these plays, as it is not in the earlier comedies, but characters who are believed dead often return to be joyfully reunited with their loved ones. The bond between father and daughter, in particular, is emphasized as a source of restorative love.

In *Pericles* the hero is separated from his wife and daughter, but a form of divine protection carries them through their many trials to a touching reunion. *Cymbeline* and *The Winter's Tale* offer parallels to *Othello.* A central figure becomes wrongly convinced that his wife is unfaithful, and it appears that his story will have a similarly tragic ending. Unlike Othello, however, the characters in these plays overcome their fears and doubts, allowing them to be happily reconciled with the wives and families they thought were lost forever. In Shakespeare's final romance, *The*

* *unrequited* not returned

Tempest, the wizard PROSPERO rules his island home with magical spells, and his mastery of illusion and reality is compared to that of a dramatist. Eventually Prospero learns to give up his urge to control and comes to terms with the outside world.

SHAKESPEARE'S LAST DAYS. Around 1611 Shakespeare appears to have left London to live in Stratford with his family but continued to be involved in the theater business. In 1613 he bought the gatehouse of BLACK-FRIARS, an indoor theater where the King's Men performed. He also interrupted his retirement at least twice. He wrote a history play, *Henry VIII,* about the troubled reign of a relatively recent monarch. This play may have been coauthored by John Fletcher, the new leading playwright of the King's Men, who also worked with Shakespeare on a romance called *The Two Noble Kinsmen.*

In February 1616 Shakespeare's daughter Judith married Thomas Quiney, who was soon caught in an affair. A Stratford physician, John Ward, wrote in his diary that around that time—perhaps at the wedding celebrations—Shakespeare had a "merry meeting" with playwrights Ben JONSON and Michael Drayton and developed a fever caused by excessive drinking. Lying ill, Shakespeare altered his will to provide for Judith, perhaps not trusting her new husband to do so. He left most of his property to Susanna's family. He mentions his wife, Anne, only to see that she receives their second-best bed, which may have been the couple's usual sleeping place. He also left money to some of his fellow actors from the King's Men—Richard Burbage, John Heminges, and Henry Condell—to buy memorial rings. On April 23, 1616, Shakespeare died. Seven years later Heminges and Condell published the FIRST FOLIO, containing 36 of Shakespeare's plays and ensuring that his art would live long after him. (*See also* **Acting Profession; Authorship, Theories About; Plays: The Comedies; Plays: The Histories; Plays: The Romances; Plays: The Tragedies.**)

SHAKESPEARE ON SCREEN

* *soliloquy* monologue in which a character reveals his or her private thoughts

In the late 1890s the new technology of motion pictures inspired a creative rush to document and represent the world. In the search for film-worthy material, some moviemakers found Shakespeare a natural. The frequent scene changes in the plays were well suited to the pace of film. In addition Shakespeare's intimate soliloquies* and conversations were perfect for camera close-ups. But actors and directors were forced to confront new challenges, such as how best to convey Shakespeare's ideas and his characters' emotions to film. This search was part of the cinema's growth into a mature medium of expression.

THE ERA OF SILENT FILMS. The first "Shakespearean" film, produced in 1899, captured a short section of Herbert Beerbohm Tree's production of *King John.* Over the next three decades dozens of silent films based on Shakespeare's plays were made. Most were straightforward documents of

stage performances, with some of the dialogue appearing in full-screen captions between sections of the performance. The lack of sound apparently did not hurt the popularity of the films, and historians are grateful to the early filmmakers for recording the acting styles of many famous actors, including Sarah Bernhardt as the young prince in *Hamlet* (1900) and Frank Benson in the title role of *Richard III* (1911). By the early 1900s filmmakers were creating new styles specifically for film and were staging scenes that would have been impossible in theater. The Italian director Enrico Guazzoni, for example, produced a spectacular *Julius Caesar* (1914) with 20,000 cast members.

EARLY SOUND FILMS. The "talkies," films with recorded sound, began to appear in theaters in the late 1920s, offering new freedom for filmmakers—if they knew how to use it. One of the first Shakespeare talkies was *The Taming of the Shrew* (1929), starring the famous Hollywood couple Mary Pickford and Douglas Fairbanks. It was a flop, as were most Shakespeare films of the 1930s. Studios and directors often failed to shake off the limitations of stage productions and sometimes made poor casting decisions. In a 1936 film version of *Romeo and Juliet,* for example, a 43-year-old actor and a 36-year-old actress played the teenage lovers.

THE FILMS OF LAURENCE OLIVIER. The first visionary director to adapt Shakespeare to film was Laurence Olivier. Olivier began his career as an actor on the British stage, but he later played in films, several of which he directed. His first cinematic success, *Henry V* (1944), was bold and patriotic and inspired English nationalism during World War II as Shakespeare's play had done during the Elizabethan era. Olivier opens and closes the film as if it is being performed in the GLOBE THEATER. The film then moves to a realistic setting, showing the London streets, the French court, and a spectacular battle scene.

In *Hamlet* (1948) Olivier created a movie that visually matched his interpretation of the play. The black-and-white scenes are full of fog and shadows, and the camera silently roams the castle, lingering on sexual images, such as the queen's bed. The sets and props are minimal, allowing room for the audience's imagination to wander in as well. In *Richard III* (1955), however, Olivier returned to a more artificial, stagelike setting. King Richard is portrayed as a complex man who murders the simple, naive characters around him. Oliver's last Shakespearean film was *Othello* (1965), which was more a showcase for his talent as an actor than for his ideas as a filmmaker.

THE FILMS OF ORSON WELLES. One of cinema's most creative pioneers, the American actor and director Orson Welles, turned his efforts to Shakespeare's plays several times. He described his film version of *Macbeth* (1948) as "a violently sketched charcoal drawing of a great play." The acting in the movie is poor, but Welles provides a wealth of striking visual images. There is a close-up of Macbeth's bloody hands, for example, and a scene in which the three weird sisters crown a clay figure of Macbeth in a mock coronation.

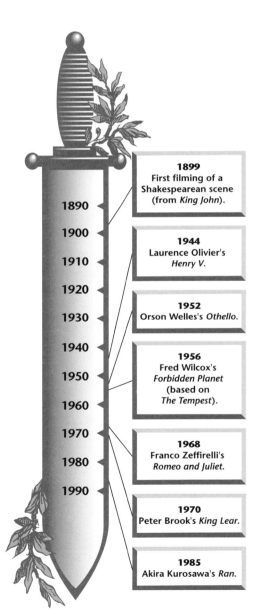

1899
First filming of a Shakespearean scene (from *King John*).

1890
1900
1910
1920
1930
1940
1950
1960
1970
1980
1990

1944
Laurence Olivier's *Henry V*.

1952
Orson Welles's *Othello*.

1956
Fred Wilcox's *Forbidden Planet* (based on *The Tempest*).

1968
Franco Zeffirelli's *Romeo and Juliet*.

1970
Peter Brook's *King Lear*.

1985
Akira Kurosawa's *Ran*.

After creating two Shakespearean films in the 1960s, Italian director Franco Zeffirelli returned to the playwright's works in 1990 with a version of *Hamlet* that featured Mel Gibson as the Danish prince and Glenn Close as Gertrude.

See color plate 3, vol. 2.

Like Olivier, Welles acted the role of Othello (1952) in dark makeup. He used images in the film to contrast the noble stature of Othello with the base, envious IAGO. Othello is seen in soaring shots with grand buildings, while Iago is filmed with harsh angles and sharp motions. Welles returned to Shakespeare with *Chimes at Midnight* (1965), an adaptation of material from *Henry IV, Part 1*; *Henry IV, Part 2*; and *Henry V*. Even without support from the Hollywood studio system, Welles succeeded in creating a highly praised film.

OTHER MAJOR SHAKESPEARE FILMS. Olivier and Welles were not the only filmmakers to find in Shakespeare a rich source of material. Hollywood threw all its resources behind major productions, such as *Julius Caesar* (1953) directed by Joseph L. Mankiewicz. Its stars included both established stage actors, such as the great Sir John Gielgud (as Cassius), and young movie stars, such as Marlon Brando (as Mark Antony). Britain's ROYAL SHAKESPEARE COMPANY contributed its best directors and actors to the cinema. Peter Hall directed members of the RSC in *A Midsummer Night's Dream* (1969), and Peter Brook did the same for *King Lear* (1970).

Filmmakers from outside the United States and England were also attracted to Shakespeare. The Italian moviemaker Franco Zeffirelli directed film versions of *The Taming of the Shrew* (1966) and *Romeo and Juliet* (1968), featuring bright colors, busy streets, rowdy humor, and flashy swordplay. The great studios of the former Soviet Union produced several magnificent films, including Grigori Kozintsev's *King Lear* (1970). In contrast to Brook's emphasis on Lear's suffering and decline, Kozintsev shows a Lear who gradually gains insight and grace.

The Japanese director Akira Kurosawa created one of the most revered Shakespearean films even while abandoning Shakespeare's dialogue, setting, and characters. Kurosawa adapted *Macbeth* for his *Castle of the Spider's Web* (1957), released abroad as *Throne of Blood*. The film translates

LEARNING WITH MOVIES

Many films and videos have been produced about Shakespeare's works to serve as educational guides. These materials can help students understand and enjoy the plays with helpful introductions, summaries, and explanations. Some of these films and videos mix educational sections with scenes from the plays themselves. Listings can be found in Andrew McLean's *Annotated Bibliographies and Media Guide for Teachers* and Barry M. Parker's *Folger Shakespeare Filmography.*

Shakespeare's vision to Japanese culture, with forest spirits instead of witches and samurai warriors instead of Scottish nobles. Few films convey Shakespeare's themes with so much power and skill. Kurosawa took up Shakespeare again with *Ran* (1985), a version of *King Lear* even less hopeful than Shakespeare's own dark tragedy.

More recently Kenneth Branagh has revived an art form that had begun to disappear. He both directed and acted in film versions of *Henry V* (1989), *Much Ado About Nothing* (1993), and *Hamlet* (1996).

ADAPTATIONS. Shakespeare's plays have inspired many films that seem to veer wildly from their original sources. They bring Shakespeare's lively plots and human insight to new settings, styles, and audiences. Movies based on musical adaptations of the playwright's work have been very popular. Among these are *The Boys from Syracuse* (1940), based on *The Comedy of Errors*; *Kiss Me, Kate* (1953), based on *The Taming of the Shrew*; and *West Side Story* (1961), based on *Romeo and Juliet*. *Love's Labor's Lost* (2000), a 1930s-style musical by Kenneth Branagh, drew on the songs of great American composers of the era, among them Irving Berlin, Ira Gershwin, Jerome Kern, and Cole Porter. Other films imagined Shakespeare in other contexts: *Joe Macbeth* (1955) recast *Macbeth* as a story about mobsters, while *Forbidden Planet* (1956) turned *The Tempest* into a science-fiction space adventure.

My Own Private Idaho (1991) updated the story of *Henry IV, Part 1* and *Part 2* to that of two troubled young men working as prostitutes. *Richard III* (1996), directed by Richard Loncraine with Ian McKellen in the title role, set the action of Shakespeare's play in an imaginary fascist England in the 1930s. *William Shakespeare's Romeo + Juliet* (1996) set the original language in a flashy, modern city with fast-paced camera work that resembled a music video. Other attempts to gain a fresh look at Shakespeare include a film version of Tom Stoppard's *Rosencrantz and Guildenstern Are Dead* (1990), which viewed *Hamlet* through the eyes of two minor characters. Several films, such as *Looking for Richard* (1996), have tried to document the making of a Shakespeare film, including footage of rehearsals and interviews with the actors. In a modern retelling of *Hamlet* (2000), a young filmmaker living in New York City struggles to deal with the death of his father and his mother's hasty remarriage. Adaptations are sure to continue as filmmakers discover new ways to bring Shakespeare's works to moviegoers. (*See also* **Actors, Shakespearean; Television.**)

SHAKESPEAREAN THEATER: 17TH CENTURY

In the late 1500s England's first permanent playhouse was constructed in the suburbs of LONDON. Called simply the Theater, it became a model for later Elizabethan playhouses, among them the GLOBE, where many of Shakespeare's plays were first performed. The structure of London's playhouses and the conventions* employed by the acting companies that performed in them were two of the features that defined Shakespearean drama during much of the 1600s.

* *convention* established practice

* *polygonal* having three or more sides

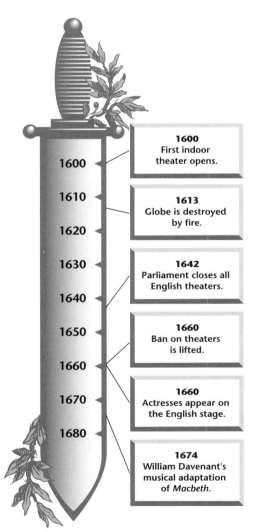

1600 ◄ 1600
First indoor
theater opens.

1610 ◄ 1613
Globe is destroyed
1620 ◄ by fire.

1630 ◄ 1642
Parliament closes all
1640 ◄ English theaters.

1650 ◄ 1660
Ban on theaters
is lifted.
1660 ◄

1670 ◄ 1660
Actresses appear on
the English stage.

1680 ◄
1674
William Davenant's
musical adaptation
of *Macbeth.*

SHAKESPEARE'S STAGE

By 1600 London boasted several public theaters, including the Curtain, the Rose, and the Swan. Shakespeare and his acting company had built the Globe in 1599. The way in which these and most other ELIZABETHAN THEATERS were constructed had a great influence on the staging of plays in the early 1600s.

THE ELIZABETHAN PLAYHOUSE. A typical Elizabethan theater was a round or polygonal* structure without a roof, more like a present-day sports stadium than a modern theater. Inside was a large open yard, at least 50 feet across, where some members of the audience stood. The stage itself was a large rectangular platform that jutted into the yard and took up almost half of the open area. The audience crowded around three sides of the stage. The back of it was a wall, behind which was the tiring house, or dressing room. Above the stage and attached to this wall was a balcony that was used for musicians and occasionally for actors playing a scene. In Shakespeare's *Romeo and Juliet,* for example, Juliet stands on the balcony while Romeo talks to her from the main stage below.

The only permanent structures on the stage were two pillars that supported a roof, which sheltered the stage from the sun and rain. Atop the roof was a hut containing machinery that could be used to lower an actor on ropes to the stage. The stage floor had a trapdoor to an area below, called the hell, that could serve as a grave, a dungeon cell, or hell itself.

The wall at the rear of the stage contained two or three doors that the actors used for entrances and exits. It also contained a curtained-off recess, called the discovery space, that served as a separate room or as a place for characters to hide. In *Hamlet,* for example, the discovery space may have been curtained off to allow Polonius to spy on the prince and Ophelia. The discovery space appears to have been used in nine of Shakespeare's plays, perhaps as many as three times in *The Merchant of Venice* (in the three scenes where Portia's suitors must choose among three metal caskets in the hope of winning her hand).

CLUES FOR THE AUDIENCE. In contrast to most modern dramatic productions, plays in the early 1600s were staged with little scenery and very few props, in part because there were no curtains across the front of the stage to hide scene changes. As a result playwrights had to devise other methods to convey information to their audiences. Shakespeare typically used words to set the scene. In the opening lines of *Hamlet,* for example, two watchmen reveal through their dialogue that they are standing guard outside the castle, that the hour is midnight, and that it is "bitter cold."

Sometimes a single piece of furniture would be employed to represent an entire set. A bed could indicate that a scene was set in a bedroom, for example, and a throne might suggest a royal court. The audience also received visual clues from COSTUMES and handheld props. If an actor was dressed in armor or carrying a sword, it was clear to the audience that he was playing a soldier. A character bearing a large ring of keys was probably a jailer.

Many stage directions in Shakespeare's plays instruct actors to enter the stage "as from" some place or activity—"as from dinner" or "as from hunting," for example. Such ambiguous directions left it up the actors to determine how to suggest the idea of a particular setting offstage. In other cases sound effects were employed to hint at action occurring behind the scenes. In a battle scene, for example, a few men might appear onstage fighting with swords, while the sounds of a larger battle—such as "alarums" (trumpet calls) and the clash of steel—could be heard in the distance offstage.

Elizabethan theaters lacked artificial lighting, so plays had to be presented during daylight hours. When a scene was supposed to occur at a particular time, the playwright might indicate this through a character's words, as in *Romeo and Juliet* (III.v), when the two lovers describe the sunrise that forces them to part. Characters could also suggest an evening scene by entering the stage dressed in nightgowns or carrying lighted torches. Whatever the playwright could not present on stage, the audience had to supply with its imagination. In the prologue to *Henry V*, Shakespeare calls on his viewers' "imaginary forces" to "piece out our [the actors'] imperfections" (18–23).

THEATER AS SPECTACLE. Spectacle was an important part of Shakespearean theater in the early 1600s. Making up for the lack of scenery and other visual effects, the curtains on the wall behind the stage were painted or embroidered with classical* figures to provide a vivid background. Moreover, the actors wore colorful apparel, or costumes, that enriched the visual

* *classical* in the tradition of ancient Greece and Rome

This fanciful engraving shows what Shakespeare's acting company may have looked like when it performed before Queen Elizabeth I and her court.

WOMEN ON THE STAGE

A significant change in Shakespearean theater that occurred between the early and late 1600s was the introduction of actresses to play the female roles. In Shakespeare's day boys and young men had performed all the female roles. As women's economic and legal position in England improved, society placed fewer restrictions on them. The first woman appeared on the Restoration stage in 1660, playing the role of Desdemona in *Othello*. By the end of the century several women had established themselves as notable Shakespearean actors.

* *Restoration* referring to the period in English history, beginning in 1660, when Charles II was restored to the throne

* *flat* backdrop composed of flat pieces of painted wood or cloth

display. Shakespeare's acting company, the KING'S MEN, is known to have spent a great deal of money assembling a lavish wardrobe for its actors.

Even more spectacular were some of the special effects that players had at their command. The large size and open design of most Elizabethan playhouses made it possible to enliven performances with such dramatic effects as fireworks and cannons. In 1600, however, the first indoor theater in London opened. This theater, BLACKFRIARS, was a much smaller space than the outdoor playhouses. It was artificially lit, and its stage was half the size of an outdoor theater's. Its small, dimly lit playing area could not accommodate spectacular effects and battle scenes. As a result wordplay and wit replaced swordplay and spectacle at Blackfriars and other indoor theaters.

THE PACE OF ELIZABETHAN PLAYS. Without elaborate scenery and props to move between scenes, Elizabethan actors could simply go out one door while other characters entered through another to appear in the next scene. Indeed, actors sometimes simply took up positions in other parts of the stage to signify scene breaks. With rapid line delivery and no pauses for set changes, Elizabethan plays proceeded quickly, and a lengthy Shakespearean script could be staged in just a couple of hours.

THE LATE 17TH CENTURY STAGE

In 1642, 26 years after Shakespeare's death, Parliament closed all the English theaters. For nearly 20 years the only plays that appeared in England were staged in private homes. In 1660, shortly after the Restoration* period began, King Charles II lifted the ban on theaters, and Shakespeare's plays were staged once again before the public. Actors such as Thomas Betterton performed in the style of the early 1600s, which they had learned from actors who had actually worked with Shakespeare. In other ways, though, Shakespearean theater in the late 1600s differed markedly from productions earlier in the century. Some changes were due to improvements in technology, others to alterations in audience taste.

CHANGES IN STAGING METHODS. Performing styles in the late 1600s differed considerably from the techniques used in Shakespeare's time. Most plays were performed in relatively small, covered theaters, such as the Dorset and Drury Lane. These spaces resembled Blackfriars rather than the large, open-air playhouses of the early 17th century.

Despite the smallness of the theaters, the trend toward visual spectacle on the stage became more pronounced toward the end of the century. Acting companies competed with each other to create spectacular effects. One major change was the introduction of more elaborate scenery, consisting of painted flats* and shutters that ran in grooves parallel to the front of the stage. Because scenery could be changed quickly by sliding new shutters into place, movement from scene to scene was still quite rapid.

OTHER CHANGES. Music became a more important part of the staging of Shakespeare's plays in the late 1600s, largely because of the influence

of English opera, which was also developing at the time. William Davenant, a leading theater owner of the late 1600s, adapted *Macbeth* by introducing music and dancing witches. Meanwhile the texts of the plays were altered to make them more courtly, reflecting the tastes of the wealthier audiences who attended the theater at the end of the century. Much of Shakespeare's imagery* was simplified, and coarse language was refined to meet a new set of audience preferences. (*See also* **Acting Companies, Elizabethan; Actors, Shakespearean; Directors and Shakespeare; Dramatic Techniques; Masques; Performances; Playhouse Structure; Settings; Shakespeare's Works, Adaptations of.**)

* *imagery* pictorial quality of a literary work, achieved through words

SHAKESPEAREAN THEATER: 18TH CENTURY

* *Restoration* referring to the period in English history, beginning in 1660, when Charles II was restored to the throne

Many changes in Shakespearean theater occurred during the 1700s. The original texts of Shakespeare's plays were gradually restored to the stage, displacing the adaptations that had held sway throughout the Restoration* period. Most 18th-century productions, however, focused not on the text but on the actors and the staging. The highly exaggerated performance style popular at the beginning of the century gradually gave way to a more natural and emotional approach. At the same time, sets and costumes grew more ornate and artificial. Productions became spectacular affairs, crowded with elaborate scenery and special effects that often distracted from the words of the play itself.

THE AGE OF THE ACTOR

English audiences of the mid-1700s flocked to the theaters to see their favorite actors in plays, much as audiences of today line up at movie theaters to see their favorite stars. Contemporary playwright Oliver Goldsmith observed, "No matter what the play may be, it is the actor who gains an audience." For this reason the late 18th century has rightfully been called the age of the actor.

ACTING STYLES. In the early 1700s Thomas Betterton was nearing the end of a highly successful 50-year acting career. Betterton, the most popular Shakespearean actor of his time, followed the grandiose* mannerisms that had been adopted from early 17th-century actors who had actually worked with Shakespeare. After Betterton's death in 1710 no actor achieved comparable fame for the next 30 years.

Then in 1741 David Garrick burst on the Shakespearean scene in the title role in *Richard III*. Unlike earlier actors who used exaggerated speech and gestures, Garrick focused on expressing strong emotions vividly and realistically. Although his style would probably seem artificial to modern viewers, when compared to the pompous and artificial style of the early 1700s, it was strikingly natural. Another early promoter of the new acting style was Charles Macklin, who appeared as SHYLOCK in a 1741 production of *The Merchant of Venice*. In the past this character

* *grandiose* characterized by an exaggerated manner

had always been portrayed as a hideously comic villain. Macklin made him a much more passionate, realistic, and human figure.

Other actors copied the naturalistic style of Garrick and Macklin with varying degrees of success. Probably the most successful was Spranger Barry, who by 1750 was seen as Garrick's equal in the role of Romeo. During that year the two actors appeared in rival performances of *Romeo and Juliet,* Garrick at the Drury Lane theater and Barry at the Covent Garden theater. Meanwhile, actresses—who had first appeared on the English stage in 1660—were coming into their own as stars. The most noteworthy female performers of the period, Susannah Cibber and Hannah Pritchard, were known for their natural and emotionally expressive portrayals of Shakespeare's heroines, especially in tragic roles.

Toward the end of the century, the Shakespearean stage was dominated by Sarah Siddons and her brother, John Philip Kemble. Their style of acting, which has been called neoclassical, was more restrained than that of Garrick and his contemporaries. Siddons and Kemble presented their characters with great dignity, delivering their lines with slow deliberation, accompanied by gestures inspired by ancient Greek and Roman sculpture. Of the two, Siddons was the more remarkable performer, with immense stage presence and superb vocal control. She was known particularly for her chilling portrayal of Lady Macbeth.

THE ACTOR-MANAGER. David Garrick's influence on Shakespearean theater extended far beyond his appearances on stage. In 1747 he became the manager of the Drury Lane theater, where he was responsible for casting plays and directing rehearsals. Garrick was one of the first in a long line of actor-managers, the forerunners of modern directors, who both performed on stage and managed the business aspects of theater production.

Samuel Johnson (right) was among the most influential critics of Shakespearean theater during the 1700s. This engraving shows him delivering a lecture to the members of his famous literary club.

SHAKESPEARE'S CHAMPION

David Garrick is considered to have been Shakespeare's greatest champion in the 1700s. Under his management about 20 percent of the plays presented at Drury Lane were Shakespeare's, far more than at the rival theater of Covent Garden. Garrick also organized the first Shakespeare festival in Stratford-upon-Avon, the Jubilee of 1769. He commissioned a statue of Shakespeare for his own home and had a special "temple" constructed to house it. Garrick's efforts helped establish a cult following for Shakespeare—and promoted his own fame as well.

See color plate 15, vol. 3.

Garrick retired from the theater in 1776, but his influence on Shakespearean drama continued to be felt for many years. Portraits of Garrick in various roles were widely distributed, inspiring later actors to copy his famous "points" (carefully crafted dramatic moments). Garrick also adapted many of Shakespeare's plays, often expanding the lead roles, which he played, at the expense of other parts. His most striking adaptation was *Romeo and Juliet*, to which he added an emotional scene between the two dying lovers. Garrick's versions of Shakespeare's plays were immensely popular, and they continued to be staged well into the 1800s.

In 1788 John Philip Kemble assumed Garrick's role as actor-manager of the Drury Lane theater. Like Garrick, Kemble wrote and presented adaptations of many of Shakespeare's plays, including *All's Well That Ends Well*, *Henry V*, *King John*, *Macbeth*, *The Tempest*, and *The Merry Wives of Windsor*. Some of these adaptations, like Garrick's, remained popular well into the 1800s.

PRODUCTION STYLES

Garrick and other actor-managers of the late 1700s made many improvements in staging techniques. Sets and lighting grew more sophisticated, resulting in visually beautiful productions, a trend that would continue into the next century. The actual words that accompanied these splendid settings, however, were often not Shakespeare's original texts but 17th- and 18th-century adaptations.

THE TEXTS OF THE PLAYS. During the late 1600s producers adapted plays to the changing tastes of their audiences, sometimes removing passages that viewers might find confusing or offensive. Such plays as *King Lear* and *Antony and Cleopatra* were so heavily altered as to become nearly unrecognizable. In the early 1700s many of these atrocities were still being staged in preference to the original texts. A few new ones also appeared during this period, such as Charles Johnson's *Love in a Forest* (1723), which combined scenes from *As You Like It* and *A Midsummer Night's Dream*.

During the late 1700s, however, the original versions of Shakespeare's dramatic works gradually returned to the stage. Two new editions of Shakespeare's collected plays helped revive interest the original texts: Nicholas ROWE's (1709) and William Warburton's (1747). Rowe's collection was the first illustrated edition of Shakespeare's plays. The images it contains are the best visual evidence available regarding 18th-century Shakespearean productions. One illustration shows a scene from *Hamlet* in which Thomas Betterton always overturned a chair on stage. This bit of stage business was adopted by nearly all other 18th-century Hamlets.

Although Garrick and other theater managers restored some of the original lines to Shakespeare's plays, they continued to use many of the adaptations that had proved to be most popular. For example, Garrick staged William Davenant's late 17th-century version of *Macbeth*, in which dancing witches and music had been introduced. Davenant's additions

provided strong visual effects that may have helped keep the attention of audiences, which were sometimes rowdy, focused on the stage.

STAGING. David Garrick was largely responsible for several important changes in the performance of Shakespeare during the 1700s. For example, since Shakespeare's day it had been possible for audience members to sit on the stage, where they distracted attention from the actors and sometimes interfered with the actors' movements. Garrick returned spectators to the customary seating areas, but he first increased the size of the theater so that no one could complain about smaller audiences.

Garrick also made changes to the stage itself. He significantly improved lighting techniques, which until that time had been generally limited to a large chandelier that hung above the stage in plain view of the audience. Garrick replaced such fixtures with more candles at the sides of the stage and brighter footlights at the front of it. Even with these modifications, however, the contrast between the lighted stage and the auditorium was not as great as it is in modern productions, which take place in a darkened theater with only the performance space illuminated. Productions in the 1700s occurred in a fully lit auditorium.

* *flat* backdrop composed of flat pieces of painted wood or cloth

Garrick also used a new type of set design in which a set of grooves running along the back of the stage held painted flats* that slid into place. With these new sliding backdrops, a scene change could be accomplished in a matter of seconds. Thanks in part to faster scene shifts, most Shakespeare plays directed by Garrick ran only a little more than two hours—a moderate length, which also reflects the fact that Garrick produced many of the plays in greatly abbreviated versions. Some aspects of set design, however, remained based on earlier conventions*. For example, a green cloth was laid on the stage to indicate that the play was a tragedy.

* *convention* established practice

Costumes and sets in the 18th-century theater were visually beautiful but not historically accurate. Most plays were performed in contemporary dress rather than in clothing of the era in which the plays were set. Scenery was designed to provide an attractive background consistent with the play's action, not to reflect the historical period in which that action took place. This would change during the 1800s, when actor-managers such as Charles Kean began insisting on historical accuracy in their set designs. (*See also* **Actors, Shakespearean; Directors and Shakespeare; Dramatic Techniques; Performances; Playhouse Structure; Shakespearean Theater: 17th Century.**)

SHAKESPEAREAN THEATER: 19TH CENTURY

Shakespeare's plays remained popular in England throughout most of the 1800s. In the early decades of the 19th century, Shakespearean productions appeared regularly at the Covent Garden and Drury Lane theaters in London. A law passed in 1843 restored competition to the theater business, and soon Shakespeare began flourishing at smaller theaters, including the Princess's, Lyceum, and Haymarket.

Two major trends characterized 19th-century Shakespearean productions. First, the previous emphasis on specific star performers shifted to a more general focus on the overall effect of a play. Second, productions grew more lavish and spectacular, with huge, expensive sets that required lengthy breaks for scenery changes. Many of these sets were careful reproductions of actual buildings from the historical period of the play's setting. This sort of attention to historical detail was matched by increasing faithfulness to Shakespeare's texts. Continuing a trend from the 1700s, actor-managers gradually eliminated the adaptations* of the 1600s in favor of Shakespeare's original words—although they continued to cut and reshape the scripts to fit their ideas of how a production should look and sound.

* *adaptation* literary composition rewritten into a new form

THE ACTOR-MANAGERS

Actor-managers, who both performed in plays and handled the financial aspects of the theater, dominated the Shakespearean scene in the 1800s. Following in the footsteps of David Garrick, the first actor-manager, Charles Kean and Henry IRVING presented their personal visions of the playwright's works to the public. Only a few 19th-century actor-managers were exceptional performers, but their business skills enabled them and their theaters to thrive.

EARLY ACTOR-MANAGERS. Charles Kemble came from a famous English acting family. He became manager of Covent Garden in 1822, taking over for his older brother, John Philip Kemble. The 19th-century interest in the historical accuracy of costume and set design began with Charles Kemble, who hired scholars to research the clothing for each play's historical period. Kemble's staging of *King John* (1823) opened with the king and his court all dressed in the style of the 1200s, a tableau* that moved the audience to thunderous applause.

* *tableau* scene in which all performers stand silent and motionless

The next actor-manager of note was William Charles Macready, who played leading roles at Covent Garden and Drury Lane in the 1820s. His acting was careful and conscientious but not especially exciting. He had a much greater influence as the manager of Covent Garden (1837–1839) and Drury Lane (1841–1843). His Shakespearean productions were very elaborate and expensive, with beautiful costumes and complicated sets. He also introduced several technical innovations that enhanced the already impressive theatrical effects. For example, Macready brought in limelight, a type of illumination that was produced by burning lime, which spread a magical glow unlike that from any other kind of lighting. Like Kemble, Macready aimed for historical accuracy in his costumes and sets. He also hired the finest artists available to paint the scenery. Macready's productions set the style for Shakespearean productions for the rest of the century.

See color plate 5, vol. 3.

One of Macready's chief goals as a theater manager was to restore parts of Shakespeare's original plays that had long been omitted from performance. For example, he revived the part of the Fool in *King Lear*, which had been cut from the play since the late 1600s. Few actor-managers of

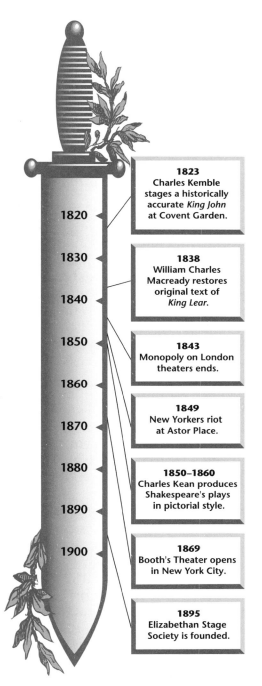

1820

1830

1840

1850

1860

1870

1880

1890

1900

1823
Charles Kemble stages a historically accurate *King John* at Covent Garden.

1838
William Charles Macready restores original text of *King Lear*.

1843
Monopoly on London theaters ends.

1849
New Yorkers riot at Astor Place.

1850–1860
Charles Kean produces Shakespeare's plays in pictorial style.

1869
Booth's Theater opens in New York City.

1895
Elizabethan Stage Society is founded.

* *canon* authentic works of a writer

the early 1800s showed such respect for the playwright's texts. Most continued to present conventional adaptations, which by that time were more familiar to audiences than the original plays.

THE PICTORIAL STYLE. Charles Kean was the son of Edmund Kean, one of the greatest actors of the early 1800s. Charles was less impressive as an actor than his father, but as the manager of London's Princess's theater he had a significant influence on Shakespearean production. He carried Macready's style of elaborate, historically accurate Shakespearean productions to great extremes. He even added detailed historical settings to plays originally meant to be fantasies. A publication called *Punch* remarked humorously that the bear used in Kean's production of *The Winter's Tale* was "an archaeological copy from the original bear of Noah's Ark."

In addition to his detailed scenery and gorgeous costumes, Kean added other forms of spectacle to his productions, including ballet and elaborate visual effects. At times he seemed to treat Shakespeare's plays as little more than background for his own glorious staging. He certainly showed little respect for the playwright's texts, because he often cut lines or rearranged scenes to make room for his elaborate special effects and to accommodate the long scene changes they required.

Kean's highly visual style of production came to be called pictorial, presenting Shakespeare's plays as a series of impressive images, or tableaux. The stage designs of the 1800s complemented the effect of the pictorial style. Instead of performing on a platform that jutted out into the auditorium, the actors were limited to the space defined by a frame called the proscenium arch. The arch formed a dividing line between the actors and the audience, creating the illusion that the spectators were viewing the action of the play through an invisible "fourth wall." Kean's productions were great successes, and his spectacular style remained the standard in Shakespearean theater for decades to come.

Kean's chief rival was Samuel Phelps, the manager of Sadler's Wells Theatre in the London suburb of Islington. Phelps adhered to the pictorial style in his productions, but unlike Kean he took care to make his tableaux enhance the overall effect of the play rather than rendering the play secondary to the pictures. During his 18 years as manager, he produced nearly every play in Shakespeare's canon*, and he favored Shakespeare's original texts over adaptations.

HENRY IRVING. Kean retired around 1860 and Phelps in 1862, and for nearly two decades no English theater focused on Shakespeare's plays. This period is known as the interregnum, meaning between reigns, because no influential actor-manager ruled the Shakespearean scene. The absence of Shakespearean productions was due in part to financial considerations. The spectacular shows that audiences had come to expect were very expensive and needed to run for a long time to recover their staging costs. Some critics have also suggested that there were no English actors at that time who were capable of meeting the demands of Shakespearean roles.

THE LEGENDARY EDMUND KEAN

Charles Kean's father, Edmund, was the best-known Shakespearean actor of the early 1800s. Although he never managed a theater like his son, he was a brilliant actor, best known for such roles as Shylock and Macbeth. Kean's acting style was vivid and intense, in contrast to the formal style of the late 1700s. His performances often involved a series of "points," brief, memorable moments that illustrated his view of a character. Kean's points were captured in drawings and imitated by other actors throughout the 1800s. Many later actors had to struggle to compete with the memory of Edmund Kean.

See color plate 3, vol. 3.

* **prompt book** annotated copy of a play, which contains instructions for entrances, exits, music, and other cues

The interregnum came to an end in 1878, when Henry Irving took over as manager of the Lyceum. From then until his retirement in 1901, Irving was the major influence on Shakespearean theater in England. He adopted Kean's attention to historical detail, his emphasis on spectacle, and his pictorial style, but he used them with greater artistry and subtlety. For his production of *Coriolanus* (1880), set in ancient Rome, Irving hired artist Lawrence Alma-Tadema to design the sets. Alma-Tadema traveled to Rome and studied ancient Roman architecture and carvings in order to create beautiful and historically accurate scenery. Like Kean, Irving regularly cut lines and rearranged scenes to accommodate his elaborate visual effects and lengthy scene changes.

Lighting was an important visual element of the pictorial approach, and by Irving's time new technology provided many new options for illuminating the stage to set the proper mood. For example, to give the impression of gloomy twilight, Irving used a combination of dim gaslights and limelight. To enhance this effect, he also darkened the auditorium, which until that time had been kept well lit during performances. Blackening the auditorium had the added bonus of helping focus the audience's attention on the stage.

Irving was the greatest Shakespearean actor of his day. Despite poor posture and a harsh voice, he had extraordinary magnetism on stage. He was especially excellent in roles that were evil or grotesque, such as that of SHYLOCK in *The Merchant of Venice*, a role he played for almost 25 years. Irving took all the leading male roles in his own productions, and the English actress Ellen Terry usually played the leading female roles—even when these parts were not particularly suited to the two of them. For example, Irving's stunning Macbeth was matched with a disappointing Lady Macbeth from Terry, while Irving's portrayal of MALVOLIO in *Twelfth Night* failed to live up to Terry's glowing performance as Viola. Despite their sometimes uneven performances, Irving's spectacular productions were immensely popular with audiences. His *Merchant of Venice*, for example, ran for more than 200 consecutive nights. In 1895 Irving became the first English actor to be knighted.

CONFLICTING STYLES. The other great advocate of the pictorial style in the late 1800s was Herbert Beerbohm Tree, a competent but not brilliant actor about 15 years younger than Irving. Tree played an astonishing variety of roles, often using elaborate makeup and minute physical details to help create his Shakespearean characters. In 1887 he became manager of the Haymarket, and he continued as a theater manager well into the 20th century.

Tree's productions were even more flamboyant than Irving's, overwhelming audiences with dazzling visual effects. With so much emphasis on the spectacular, Tree sometimes had to cut the scripts of Shakespeare's plays quite drastically. At the same time he was known to add lines to his own roles to increase their importance. The prompt book* for a production in which he played FALSTAFF shows the lines and stage business he devised to make his character the focus of attention. Although Tree's elaborate productions were extremely expensive, they were wildly popular,

earning huge profits. Tree's rendering of *King John* (1899), for example, was seen by nearly 200,000 people.

A contrasting approach to Shakespearean theater was favored by William Poel, who felt that the visual displays and drastic cutting of Shakespeare's texts violated the playwright's vision. Poel aimed to present the dramas as they had appeared in Shakespeare's time, more than 200 years earlier. In 1881 he presented a version of *Hamlet* based on the First Quarto edition (long seen as too flawed to perform) on a bare stage with no intermission. Rapid delivery of lines and quick scene changes made the performance only two hours long.

In 1895 Poel founded the Elizabethan Stage Society, producing Shakespeare's plays on a bare platform stage with close contact between the actors and the audience, little scenery, and Elizabethan costumes. He was not strict about using Shakespeare's original, uncut texts, but he did eliminate the textual rearrangements required by the pictorial style. In Poel's theater, the focus was on the actors and the language of the plays rather than on theatrical spectacle. The Elizabethan Stage Society's productions suffered from amateurish acting, however, and were not commercially successful. Nonetheless, Poel's approach to Shakespeare had a significant influence on 20th-century directors, who focused increasingly on Shakespeare's original words and ideas.

SHAKESPEAREAN THEATER ABROAD

By the mid-1800s it had become common for acting companies to travel abroad. Every English actor-manager took his company on tour in the hope of recovering the money lost on costly London productions. Such tours were generally popular in the United States. Some American acting companies also staged commercially successful productions of Shakespeare's plays in the United States during the 1800s. In addition a few American actors gained international fame for their Shakespearean roles.

Many 19th-century American Shakespearean actors were especially eager to prove themselves in London, the home of Shakespearean theater. One of the first American actors to appear on the English stage was Ira Frederick Aldridge, an African American actor from New York. He made his English debut as Othello in 1826. He also won praise for his portrayals of King Lear and Macbeth. Another American Shakespearean actor to play in England in the 1820s was Edwin Forrest, who focused on roles that put him in direct competition with Macready. The rivalry between the two became so intense that it eventually resulted in an anti-British riot outside a theater in New York's Astor Place. In the 1840s, the American actress Charlotte Cushman also played several Shakespearean roles in England, including Romeo in *Romeo and Juliet,* much to the amazement of her audience.

None of these early 19th-century American actors, although favorites in the United States and Europe, enjoyed much popularity in England. Even during the interregnum—that period from about 1660 to 1880 when no English actor-managers dominated Shakespearean theater—American actors were unable to gain prominence on the English stage.

Apparently the legacy of Charles Kean and his expensive, spectacular productions was too hard to overcome.

It was not until the late 1800s that an American Shakespearean actor finally established a firm reputation on the English stage. His name was Edwin Booth. Booth was the leading American Shakespearean actor of the 1860s and probably the greatest Hamlet of the 19th century. He enjoyed his first appearance on the English stage in 1861, and he made many repeat appearances over the next two decades. In 1869 he opened Booth's Theater in New York City. Under his management eight Shakespearean plays were successfully staged, with Booth himself in each of the leading roles. At first he attempted to mimic the grand pictorial style of Kean and Irving, but the expense of such productions soon bankrupted him. He lost his theater and went on tour as an actor, performing in London, the American South, California, and Germany. In 1884 Booth and Henry Irving alternated the roles of Othello and IAGO in a London production of *Othello*. (*See also* **Actors, Shakespearean; Astor Place Riot; Directors and Shakespeare; Performances; Shakespearean Theater: 18th Century; Shakespearean Theater: 20th Century; Shakespeare's Works, Adaptations of.**)

SHAKESPEAREAN THEATER: 20TH CENTURY

During the 1900s Shakespearean productions branched out in many new directions at once. Advances in technology, such as sophisticated machinery and electric lighting, opened up new possibilities for staging the plays. Directors also took on greater importance than ever before, allowing their personal interpretations of the plays to influence entire productions. Meanwhile a wider variety of styles, interpretations, and techniques were being used in the presentation of Shakespeare's plays during the 20th century than at any other period in the history of theater.

THE AGE OF THE DIRECTOR

The early 1900s can be seen as the age of the director. Directors made all the artistic decisions about a play, and each had a unique vision of how it should be presented. During this period scores of notable directors presented novel approaches to Shakespeare.

THE OLD STYLE. At the beginning of the century, the best-known director was Herbert Beerbohm Tree, manager of Her Majesty's Theatre in London. Tree's lavish, showy productions of Shakespeare reflected the pictorial style of the late 1800s, in which the plays were presented as a series of colorful images with little attention to the text. Sets were beautiful, complex, and expensive. An extreme example is Tree's *A Midsummer Night's Dream* (1900), with live rabbits scampering about in a realistic-looking forest. This staging also featured elaborate, historically accurate costumes and lush Romantic* music. To allow time to change the elaborate sets,

* **Romantic** referring to a school of thought, prominent in the 1800s, that emphasized the importance of emotion in art

Tyrone Guthrie was one of the leading Shakespearean directors of the 1900s. His productions at the Old Vic and Sadler's Wells theaters featured dazzling performances, contemporary costumes, and minimal scenery. Guthrie was knighted in 1961 and founded the Tyrone Guthrie Theater in Minneapolis in 1963.

Tree had to cut out some of Shakespeare's lines, a practice that had been common in the 1800s.

Tree's most ambitious production was *Henry VIII*, presented in 1910, in which he attempted to create "an absolute reproduction of the Renaissance." This dazzling pageant was a huge success with audiences. Spectacular productions such as Tree's, which depended on the overall artistic supervision of a single individual, helped make directors the most important figures in Shakespearean theater during the early 1900s.

While Tree was staging his spectacles in London, actor-manager Frank Benson was touring the English countryside with old-fashioned, beautifully spoken performances of Shakespeare's plays. Benson was in charge of the annual SHAKESPEARE FESTIVAL at STRATFORD-UPON-AVON, a position he held until 1919. He also presented plays at London's Lyceum Theatre. He produced a broad range of Shakespeare's plays, including some that were rarely performed at that time. His renderings focused on the language of the scripts and the use of simple scenery, such as painted cloths.

NEW SIMPLICITY. In the meantime other directors were experimenting with other ways of presenting the plays. One of these was William Poel, founder of the Elizabethan Stage Society, who adopted a far simpler style that concentrated on Shakespeare's words. Poel attempted to present Shakespeare's plays as they might have been played in the playwright's time, on a bare platform stage and in costumes of the Elizabethan period. He had all his actors deliver their lines rapidly, as he believed they had been spoken in the playwright's own theater.

Although Poel's productions were not commercially successful, they nonetheless had a tremendous influence on Shakespearean theater in the 20th century. Many directors adopted aspects of Poel's approach, focusing on the playwright's words rather than on spectacular effects. In addition many of the Shakespearean stages that were built in the 1900s, such as the one at the Tyrone Guthrie Theater in Minneapolis, were modeled on the type of Elizabethan stage that Poel advocated.

Poel's contemporary, Edward Gordon Craig, favored a different kind of simplicity in his set designs. Craig, the son of legendary actress Ellen Terry, created sets unlike anything that had been seen in Shakespearean theater before his time, defining the performance space with sweeping draperies, huge movable screens, and lighting effects that were quite striking. Craig's ideas about set design were tremendously influential. Later directors, especially in Europe, quickly adopted his style in place of the highly realistic and historically accurate sets that were favored by Tree and other earlier designers.

FLIGHTS OF FANCY. Both Poel and Craig inspired Harley Granville-Barker, an actor who had worked under Poel's direction. Around 1912 Granville-Barker began producing plays at London's Savoy Theatre in which he attempted to combine Poel's platform stage and rapid delivery of lines with Craig's innovative use of curtains and lighting. Like Poel, Granville-Barker sought to direct the audience's attention away from

scenery and special effects and toward the text, which he kept unedited and uncut. Instead of trying to re-create the exact conditions of the Elizabethan theater, however, Granville-Barker aimed to capture the overall effect of Elizabethan staging methods by other means.

Granville-Barker introduced startlingly original designs, such as a set for *The Winter's Tale* that consisted solely of white pillars on a white stage under white lights. His most famous staging was of *A Midsummer Night's Dream* (1914), notable for its golden fairies. Not surprisingly, Granville-Barker's productions were highly controversial. Although some of his creations helped audiences focus on the text, others were so outlandish that they distracted from the words. A scholar as well as a director, Granville-Barker wrote a series of *Prefaces to Shakespeare* (1923–1947) that discuss the plays as theater rather than as literature.

SHAKESPEAREAN THEATER AFTER WORLD WAR I

After World War I innovative directors continued to dominate Shakespearean theater in England. As the decades progressed, however, actors began to exert a greater influence on artistic trends. The late 1900s were in a way a return to the age of the actor and thus a return of sorts to the late 1700s.

VARIETY ON THE ENGLISH STAGE. After World War I various directors took diverse and novel approaches to Shakespeare. At one extreme was Nugent Monck. Influenced by William Poel, he presented Shakespeare's plays with amateur actors and simple Elizabethan sets. Between 1921 and 1958 he directed the entire Shakespeare canon* at the Maddermarket Theatre in Norwich.

At the other extreme were the outrageously flamboyant Shakespearean productions of Terence Gray at the Festival Theatre in Cambridge (1926–1933). In Gray's production of *Twelfth Night,* for example, two actors entered on roller skates. One of his best-remembered productions was a *Henry VIII* in which the actors were dressed to look like the kings and queens in a deck of playing cards. A baby doll, representing the newborn Princess Elizabeth, was tossed out to the audience at the end of the show.

One of the more influential experiments of the period was initiated by Barry Jackson, director of the Birmingham Repertory Theatre in the 1920s. Jackson is known for his modern-dress productions of *Hamlet, Macbeth,* and *The Taming of the Shrew*. His goal was to make the plays more accessible to 20th-century audiences. Many other directors followed this trend throughout the century.

A Russian director, Theodore Komisarjevsky, staged several unusual productions of Shakespeare's plays at Stratford-upon-Avon in the 1930s. He set *Macbeth* in a nightmarish modern world, complete with steel helmets and machine guns. He staged several of Shakespeare's comedies with costumes and sets from a wild jumble of different time periods. This

* *canon* authentic works of a writer

Golden Fairies

Among Harley Granville-Barker's most daring creations were the golden fairies in his 1914 production of *A Midsummer Night's Dream.* They were dressed in shimmering gold from head to toe, with gold paint on their skin and their eyebrows outlined in red. They also wore masks and elaborate wigs and mustaches made of raveled rope and curls of metal. Instead of skipping and frolicking like fairies in most earlier productions of the play, Granville-Barker's fairies moved stiffly and stood in poses inspired by the art of the Far East. These bizarre creatures shocked audiences, and many critics felt that they distracted from the play rather than enhancing its effect.

blending of costumes from several eras is one of the most popular approaches of modern Shakespeare productions.

THE OLD VIC. Shortly before World War I, Lilian Baylis, manager of the Old Vic in London, hired Matheson Lang to direct some of Shakespeare's plays on the Old Vic stage. With his wife, Hutin Britton, Lang produced 25 of Shakespeare's works during the war. From this modest beginning, the Old Vic company would go on to play a lasting role in 20th-century Shakespearean theater, eventually becoming the National Theatre Company.

The Old Vic company began to attract attention with the arrival of Edith Evans, a noteworthy English actress, in 1925. Other superb actors joined the company over the next decade, most notably John Gielgud and Laurence Olivier. Evans, Gielgud, and Olivier were among the greatest dramatic artists of the 20th century, and their Shakespearean roles were admired and imitated the world over. All three were eventually knighted for their outstanding contributions to English theater.

In 1933 Tyrone Guthrie took over as director of the Old Vic company. He also ran London's Sadler's Wells, where he had a permanent Shakespearean set installed. At these two theaters Guthrie directed some of the finest Shakespearean productions of the 20th century, featuring minimal scenery and outstanding performances. One of his greatest achievements was to reestablish *Love's Labor's Lost,* after centuries of neglect, as one of Shakespeare's major plays. Guthrie's 1936 production conveyed the full force of the idea that death and tragedy are ever present in Shakespeare's lighthearted comedies. Other directors followed Guthrie's lead, probing deep below the surface of this forgotten classic.

THE NEW AGE OF THE ACTOR. John Gielgud and Laurence Olivier represented two major acting styles, sometimes described as the lyrical and the realistic. Gielgud had an exquisite voice, perfectly suited to bringing out the musical qualities of Shakespeare's verse. Olivier was a far more physical actor who excelled at playing scenes of intense emotion, concentrating on the meaning behind the words. As exemplars of contrasting styles, Olivier and Gielgud dominated Shakespearean theater through the 1950s. Both of them directed, as well as performed in, Shakespeare plays. Gielgud's production of *Much Ado About Nothing* (1949) at London's Haymarket Theatre was so successful that it was revived frequently over the following decade. Olivier directed four Shakespearean films—*Hamlet, Henry V, Richard III,* and *Othello*—with himself in each of the title roles. Other actors who made their mark on Shakespearean theater in the 1900s included Peggy Ashcroft, Ralph Richardson, Paul Scofield, Maggie Smith, Ian McKellen, Judi Dench, Derek Jacobi, and Kenneth Branagh.

THE ROYAL SHAKESPEARE COMPANY. Since the founding of the annual Shakespeare festival at Stratford-upon-Avon in the late 1800s, a different group of actors have assembled each season for a series of plays. In 1960 festival director Peter Hall decided to form a permanent ensemble

instead. He hired a group of actors, directors, and designers to form the core of the company, which he named the ROYAL SHAKESPEARE COMPANY (RSC). Hall also took over the Aldwych Theatre in London so that the troupe could continue to perform when the theater at Stratford-upon-Avon was closed for the season.

Peter Hall and the directors of the RSC who followed him developed a flashy, quick-moving, and original style. They struck a fine balance between innovative productions and outstanding acting. In 1982 the RSC moved its London base from the Aldwych to the Barbican. The company now performs regularly at the Barbican Theatre as well as at Stratford-upon-Avon. It also tours internationally. Today it is the most highly regarded Shakespearean acting company in the world.

The RSC was one of the main forces behind the revival of Shakespeare's histories, which until 1950 had been less popular than his other works. Even before the official founding of the permanent company, the Stratford actors had taken a giant step by presenting several Shakespearean histories in chronological order, from *Richard II* through *Henry V*. In 1964 the RSC went even farther, staging the eight histories from *Richard II* through *Richard III* in sequence. Presenting these works as a group displayed the full development of the plot and characters in a way that individual plays, taken out of context, could not.

TRENDS IN 20TH-CENTURY SHAKESPEAREAN THEATER

During the 1900s Shakespeare's plays assumed new forms. On the stage new technology enabled directors to produce a greater range of special effects. Even more can be achieved on the screen, and all of Shakespeare's plays have now been adapted for film or television. The plays have been rendered in other ways as well, inspiring a variety of musical versions and original takes on Shakespeare's themes. Directors have also used the playwright's scripts to examine or support a variety of political and artistic issues. Finally, Shakespeare has spread around the globe, with more productions outside of England than ever before.

NEW TECHNOLOGY AND THEATRICAL EFFECTS. Advances in technology made many new theatrical effects possible during the 1900s. One of the most important innovations was the development of electric lighting, which could create effects far more subtle than anything achieved in theaters before this time. One particularly skillful use of modern lighting techniques occurred in a production of *A Midsummer Night's Dream* (1984) at Stratford, Ontario. When the fairies blessed the palace at the end of the play, the dew they sprinkled was reflected in shimmering light, not only on the stage but over the entire ceiling of the theater.

Other technical advances allowed a greater variety of arrangements for the stage. A major development was the revolving set, first used at the Residenz Theater in Munich, Germany, in 1896. German director Max Reinhardt put this new technology to effective use with his production of

1910
Herbert Beerbohm Tree stages an elaborate *A Midsummer Night's Dream.*

1914
Lillian Baylis begins productions of Shakespeare's plays at the Old Vic.

1920s
Barry Jackson introduces modern-dress costuming.

1930s
Theodore Komisarjevsky introduces mixed-period costuming.

1944
Laurence Olivier produces popular film of *Henry V.*

1960
Royal Shakespeare Company is founded.

1910
1920
1930
1940
1950
1960

A *Midsummer Night's Dream* in the early 1900s. An even more advanced moving set was constructed at Stratford-upon Avon in 1972. Operated by hydraulic machinery, it is capable of an almost infinite number of different arrangements. Its potential has not been fully utilized, however, perhaps because it is too complex or too expensive.

Modern technology also facilitated much more rapid set changes. Early in the century, Tree's elaborate backdrops had required him to cut lines from the plays in order to make time for lengthy scene shifts. Later productions, such as William Poel's, overcame this problem with simplified sets that could be altered more quickly. As electronics and other sophisticated technologies developed over the course of the 1900s, it became possible for directors to have it both ways. With the help of machinery, even elaborate sets could be rapidly transformed, and Shakespeare's plays could be presented at full length without sacrificing either scenery or special effects.

NEW INTERPRETATIONS. During the 1900s directors frequently used Shakespeare's plays to express artistic and political viewpoints. For example, Salvador Dali's designs for a production of *As You Like It* reflected the artistic philosophy known as surrealism, which draws on dreamlike images to illustrate the strangeness of everyday life. Similarly, it has become common for productions of *Henry V,* a play that was formerly viewed as a celebration of military conquest, to reinterpret the work as a criticism of war and monarchy.

See color plate 8, vol. 3.

Modern playwrights such as Bertolt Brecht, Samuel Beckett, and Tom Stoppard have either adapted Shakespeare's plays or incorporated Shakespeare's ideas or words into their own works. Shakespeare's scripts have also been converted into operas, musicals, and ballets. For example, the musical *West Side Story* transfers the conflicts of *Romeo and Juliet* to New York City in the 1950s, with the feuding families portrayed as two rival gangs. Reinterpreting the play in this fashion helped bring the tragedy to life for a new generation of viewers. Many recent adaptations* have been films, such as *Forbidden Planet* (1956), which recast *The Tempest* as an outer-space adventure, and *Prospero's Books* (1991), which approached the same play as a meditation from the mind of Shakespeare's central figure. The plays in their original forms have also been preserved many times on film.

* *adaptation* literary composition rewritten into a new form

SHAKESPEARE ABROAD. During the 1900s Shakespeare's plays were translated into more languages and presented in more countries than ever before, with such notable events as the first-ever performances in China and Japan. European directors who made a mark in Shakespearean theater in the 20th century included Max Reinhardt from Germany, Franco Zeffirelli from Italy, Michel Saint-Denis from France, and Grigori Kozintsev from Russia. (*See also* **Acting Companies, Modern; Actors, Shakespearean; Directors and Shakespeare; Shakespeare Festivals; Shakespeare on Screen; Shakespearean Theater: 19th Century; Shakespeare's Works, Adaptations of; Television; Translations of Shakespeare.**)

SHAKESPEARE'S CANON

The term *Shakespeare's canon* refers to all the works generally believed to have been written by Shakespeare. Scholars disagree about which titles belong in Shakespeare's canon, and the list of plays usually numbers from 36 to 38 titles. The most widely accepted authority is the FIRST FOLIO, which includes 36 works and is considered reliable because it was compiled by John Heminges and Henry Condell, two actors who had worked with Shakespeare as fellow members of his acting company.

Over the years many non-Folio plays have been suggested for inclusion in the canon, but only two have been accepted by a majority of scholars: *Pericles* and *The Two Noble Kinsmen.* Supporters for the inclusion of *Pericles* argue that Acts III, IV, and V were principally authored by Shakespeare even if he did not write the entire play. Supporters of *The Two Noble Kinsmen* contend that Shakespeare wrote a substantial part of that drama, which was published after the playwright's death as a joint labor by William Shakespeare and John Fletcher. Critics argue, however, that these plays were excluded from the First Folio because Heminges and Condell knew that other playwrights had written most of the lines. In fact some argue that other authors had written at least portions of some of the plays that were included in the First Folio, such as *Henry VIII*. Scholars who deny Shakespeare's sole authorship of plays within the accepted canon are sometimes referred to as "disintegrationists."

The term *canon* frequently refers only to the plays, but most scholars include Shakespeare's sonnets and his other poems as well. Over the centuries new works have been nominated for the list, and to this day scholars continue to argue about which ones should be included in Shakespeare's definitive canon. (*See also* **Lost Plays.**)

SHAKESPEARE'S REPUTATION

More than any other English writer, Shakespeare has continued to attract readers and viewers through the ages. His works have probably been more widely studied, viewed, and admired than those of any other author. His fame has spanned the globe, and recent polls in Great Britain and the United States have found him to be the most significant person of the last thousand years. (In 1991 he was named Britain's "Man of the Milennium" in an audience survey.)

A LEGEND IN HIS TIME. Even during his lifetime some of Shakespeare's contemporaries recognized his genius. In 1598, before the poet had written what are now considered his greatest tragedies, Francis Meres wrote, "As Plautus and Seneca are accounted the best for Comedy and Tragedy among the Latines: so Shakespeare among the English is the most excellent in both kinds for the stage." His plays were performed not only in the public theaters but also at Queen Elizabeth's court. After her death the new king, JAMES I, adopted Shakespeare's acting company as his own, changing its name from the Chamberlain's Men to the KING'S MEN. The company toured the English countryside and occasionally performed

at the universities. *Hamlet* was so popular that a British sea captain ordered the play acted on his ship, which lay off the African coast, "to keep my people from idleness and unlawful games, or sleep." Shakespeare's success as a playwright, actor, and shareholder earned him enough wealth to purchase for his family the second largest property in his native town of Stratford-upon-Avon.

Seven years after his death Shakespeare's collected plays were published with tributes from fellow poets who predicted that this book "shall make thee looke / Fresh to all ages." Ben Jonson, his friend and fellow playwright, claimed that there had not been a playwright equal to Shakespeare since the time of the great Greek tragedians Aeschylus, Sophocles, and Euripides, 2500 years before. In what is probably his most often quoted line, Jonson declared that Shakespeare was "not of an age, but for all time!"

Throughout the 1600s and 1700s literary giants continued to proclaim Shakespeare's greatness. John Dryden, an English poet, playwright, and critic, wrote in 1668, "He was the man who of all modern, and perhaps ancient poets, had the largest and most comprehensive soul." In 1725 poet Alexander Pope maintained that "Every single character in Shakespeare is as much an individual, as those in life itself." Dr. Samuel Johnson, the noted author and journalist, described Shakespeare's drama as "the mirror of life." Perhaps the highest praise of the playwright's genius is a passage from a letter written in 1664. The author, Margaret Cavendish, explained Shakespeare's success in a way that would be echoed in later critical works and theatrical reviews:

> So well he hath expressed in his plays all sorts of persons, as one would think he had been transformed into every one of those persons he hath described. He presents passions so naturally, and misfortunes so probably, as he pierces the souls of his readers with such a true sense and feeling thereof, that it forces tears through their eyes.

Shakespeare on the Stage. Despite the praise of these literary figures, Shakespeare's works fell out of favor in the theater in the late 1600s and early 1700s. His comedies were thought too romantic, too poetic, and even too moral for an age that delighted in naughty dialogue, secret love affairs, and social satire*. The same critics who praised Shakespeare's "natural genius" blamed him for violating their rules of order and style. When his works were performed they were often adapted to conform to the standards of the day. Perhaps the most outrageous of these adaptations was Nahum Tate's version of *King Lear,* in which the king lives happily ever after with his daughter Cordelia and her heroic husband, Edgar. This adaptation was performed for 150 years before the original text of Shakespeare's tragedy was restored to the stage.

Beginning around 1720 the theater's interest in Shakespeare's plays gradually revived, and by 1740 his works accounted for about 25 percent of all London productions. In 1741 the young actor David Garrick made a sensational success of his first London appearance in the role of Richard III. For the next 35 years Garrick dominated the stage, adapting and

* *satire* literary work ridiculing human wickedness and foolishness

Shakespeare's Reputation

* Romantic referring to a school of thought, prominent in the 1800s, that emphasized the importance of emotion in art

* genre literary form

SHAKESPEARE'S TIMELESS APPEAL

Ben Jonson's claim that Shakespeare was "not of an age, but for all time" seems to have been prophetic. Many critics have wondered about the source of Shakespeare's lasting appeal. Some focus on the complexity of his characters and the beauty of his language. Others believe that England, as a major world power, spread the bard's works to many cultures. Still others note that Shakespeare's era was much like the present day—a time of dramatic change, hope, and uncertainty.

directing Shakespeare's plays as well as performing in them. By the time of his retirement, he had made Shakespeare into the idealized figure he remains today.

The 19th century is sometimes referred to as the age of "bardolatry." Romantic* poets such as John Keats and Samuel Taylor COLERIDGE treated the playwright as if he were divine. Essayist Charles LAMB (who, with his sister Mary, wrote the first set of children's stories based on Shakespeare) protested against the adaptation of Shakespeare's works, saying that if they were staged at all they should be presented only in their original form. Actors throughout the 1800s made their reputations by identifying themselves with particular Shakespearean roles. In America, for example, Edwin Booth's performance as Hamlet became legendary. In England audiences flocked to the theaters to see actors such as Charles Kemble, Charles Kean, William Charles Macready, and Henry IRVING compete for stardom. They also came to admire the great actresses of the day, among them Sarah Siddons, Fanny Kemble, and Ellen Terry. Countless editions of the plays were published. Average citizens founded Shakespeare clubs and copied out their favorite passages to refer to and recite. Shakespeare's works also began to be taught in schools.

MODERN VIEWS. During the first half of the 20th century, literary criticism dominated what has become known as the Shakespeare industry. Every detail of his plays was analyzed—his IMAGERY, his plots and characters, and his dramatic LANGUAGE. Scholars divided the plays into genres* and discussed the distinctive characteristics of his histories, tragedies, comedies, and romances. He and his characters were psychoanalyzed as if they were alive, even by Sigmund Freud himself, the founder of psychoanalysis. This practice led to such studies as *Hamlet and Oedipus,* in which Dr. Ernest Jones argues that Hamlet is in love with his mother. Several stage and film versions of *Hamlet* reflected this theory. Shakespeare's characters took on a life of their own, independent from the plays, and became symbolic figures to rival the gods of Greek and Roman mythology. Even people who had never read the plays recognized Hamlet as a personification of indecision, Lady Macbeth as an embodiment of ruthless ambition, and Romeo and Juliet as tragic emblems of young love. Shakespeare's characters had become part of popular culture.

Although critics and scholars of Shakespeare sometimes overshadowed performers in the theater during this period, his plays were still produced each year in the theater at Stratford-upon-Avon. Audiences at London's Old Vic viewed Shakespearean performances by young actors and actresses who would go on to become stars of stage and film: John Gielgud, Ralph Richardson, Laurence Olivier, Peggy Ashcroft, and Vivien Leigh. In America both Broadway and regional theaters fed the growing interest in Shakespeare. On both sides of the Atlantic, this enthusiasm was enlivened by modern-dress productions of Shakespeare, which led the way to daring film adaptations in the second half of the 20th century.

Since World War II, Shakespeare's stature has grown as numerous productions on stage, screen, and television have brought his plays to an ever-expanding audience. All 37 of his plays have been shown on television,

making them available to many viewers who had never seen a Shakespearean performance before. Across America almost every state has a summer festival that highlights Shakespeare. There are major theaters in New York, Washington, San Diego, Ashland (Oregon), and Cedar City (Utah) devoted to Shakespearean performances. It is now possible for those who love the playwright's works to see every one of his plays on stage, something that few people if any from Shakespeare's time to the mid-20th century could have hoped to do. His popularity with mass audiences has soared with movies that have been box-office successes and Academy Award winners. Films of his plays have been produced not only in Great Britain and the United States but also in Russia, Japan, Germany, Italy, Poland, and the Czech Republic.

The educational system has played a major role in making Shakespeare the prominent figure he is today. Elementary school students recite lines from Shakespeare and act out short scenes. High school students study *Romeo and Juliet, Julius Caesar,* and *Hamlet* as part of their required curriculum, and nearly every drama department has attempted at least one Shakespeare play. On the college level Shakespeare is an essential part of a liberal arts education, and every educated person is expected to have some familiarity with the playwright's works. Throughout the world, including non-English-speaking countries, Shakespeare is taught as a guide to understanding human conflicts and emotions.

SHAKESPEARE ACROSS THE GLOBE. Countries throughout the world, from Europe to the Far East, have claimed Shakespeare as their own and used him to support their social ideologies*. In 19th-century Germany, political dissatisfaction was summed up in the phrase "Deutschland ist Hamlet" (Germany is Hamlet). In Eastern Europe under communism, Rumania reported that "Shakespeare's theater represents a heritage of patriotic education." In the former Czechoslovakia, Shakespeare was hailed as "the greatest playwright and the most human poet the history of culture has known." Today Japan claims the second largest Shakespeare association; only the Shakespeare Association of America has more members. India has had a long history of Shakespearean theater and scholarship. Even China, which had banned Western writers for decades, sponsored its first SHAKESPEARE FESTIVAL in 1986.

The most astonishing evidence of Shakespeare's global influence is the way that communist* nations, such as the former Soviet Union, have used his writings to educate their citizens and foster political ideology. Karl Marx, the principal author of the communist belief system, praised Shakespeare as one of the world's geniuses. His daughter wrote that Shakespeare was the bible of their house and that by the age of six she knew scene after scene of his plays by heart. When Russia became a Marxist state, Shakespeare was used to promote and popularize the government's doctrines through theater and other media. Between 1917 and 1939, 5 million copies of Shakespeare's plays were published in the 28 languages of the Soviet Union. There were more productions of his plays in Soviet theaters than in the theaters of Britain and America combined, according to one estimate. A production of *The Taming of the Shrew* at the

* *ideology* belief system

* *communist* referring to an economic system in which the state owns all property and all goods are shared equally among the people

Central Theater of the Red Army ran all the way through World War II. One hundred and fifty productions of *Othello* were presented during the same period.

Today the annual *World Shakespeare Bibliography*, published in *Shakespeare Quarterly*, informs scholars in every country of the world about critical and theatrical Shakespearean activities in their regions. In 1998, a typical year, the publication contained 4,278 entries, all devoted to books, articles, performances, recordings, and educational materials on Shakespeare. With such international influence, perhaps William Shakespeare can rightly be called the Man of the Millennium. (*See also* **Acting Companies, Elizabethan; Acting Companies, Modern; Actors, Shakespearean; Museums and Archives; Playwrights and Poets; Shakespeare on Screen; Shakespeare's Sources; Shakespeare's Works, Adaptations of; Shakespeare's Works, Changing Views.**)

SHAKESPEARE'S SOURCES

Like most playwrights of his day, Shakespeare borrowed from an immense variety of historical, dramatic, and literary sources. He drew plots, characters, and themes from collections of histories, essays, and poems, as well as from such familiar works as the BIBLE and the writings of several ancient Greek and Roman authors. In fact there are only three Shakespearean plays (*Titus Andronicus, Love's Labor's Lost,* and *The Tempest*) for which scholars cannot identify a specific primary source. A major part of Shakespeare's genius was his ability to combine material from what he had read and what he had personally experienced into a unique creation all his own.

ANCIENT INFLUENCES. Shakespeare was probably educated at a grammar school in STRATFORD-UPON-AVON and was therefore familiar with the classics of ancient Greek and Roman literature. He may have read these works in Latin or in contemporary French and English translations, and there is some evidence that he could read Italian as well. One of the most important of these ancient sources was the *Metamorphoses* by the ancient Roman poet OVID. This collection of fanciful tales provided Shakespeare with a broad field of inspiration rather than with specific plots. Themes drawn from the *Metamorphoses* include magic and transformation, as seen in *A Midsummer Night's Dream* and *The Tempest.* Ovid also inspired two of Shakespeare's major poems, *Venus and Adonis* and *The Rape of Lucrece.*

Two other Roman writers who influenced Shakespeare were the comic playwrights Plautus (ca. 254 B.C.–184 B.C.) and Terence (ca. 190 B.C.–ca. 159 B.C.). The plays of Plautus are mostly broad farce*, but they also contain clever puns and other wordplay. Elements of Plautus's style appear in *The Comedy of Errors, The Taming of the Shrew,* and *The Merry Wives of Windsor.* Both Terence and Plautus used stock characters, such as the braggart soldier, whom Shakespeare expanded into the unforgettable Sir John FALSTAFF. Terence's most significant influence was the five-act

Shakespeare's primary source for his history plays was Raphael Holinshed's *Chronicles of England, Scotland, and Ireland.* Originally published in 1577, the work was intended to be the first book in a multivolume history of the entire world. It was never completed.

* **farce** light dramatic composition that features broad satiric comedy, improbable situations, stereotyped characters, and exaggerated physical action

* **tetralogy** four-part series of literary or dramatic works
* **humanist** referring to a philosophy that emphasizes the value of everyday life and individual achievement

THE BIBLE AND THE BARD

Although Shakespeare mentions the Bible by name only once (in *The Merry Wives of Windsor*), nearly every scene in his plays contains some biblical quotation or reference. For example, many references to the Old Testament appear in the speeches of the Jewish moneylender Shylock in *The Merchant of Venice.* The playwright used both the 1560 Geneva Bible and the 1568 Bishops' Bible as references, and he probably also knew the Vulgate of St. Jerome, a Latin version that had been used throughout western Europe from the 400s to the 1500s. The King James version familiar to modern readers was not published until 1611, around the time that Shakespeare retired from the theater.

structure he used for his plays. Shakespeare would have been familiar with it from grammar school, and it became the standard dramatic form in Shakespeare's day.

Parallel Lives, a collection of biographies by the Greek philosopher Plutarch (ca. A.D. 56–ca. A.D. 130) provided background for the plays Shakespeare set in ancient Greece and Rome. The playwright is believed to have used Thomas North's translation of PLUTARCH'S LIVES (1570), which is considered to be one of the finest translations in the English language. Several of the Roman plays, especially *Titus Andronicus,* also show the influence of the ancient tragedian Seneca (ca. 4 B.C.–A.D. 65).

LATER SOURCES. For his English history plays, Shakespeare borrowed mostly from the work of two English historians: Raphael Holinshed and Edward Halle. Halle's *The Union of the Two Noble and Illustre Famelies of Lancastre and York* (1548) was the primary source for Shakespeare's tetralogy* about the WARS OF THE ROSES. HOLINSHED'S CHRONICLES (1577) influenced fully a third of his plays, including all the histories, the tragedies *King Lear* and *Macbeth,* and the romance *Cymbeline.*

For additional information about the Wars of the Roses, Shakespeare turned to the writings of Sir Thomas Elyot (ca. 1490–1546). Elyot's best-known work, *The Boke Called the Governour,* dealt with the morals and education of political leaders. Echoes of the work can be found in *The Two Gentlemen of Verona* and in *Henry IV, Part 2.* The histories also show the influence of *A Mirror for Magistrates,* a collection of biographies of kings and other important political figures. Seven editions of this popular book were published between 1559 and 1619. Most of the figures depicted in *A Mirror for Magistrates* were tyrannical rulers who met with tragic ends. The collection also provided material for two of Shakespeare's tragedies, *King Lear* and *Julius Caesar.*

Two Italian authors provided material for Shakespeare's plays and poems. Francesco Petrarca, known as Petrarch (1304–1374), was a humanist* who edited and commented on many ancient Latin classics. He also wrote original works of poetry and prose in both Latin and Italian. His sonnets, in which the poet idealizes his beloved Laura, influenced Shakespeare's own sonnets in both form and subject matter. Giambattista Giraldi, known as Cinthio (1504–1573), provided some of the plot details for *Measure for Measure* and *Othello.* Cinthio's plays examine the relationship between love and justice, two subjects close to Shakespeare's heart.

Many passages in Shakespeare's dramatic works and poems are drawn from the writings of the Dutch humanist author Desiderius Erasmus (ca. 1466–1536). His *Adagia,* a collection of famous quotations that had been translated into English in 1539, provided Shakespeare with material for *The Rape of Lucrece* and for parts of *Love's Labor's Lost* and the *Henry IV* plays. Many scholars also believe that Erasmus's *The Praise of Folie* supplied material for *Julius Caesar, Troilus and Cressida,* and *As You Like It,* including Jaques's famous speech on the SEVEN AGES OF MAN. (*See also* **History in Shakespeare's Plays: Ancient Greece and Rome; History in Shakespeare's Plays: England; Playwrights and Poets.**)

SHAKESPEARE'S WILL

When Shakespeare died on April 23, 1616, he left his property to his family and friends according to a will drawn up in January of that year. This will, which still survives, is three pages long, with the playwright's signature on each page. It is the most extensive document scholars have relating to Shakespeare's life, but its contents are mostly unremarkable. The will leaves the majority of the playwright's property to his older daughter, Susanna Hall, and indicates who is to receive certain personal items.

One of the most intriguing items for scholars is the playwright's "second best bed," which he left to his wife, along with the accompanying "furniture" (bed linens and hangings). Some critics have seen this as an insult to his wife, Anne—as if he had left her nothing else—but English common law ensured that all widows automatically received a third of the income from their husbands' estates. For this reason other interpreters believe that the bed Shakespeare left to Anne may have had sentimental value for the couple.

Shakespeare revised his will on March 25, 1616, shortly before his death. His younger daughter, Judith, had been married in February to a man who was caught in an affair soon afterward. Historians speculate that Shakespeare, not trusting his new son-in-law, carefully arranged an inheritance for her that would guarantee an income to Judith and to her heirs.

Shakespeare mentions several of his fellow actors from the KING'S MEN in his will, leaving them money to buy memorial rings. He did not, however, leave his plays to anyone, because legally they were the property of the King's Men and of the publishers who had laid claim to them in the Stationers' Register during his lifetime. (*See also* **Hathaway, Anne; Shakespeare, Life and Career.**)

SHAKESPEARE'S WORKS, ADAPTATIONS OF

* **classical** in the tradition of ancient Greece and Rome

* **Restoration** referring to the period in English history, beginning in 1660, when Charles II was restored to the throne

For nearly 200 years, many of Shakespeare's plays were replaced on the stage by adaptations. These heavily rewritten versions gained favor for a variety of reasons. During the political turmoil of the English Civil War (1642–1660), the English theaters were closed, and by the time they reopened tastes had changed. Many critics objected to Shakespeare's plots, which violated the rules of classical* drama that insisted on continuity of action, time, and location. They also found fault with the complex morality of the plays, in which heroes tend to be flawed, villains are sometimes sympathetic, and justice is not always apparent in the doling out of rewards and punishments. Many authors of the period therefore attempted to "improve" Shakespeare's plays, making them conform more completely to the values of Restoration* society.

One of the first adapters of Shakespeare's work was William Davenant, the playwright's godson. In 1663 he created a spectacular version of *Macbeth* with music and dancing witches, cutting and rearranging many of Shakespeare's scenes and expanding the roles of Macduff and Lady Macduff. Davenant's version became so popular that Shakespeare's

Shakespeare's plays have inspired many musical adaptations. One of the best known is *West Side Story,* which casts *Romeo and Juliet* in the middle of a gang war in New York City.

* *satirical* ridiculing human wickedness and foolishness

original *Macbeth* was not performed again until 1744. Davenant also combined *Measure for Measure* and *Much Ado About Nothing* into a single play called *The Law Against Lovers.* Like Davenant's other adaptations, this work removed any language that might have been considered either unclear or improper.

Another early adapter was the poet and playwright John Dryden, an outstanding author in his own right. Although an admitted admirer of Shakespeare, Dryden criticized the plots and language of many of the plays. In 1667 he collaborated with Davenant on *The Enchanted Island*, an adaptation of *The Tempest* that added several new characters and reduced the role of the central figure, PROSPERO. Dryden also penned a version of *Antony and Cleopatra*, which he retitled *All for Love,* and changed the language in *Troilus and Cressida,* with the result that a satirical* play condemning war and lechery turned into one that glorified the heroes of ancient Greece.

One of the most successful adaptations of a Shakespeare play was *King Lear,* as rewritten in 1681 by the playwright Nahum Tate. Tate changed Shakespeare's play almost completely, creating a love affair between the CORDELIA and Edgar and constructing a happy ending to one of the most tragic plays ever written. Instead of dying at the conclusion of a tragedy, Lear and Cordelia kill their captors, Cordelia marries Edgar, and Lear retires peacefully. Although this revised plot destroys most of the power of the original play, it proved hugely successful, replacing the original version on stage for more than 150 years. Less popular were Tate's adaptations of *Richard II* and *Coriolanus,* both of which closed soon after their initial performances.

New adaptations continued to appear until the early 1800s. At the same time, however, actors who managed theaters were gradually beginning to restore Shakespeare's original plays to the stage. Some made only slight changes, putting a few of the playwright's lines back into the script of an adapted version, but over time more and more of the original texts crept back into performances. The "improved" versions finally disappeared in the late 1800s, and for the most part Shakespeare as written by Shakespeare has held the stage ever since. (*See also* **Shakespearean Theater: 17th Century; Shakespearean Theater: 18th Century; Shakespeare's Reputation.**)

SHAKESPEARE'S WORKS, CHANGING VIEWS

Ben JONSON's claim, in a poem praising Shakespeare that appears in the FIRST FOLIO, that Shakespeare was "not of an age, but for all time" has proved prophetic in many respects. In the years since Shakespeare's death, numerous books and movies have been based on his life and plays. College courses and scholarly journals are dedicated to the study of his works, and conferences are held in his honor throughout the world. Clearly Shakespeare's works continue to speak to readers, scholars, and audiences in the modern world. In fact Shakespeare has become so central to Western literature and culture that it is easy to assume he has always been universally admired. But in reality, Shakespeare's reputation and the ways in which his plays are interpreted have changed dramatically over time—and continue to change today. Shakespeare may be "for all time," but he means decidedly different things to different generations of readers.

CONTRASTING VIEWS. Since his plays first appeared on the London stage, Shakespeare has attracted the attention of leading poets, scholars, and thinkers. The differences in their responses to the playwright's works reflect the changes in society, culture, and literature over the past four centuries.

The famous diarist Samuel PEPYS, for instance, saw a production of *A Midsummer Night's Dream* in 1662 and recorded afterward that it was "the most insipid* ridiculous play that ever I saw in my life." The only aspects of the performance he enjoyed were "some good dancing and some handsome women." In the 1980s, on the other hand, literary critic Louis Montrose described the same play as a highly complex presentation of "personal and public images of gender and power" that offers valuable insight into Elizabethan culture. In the early 1690s Thomas Rymer labeled the tragedy *Othello* a "Bloody Farce," and remarked that if Desdemona had lost her garter instead of her handkerchief in *Othello*, her husband "might have smelled a rat." Today the same play is viewed as a key text for examining Renaissance attitudes about sex and race.

Views of Shakespeare's characters have also shifted over time. Some productions of *The Merchant of Venice* have presented SHYLOCK as a bloodthirsty villain, while others have made him an unfortunate victim of

* *insipid* dull and lifeless

78

Christian persecution. Lady Macbeth has traditionally been regarded as an evil temptress, but feminist scholar Cristina León Alfar sees her as a properly submissive wife who merely reflects her husband's bloody and criminal desires. Many critics have echoed the Chorus's description of Henry V as the "mirror of all Christian kings," but an influential modern critic, Stephen Greenblatt, calls him a "conniving hypocrite" whose royal power stems from "glorified usurpation* and theft."

Hamlet has provoked an immense variety of critical reactions. The Romantic* poet Samuel Taylor COLERIDGE admired the prince as a deep thinker, and declared with some pride that "I have a smack of Hamlet myself." On the other hand 20th-century psychoanalytic critic Ernest Jones argued that Hamlet's indecisiveness resulted from an unresolved Oedipal conflict, a secret desire to murder his father and marry his mother. Modernist* poet T. S. Eliot proclaimed *Hamlet* an "artistic failure" because it is "full of stuff" that Shakespeare was unable to "manipulate into art." More recently, critic Harold Bloom praised the character of Hamlet and his creator for "the invention of the human, the inauguration of personality as we have come to recognize it."

EARLY CRITICS. Ben Jonson attached some qualifications to his praise of Shakespeare. His poem in the First Folio claimed that Shakespeare knew "small [little] Latin and less Greek" and that his poetic genius was due more to natural ability than to learning, labor, and craft (which characterize Jonson's own verse).

Jonson's mixed reaction to Shakespeare was echoed by the Restoration* poet and playwright John Dryden. In his *Essay of Dramatic Poesy*, published in the late 1660s, Dryden professed to "love Shakespeare" and asserted that when Shakespeare describes something "you more than see it, you feel it too." Nonetheless, Dryden considered Jonson a more "correct playwright" than Shakespeare because the former followed the ideals of classical* drama, including the three "unities" of time, place, and action. Shakespeare, by contrast, often allowed a single scene shift to bridge vast distances (*Antony and Cleopatra*) or the passage of several years (*The Winter's Tale*). Jonson also maintained the "decorum* of the stage," while Shakespeare filled his comedies with bawdy passages and his tragedies with overblown speeches that Dryden described as "bombast*." But despite his distaste for the unruliness of Shakespeare's plays Dryden judged him "the Man who of all Modern, and perhaps Ancient Poets, had the largest and most comprehensive soul."

The next major critic of Shakespeare was Dr. Samuel Johnson, a celebrated literary figure of the 1700s who compiled an edition of Shakespeare's plays. In his influential "Preface to Shakespeare," Johnson described the dramatist's work as the "mirrour of life" that captures "common humanity." But, like Dryden, he criticized Shakespeare's careless plotting, his endless puns, and his bawdy humor. He also accused the playwright of lacking "moral purpose" because he did not always punish the wicked and reward the good. This was quite unacceptable to an 18th-century reader who believed firmly in classical ideals of order and justice, good and evil.

* *usurpation* seizing of power from a rightful ruler

* *Romantic* referring to a school of thought, prominent in the 1800s, that emphasized the importance of emotion in art

* *modernist* referring to a literary and artistic style that emphasized new and different forms of expression appropriate to modern society

* *Restoration* referring to the period in English history, beginning in 1660, when Charles II was restored to the throne

* *classical* in the tradition of ancient Greece and Rome

* *decorum* proper behavior

* *bombast* heavy padding used in Elizabethan clothing

Johnson felt, for example, that Angelo should not have been spared from punishment in *Measure for Measure* and that Bertram, whom Johnson saw as a selfish coward and a liar, should not be "dismissed to happiness" at the end of *All's Well That Ends Well*. Johnson was so "shocked" by the death of the innocent CORDELIA at the end of *King Lear* that he did not know "whether I ever endured to read again the last scenes of the play till I undertook to revise them as editor."

Samuel Johnson was not the only critic to object to the lack of poetic justice in *King Lear*. Nahum Tate, the Restoration dramatist, saw the play as "a Heap of Jewels unstrung and unpolish'd," which he took upon himself to turn into beautiful jewelry. He added a love story between Edgar and Cordelia, whose husband, the king of France, is conveniently dropped from the play. He then drastically revised the play's ending, allowing Lear to be restored to the throne, while Cordelia lives happily ever after with Edgar.

THE ROMANTICS. The rise of the Romantic poets in the late 1700s changed the face of literary criticism as well as poetry. The neoclassical* emphasis on structure, decorum, and moral instruction gave way to a growing interest in the psychology of individual characters. Earlier critics, such as John Dryden, Samuel Johnson, and Alexander Pope, had recognized the power of Shakespeare's imagination but believed he should have restrained it more. The Romantic poet and critic Samuel Taylor Coleridge, by contrast, was enraptured with it. He felt that Shakespeare's poetic intellect gave "organic form" to seemingly disconnected elements in the plays. Instead of praising Shakespeare for mirroring life, Coleridge applauded him for writing plays that were the products of his own imagination.

Coleridge focused much of his critical attention on analyzing the minds of specific characters, such as Hamlet and IAGO. His psychological approach was later adapted by 20th-century scholar A. C. Bradley. Bradley's Romantic fascination with character psychology led him and several of his contemporaries to treat Shakespeare's dramatic creations as "real" people whose lives extend beyond the plays in which they appear. This development in turn paved the way for psychoanalytic criticism, which subjected Shakespeare's characters to Freudian* analysis.

MODERN VIEWS. The 1900s, especially after World War II, witnessed an explosion in Shakespeare criticism. Between 1945 and the late 1960s, there were two main schools of critical thought. The first was Historicism, which focused on the historical context of Shakespeare's works. Historicists read the plays as products of an Elizabethan culture that stressed order, rank, tradition, and stability. Ulysses' famous speech in *Troilus and Cressida* on the importance of order in the universe and in society (I.iii.75–137) best illustrates the Historicists' understanding of Renaissance history. The other major school, New Criticism, took the opposite approach. It focused on the text itself, outside of any personal or social context that might have gone into its writing. The New Critics tended to focus on Shakespeare's poetic language and imagery rather

* *neoclassical* referring to a school of thought, prominent in the 1800s, that focused on restoring the traditions of ancient Greece and Rome

* *Freudian* based on the theories of Sigmund Freud, a doctor in Vienna during the late 1800s and early 1900s who developed the practice of modern psychotherapy

* *Marxist* based on the ideas of communist reformer Karl Marx

* *illegitimate* born to parents who are not married to each other
* *misogyny* distrust or hatred of women
* *hierarchical* ordered according to rank

VIEWS ON FILM

Directors, as well as scholars, have reinterpreted Shakespeare's works to focus on the aspects most in tune with their own times. Modern film versions of Shakespeare's plays illustrate how directors shape the playwright's works to their society. In a 1996 film Baz Luhrmann set *Romeo and Juliet* in modern Los Angeles, with the Montagues and Capulets as members of rival gangs. *Hamlet* has been set in the business world of 2000, *Macbeth* in the realm of high school football, and *Othello* as a college basketball story. The fact that Shakespeare's works can sustain so many interpretations highlights their richness and complexity.

than on plot, character, or historical background. Indeed, it has been said that for the New Critics plays became poems.

Both the New Criticism and the "old" Historicism of the 1960s were politically and socially conservative in their approaches to Shakespeare. In the 1980s two new schools of Marxist*-influenced criticism emerged: cultural materialism and New Historicism. Both are schools of leftist literary criticism that reject the study of Shakespeare's texts in isolation from history (as did the New Critics) or as a passive reflection of a society's beliefs (did the "old" Historicists). Instead they maintain that literary texts both influence and are influenced by historical, cultural, and economic conditions.

This generation of critics differed dramatically from 18th-century critics, such as Johnson and Dryden, who had lamented the lack of order and poetic justice in *King Lear*. Cultural materialists and New Historicists applauded Shakespeare's willingness to confront the reality of a cold and uncaring universe in which there is neither God nor divine justice.

This shift in critical emphasis led to new understandings of major Shakespearean characters. In Jonathan Dollimore's reading of *King Lear*, for instance, Edmund—the earl of Gloucester's illegitimate* son, who schemes against his father and brother—becomes a more sympathetic character, a victim of prejudice and government oppression. By contrast the king, traditionally seen as a tragic victim whose faults pale in comparison to his majesty, is viewed with a more critical eye. Marxist-feminist critic Kathleen McLuskie cautions against any glorification of Lear that overlooks, or even embraces, his frenzied misogyny*.

Critic Terry Eagleton makes an even bolder claim in his reading of *Macbeth*, describing the witches—seen as evil spirits by generations of readers—as "the heroines of the piece, however little the play itself recognizes the fact." Eagleton argues that by triggering Macbeth's ambition, the witches help expose the idea of "hierarchical* social order" as a way of justifying "routine oppression and incessant warfare." The witches reveal that evil is not some supernatural power lurking on the heath but a material force at the very heart of the play's social structure.

Another major change in Shakespearean criticism was the birth of feminist criticism in the late 1970s. This school of interpretation was one of the products of the feminist movement, which in turn reflected the changing perceptions of women in society. Feminist critics were the first to seriously examine some of Shakespeare's female characters, who had been ignored or slighted by male critics. They also applied a feminist perspective to Shakespeare's male characters and to the male-dominated societies in which many of his plays are set. Feminist literary critics such as Jean Howard, Catherine Belsey, and Coppélia Kahn conducted historical research to learn more about the conditions of women's lives in Shakespeare's time and reread the plays in the context of this new information.

Feminist criticism completely revitalized and transformed Shakespeare in the 1970s and 1980s. It is hard to imagine any approach to Shakespeare today that does not draw, consciously or unconsciously, on the basic assumptions and insights of this school of criticism. It should be

clear by now that even though Shakespeare may be for all time, each generation creates him anew. (*See also* **Characters in Shakespeare's Plays; Feminist Interpretations; Marxist Interpretations; Shakespeare on Screen; Shakespeare's Reputation.**)

SHAKESPEARE'S WORKS, INFLUENTIAL EDITIONS

Countless editions of Shakespeare's works have been published in the nearly 400 years since his death, but scholars consider only a handful of them to be particularly important. The earliest of these is the FIRST FOLIO, the very first printed collection of Shakespeare's plays. Published in 1623 the First Folio was compiled by John Heminges and Henry Condell, two of Shakespeare's fellow actors from the KING'S MEN. It included 36 plays, half of which had never before been published in any form. However, it omitted two others, *Pericles* and *The Two Noble Kinsman*, which would not appear in any collection of Shakespeare's works for many years.

The next significant collection of Shakespeare was published in 1709 by the poet Nicholas ROWE. This edition featured Rowe's biography of Shakespeare, based on the recollections of actor Thomas Betterton, who had compiled stories about the playwright. Rowe's was the standard Shakespeare biography for the next century. His edition was the first to include a list of the characters (dramatis personae) for each play, as well as a systematic approach to the entrances and exits of various characters. Rowe also supplied act and scene divisions for the plays. Most of the designations in his volumes are still used in modern editions.

In 1725 the poet Alexander Pope published a Shakespeare collection that proved to be quite disappointing. Pope changed much of the wording in the plays to suit his own poetic tastes and omitted entire sections that he did not believe were Shakespeare's original writing. His most important contribution was in his decision to reject six plays not by Shakespeare that had been included in the Third Folio.

The most noteworthy edition published during the late 1700s was Samuel Johnson's, prepared in 1765. Unlike many previous editors, Johnson did not make extensive changes to the text of the plays, stating that "after I had printed a few plays, [I] resolved to insert none of my own readings in the text." Johnson added some new stage directions, however, and altered some punctuation. The primary strengths of his work are its critical notes and its preface, considered by many scholars to be the finest evaluation of Shakespeare ever produced.

In 1778 George Steevens published an edition that attempted to list all of the plays in the order in which they were written. This chronology was prepared by scholar Edmond Malone, who published the first critical edition of the sonnets two years later. Steevens went on to prepare most of the material in the First Variorum edition, published in 1803 by Isaac Reed. The variorum contained not only the full texts of the plays, but also a collection of notes and comments added by earlier editors. It also listed different versions of certain lines in the texts that varied from edition to edition. A reprint of this volume, called the Second Variorum, was published in 1813, and a Third Variorum—based on the work of Malone—was released in 1821. The fourth, or New Variorum, was published in a series of volumes, beginning in 1871 and continuing to the present.

The *Globe Shakespeare,* a single-volume work published in 1864, was influential because of its system for numbering the lines in Shakespeare's text. This edition is still considered standard for line numbering. The most widely accepted scholarly edition of the plays is the *Arden Shakespeare,* a 37-volume edition begun in 1899 and revised in 1951 as the *New Arden Shakespeare.* The third Arden edition is in progress. (*See also* **Printing and Publishing; Quartos and Folios.**)

SHIPS

By defeating the Spanish Armada in 1588, England replaced Spain as the greatest naval power in Europe. While England's armed naval vessels were gaining control of the seas, its merchant fleet was playing a key role in expanding the nation's trade and commerce. Together the men-of-war and the cargo carriers of Elizabethan England laid the foundation of British sea power that would dominate the waves for the next 350 years.

The Elizabethan era was the age of sails, and a ship's size, its shape, and the types of sails it carried determined its use. The most common English ships were cargo carriers. At the time, however, there was little distinction between a cargo ship and a fighting vessel. The widespread threat of piracy meant that most ships carried at least a few small cannons for self-defense, and merchant ships were often pressed into military service. Nearly five-sixths of the ships that fought against the Spanish Armada were English merchant vessels.

The smallest and slowest cargo ships, called crayers, had a single mast carrying a square sail. A crayer could travel slowly along the coast, but it was unsuited for sailing the open sea. A larger cargo craft was the flat-bottomed hoy, which might carry either one or two masts. Also built for use in shallow waters, hoys could make longer journeys by using a large leeboard* for stability in deeper, rougher waters.

The most popular oceangoing merchant ships were the caravel and the hulk. The caravel, originally designed by the Portuguese, had a long, deep hull that enabled it to carry significantly more cargo than a crayer or a hoy. Its deep hull also made it much more stable in the violent seas of the open ocean. A caravel typically had four masts carrying both square and lateen (triangular) sails. Square sails caught more wind, enabling ships to sail faster. The advantage of lateen sails was that they could be adjusted to sail against the wind. A ship with lateen sails was much more maneuverable than one that carried only square sails.

More common than the caravels were the larger ships called hulks. Like caravels, hulks had deep hulls and four masts carrying both square and lateen sails. Hulks were two to three times as large as caravels (300 to

* *leeboard* board attached to the side of a sailing ship that prevents the vessel from drifting off course

Ships

Because piracy was a constant threat, most ships carried weapons for self-defense. This woodcut from 1619 shows cannons protruding from the side of an English galleon.

See color plate 14, vol. 1.

400 tons, as compared to 100 to 150 tons) and carried considerably more cargo. While a caravel was relatively long compared to its width, the hulk was only about twice as long as it was wide. It was thus much slower and less maneuverable than the smaller caravel.

Although merchant vessels could be used for military purposes, there were also ships designed specifically for naval warfare. The smallest sail-driven warships were called pinnaces. They were large enough to navigate the open sea but small enough to be propelled by oars in the absence of wind. Spain and other Mediterranean countries made much use of galleys, which were low, sleek, speedy vessels powered by both sails and oars. Galleys attacked enemy ships by ramming them or pulling alongside so that sailors from the galleys could board the enemy vessels. Galleys were unsuited to rougher seas, however, because they were easily swamped by large waves.

Galleons were the largest battleships, weighing 800 tons or more. The length of a galleon was about three times its width, making it faster than the broader merchant ships. Galleons carried heavy cannons that enabled them to fight from long range rather than close up like galleys. The Spanish originally used galleons to guard merchant vessels that carried American gold back to Europe. Because of their speed and powerful armament, however, galleons were eventually used to carry the gold themselves. English galleons were typically more agile and better armed than their Spanish counterparts. Their greater maneuverability was decisive in the 1588 battle with the Spanish Armada. English ships easily outran the heavier Spanish vessels, preventing the Spanish from boarding the galleons while at the same time causing heavy damage with their long-range missiles. (*See also* **Exploration; Navigation; Trade; Transportation and Travel.**)

SHYLOCK

* **medieval** referring to the Middle Ages, a period roughly between A.D. 500 and 1500

* **aside** remark made by a character onstage to the audience or to another character, unheard by other characters present in the same scene

See color plate 11, vol. 3.

* **anti-Semitic** referring to prejudice against Jews

Shylock, the Jewish moneylender in *The Merchant of Venice,* is one of Shakespeare's most controversial characters. Over the years, he has been portrayed as a comic scoundrel, a bloodthirsty villain, and a tragic victim—sometimes all three at once. These conflicting interpretations reflect the history behind this complex figure.

Shakespeare based Shylock on the miser, a stock character from medieval* literature. Although the miser was traditionally a comical villain, the playwright made his character more human by giving him sympathetic qualities. When Shylock first appears in the play, his greediness is firmly established when he says in an aside* that he hates Antonio, a Christian merchant, mostly because "He lends out money gratis [free], and brings down / The rate of usance [interest rate]" (I.iii.44–45). Shylock soon reveals that he also has a more personal reason to hate Antonio: "You call me misbeliever, cut-throat dog, / And spet [spit] upon my Jewish gaberdine [cloak]" (I.iii.111–12). In other words Shylock is not only hateful but a victim of others' hate.

Shylock agrees to lend Antonio money on the condition that the merchant will surrender a pound of his flesh if he cannot pay the debt within three months. Shylock attempts to justify his thirst for revenge with a speech in Act III that emphasizes his humanity:

> I am a Jew. Hath not a Jew eyes? Hath not a Jew hands, organs, dimensions, senses, affections, passions; fed with the same food, hurt with the same weapons, subject to the same diseases, heal'd by the same means, warm'd and cool'd by the same winter and summer, as a Christian is? If you prick us, do we not bleed? If you tickle us, do we not laugh? If you poison us, do we not die? And if you wrong us, shall we not revenge?

(i.58–67)

This speech perhaps best illustrates the complexity of Shylock's character. On the one hand it is an eloquent argument against the unfair treatment of Jews by an unfeeling Christian majority. On the other it reveals Shylock's cold-blooded plan to end Antonio's life.

Some critics have argued that Shakespeare's portrayal of Shylock is anti-Semitic*. Others contend that *The Merchant of Venice* is more critical of the anti-Semitic Christians than it is of the vengeful Shylock. In any case it seems likely that Shakespeare knew very few Jewish people; Jews had been banished from England as far back as 1290 and were not allowed to return to the country until 1655. The law was not strictly enforced, but only a small community of Jews lived in London (*See also* **Jews; Race and Ethnicity; Religion.**)

SICKNESS

See *Disease; Medici*

SIDNEY, SIR PHILIP

1554–1586
Poet, scholar, soldier

* **courtier** person in attendance at a royal court
* **genre** literary form
* **romance** story of love and adventure, the forerunner of the modern novel
* **pastoral** relating to the countryside; often used to draw a contrast between the innocence and serenity of rural life and the corruption and extravagance of court life
* **sonnet** poem of 14 lines with a fixed pattern of meter and rhyme
* **classical** in the tradition of ancient Greece and Rome

Sir Philip Sidney, a courtier* of Queen Elizabeth, was a true "Renaissance man." He excelled as a soldier, a scholar, a diplomat, and a poet, winning the admiration of his contemporaries. He died young, killed at the battle of Zutphen in the Netherlands, but his fame endured. His writings, which were not published until after his death, were popular, and they greatly influenced other Elizabethan writers, including Shakespeare.

Sidney is most widely remembered for introducing the genre* known as the romance* to the English reading public. Shakespeare's romances, four plays written late in his career, build on Sidney's literary endeavors. Sidney's great, unfinished romance *Arcadia,* first published in 1590, inspired several of Shakespeare's plots, among them the story of King Lear and his three daughters. Echoes of *Arcadia* also appear in *As You Like It,* a humorous and frequently skeptical look at the pastoral* style.

Sidney's famous collection of sonnets*, *Astrophel and Stella,* was probably responsible for the sonnet-writing fad of the 1590s. The story Sidney narrated in his poems may also have inspired the plot of *Romeo and Juliet.* In addition Sidney was one of the greatest literary scholars of his day. His *Apologie for Poetrie,* published in 1595, defended the principles of classical* literature. Moreover, his comments on drama in the *Apologie* made Sidney England's first significant dramatic critic. (*See also* **Pastoralism; Plays: The Romances; Sonnets.**)

SOCIAL CLASSES

* **hierarchy** ordered structure based on rank

Elizabethan society was highly class conscious. Group distinctions based on occupation, wealth, and family history were fairly rigid and strictly observed. Elizabethans saw such differences as the natural reflection of a divine order, known as the Great Chain of Being, a vast hierarchy* that contained everything in the universe. People generally tried to live according to their "proper" station in life. Occasionally, however, an individual could rise in social status by gaining wealth and standing in the community.

The book *The Description of England,* published by clergyman William Harrison as part of HOLINSHED'S CHRONICLES, listed four basic social classes in Elizabethan England: gentlemen (collectively known as the gentry), citizens, yeomen, and laborers. Each of these broad categories included a large variety of people.

THE GENTRY. Harrison's first category, the gentry, was divided into two subcategories: the ARISTOCRACY and the minor gentry. The aristocracy, or peerage, consisted of everyone with a hereditary title—such as duke, earl, marquess, viscount, or baron—that could be passed down from one generation to the next. Monarchs occasionally granted such titles to commoners (nonnobles) as a mark of favor or as a reward for some particularly valuable service. When ELIZABETH I took the throne in 1558, there were only 57 peers in England; she created 18 more during her 45-year reign. Her successor, JAMES I, was more generous, advancing 46 of

See color plate 2, vol. 1.

his subjects to the peerage over a period of about 20 years. Aristocrats controlled most of the country's land, wealth, and power. Every noble owned a significant amount of land, known as a country estate. Aristocrats were also entitled to seats in the House of Lords (the upper house of Parliament) and thus held a share in the nation's political power.

The minor gentry included all those who did not have noble titles but who could, as Harrison put it, "live without manual labor, and . . . bear the port, charge, and countenance of a gentleman." The "countenance of a gentleman" meant both the manners and bearing suited to the title and the wealth to support oneself in the style appropriate for the gentry. Gentlemen were expected to dress fashionably, maintain elegant households, and provide charity to the poor. Members of the gentry were entitled to display a family coat of arms if they had one and to have one created if they did not.

Most of the gentry were not nobles and could not serve in the House of Lords. Nonnoble members of the gentry included knights, doctors, professors, military captains, and other professionals. The minor gentry was a much larger class than the aristocracy, consisting of more than 16,000 families between 1590 and 1642.

CITIZENS AND YEOMEN. Below the gentry were several distinct classes of working people: citizens, yeomen, and laborers. During Elizabethan times the word *citizen* had a more specific definition than its modern meaning. Citizens were tradespeople—such as merchants, traders, clothiers, and printers—who made and sold goods, as well as some who provided services, such as innkeepers. Citizens who were particularly successful or influential could become burgesses, holders of political positions either on local town councils or in the House of Commons (the lower house of Parliament).

Although they were often quite prosperous, citizens were distinct from the gentry because they had to work for a living. A successful citizen could enter the gentry, however, by retiring from his trade and buying a country estate. Because of lingering class prejudices, it was usually the children of such retired citizens, rather than the citizens themselves, who were considered gentlemen. Daughters of citizens could also rise in status by marrying into the gentry.

The word *citizen* refers to city and town dwellers. Yeomen, a separate group, were roughly equivalent to citizens in wealth and status but lived and worked in the country. Yeomen were lower in status than gentlemen because they did not own their land but leased it from members of the gentry. They were not considered laborers, however, because they usually did not perform the manual tasks involved in running a farm, such as plowing, planting, harvesting, and carrying the crops to market. Instead they hired and oversaw the work of others. Like citizens, yeomen were often very prosperous. Sometimes they were able to buy land of their own—often from gentlemen who had fallen on hard times—and enter the ranks of the gentry. They could also help their children become gentlemen by educating them to enter such professions as law and medicine. Shakespeare comments on this fact in *King Lear*, remarking

PEER FOR A PRICE

King James I not only created many new nobles but considerably broadened the class of the aristocracy. In 1611 he created a new hereditary title—baronet—and offered it to 200 gentlemen for a payment of £1,095. He also sold baronies, higher ranking titles, to wealthier gentlemen at a price of £10,000 apiece. One gentlewoman paid the crown £12,000 to become a viscountess, and five years later she was elevated to the rank of countess after making another payment.

Social Classes

Most Elizabethans recognized and respected class distinctions. The "countryman" shown in this woodcut from Robert Greene's *A Quip for an Upstart Courtier* (1592) would naturally defer to the "courtier" who outranks him socially.

that "he's a mad yeoman that sees his son a gentleman before him" (III.vi.13–14).

LABORERS AND SERVANTS. The vast majority of the population in Elizabethan England were members of the lowest recognized social group, "artificers and laborers." Artificers were manual workers employed by citizens. This group included skilled craftspeople (such as carpenters) who were distinct from citizens because they did not own the shops they worked in. With hard work and a bit of luck, skilled artificers could rise to the citizenry. Agricultural laborers had fewer possibilities for economic and social advancement. Their prospects depended on the availability of work and the goodwill of their employers. As Harrison put it, they had "neither voice nor authority in the commonwealth" and were "to be ruled and not to rule others."

This class also included servants. The social status of servants depended both on the position they held and on the status of those they served. A servant in a noble household, for example, could consider himself the superior of a servant in a more humble home. Servants generally could not rise to a different social class, but they could become higher-ranking servants. For example, a kitchen servant might hope to become chief cook. A good servant was a credit to his master and vice versa.

"CLASSLESS" PEOPLE. Many individuals in Elizabethan England did not fit neatly into Harrison's basic categories. Some, such as lawyers,

soldiers, and sailors, held respectable positions that were not officially recognized as part of a specific social class. Their unofficial social position depended mainly on how much money they had. Most of those who fell outside the recognized class structure, however, were social outsiders such as beggars, prostitutes, and criminals. This group also included "masterless men," such as ex-soldiers, who traveled about the kingdom finding employment where they could—and sometimes thieving when they could not support themselves otherwise. Laws passed during the reign of Henry VIII made masterless men subject to whipping wherever they went.

The laws against masterless men were an important concern for actors, who spent much of their time touring the countryside. To avoid legal difficulties Elizabethan acting companies sought aristocratic patrons*. A patron became a company's "master," often providing the actors with livery* that carried his personal colors or coat of arms. Patrons usually paid some of a company's expenses as well. In return for protection and support, the acting troupes performed on demand for their patrons and their guests.

* **patron** supporter or financial sponsor of an artist or writer
* **livery** distinctive clothing worn on formal occasions

CLASS DISTINCTIONS. In addition to the law governing masterless men, Elizabethan society had several formal structures to enforce class distinctions. Among these were the sumptuary laws, which required individuals to dress according to their station. For example, only countesses or ladies with higher titles were allowed to wear purple silk. Another mechanism was the granting of coats of arms to upper-class families. To obtain a coat of arms, the head of a family had to submit an application to the College of Arms (or the Herald's College). The heralds decided whether an applicant's family background entitled him to a coat of arms and to be officially identified as a gentleman.

By Shakespeare's time this rigid class system was beginning to fall apart. The feudal* system, the source of England's class structure, was giving way to a capitalist* economy that increased personal prosperity and social mobility. Shakespeare himself is a good example of an individual who was able to break through class barriers. His professional success in the theater enabled him to obtain a coat of arms for his family, purchase land, and become a prominent gentleman in his hometown, STRATFORD-UPON-AVON.

* **feudal** referring to the medieval system of government and landowning based on rank and loyalty
* **capitalist** referring to an economic system in which individuals own property

Shakespeare's characters come from all social classes. Many works show upper-class and lower-class characters interacting, as Prince Hal does with his companions at the Boar's Head tavern in *Henry IV, Part 1*. The central figures in the plays, however, are typically members of the gentry or wealthy citizens, such as the title character in *The Merchant of Venice*. Members of the lower classes are commonly minor characters, such as servants, or humorous figures, such as the "rude mechanicals" in *A Midsummer Night's Dream* and the bumbling watchmen in *Much Ado About Nothing*. (*See also* **Acting Companies, Elizabethan; Agriculture; Clothing; Craftworkers; Education and Literacy; Government and Politics; Heraldry; Patronage of the Arts; Poverty and Wealth; Royalty and Nobility; Vagabonds, Beggars, and Rogues.**)

SOLDIERS

See *Warfare; Work.*

SOLILOQUY

* *monologue* long speech by one character

Shakespeare's characters are frequently not what they seem. The thoughts and feelings they express in conversation with other characters may be considerably different from their true ones. When they address the audience, however, Shakespearean figures often reveal their private, inner thoughts through asides and soliloquies. An aside is a short speech—perhaps one line—that is spoken in the presence of other characters but not heard by them. A soliloquy is an extended monologue* delivered by a speaker who is either alone on the stage or temporarily detached from other characters. Shakespeare and other Elizabethan playwrights often used asides and soliloquies to provide the audience with information that could not reasonably be revealed through dialogue.

THE USES OF SOLILOQUY. Like many dramatic techniques of the time, soliloquies originated in ancient Greek and Roman theater. In Shakespeare's plays they serve two main functions. One is to provide information that helps the audience follow the plot. In the three *Henry VI* plays, for example, soliloquies describe events that have occurred offstage. They also reveal the intentions of certain characters so that audience members will understand what is happening as they observe these characters. The more complicated type of soliloquy reveals information about a character's thoughts, feelings, and motivations, helping the audience perceive a speaker's true nature in ways that other characters in the play cannot.

Shakespeare's use of the soliloquy developed over the course of his career. The soliloquies in his early plays are generally of the simpler type. In *Titus Andronicus,* the playwright's first tragedy, the villain Aaron informs the audience of his evil plans through soliloquies. These monologues also reveal his personality, but only in the most basic way. He gloats about his plots and takes delight in his own wickedness; there is no inner conflict or uncertainty in his character.

Gradually, however, Shakespeare mastered the soliloquy as a tool for revealing and developing character. In his later plays the soliloquy usually enables the audience to share a character's immediate thoughts, conflicts, and decisions. This technique reaches its fullest expression in the tortured speeches of Hamlet and Macbeth. Monologues of this type, in which a speaker shares his mental and emotional state with the audience, appear most often in the tragedies. A few are spoken by comic characters, such as FALSTAFF in the *Henry IV* plays, MALVOLIO in *Twelfth Night,* and Benedick in *Much Ado About Nothing.* Unlike tragic characters, who usually soliloquize in verse, these comic figures ordinarily reveal themselves to the audience in prose.

Many of Shakespeare's monologues combine the two primary purposes of soliloquy: plot explanation and character development. For example, villains often use soliloquies to explain how they will accomplish their goals while at the same time exposing the wicked motives behind them. In *Henry VI, Part 3*, the unscrupulous nobleman who will eventually become King Richard III reveals his ruthless ambition in a soliloquy, declaring his intention to "pluck" the crown from the present king. His speeches in *Richard III* disclose his schemes more fully, beginning with the play's opening lines, in which Richard explains that he is "determined to be a villain" (I.i.30). Most of his monologues serve primarily to explain his plans, but his final soliloquy is one of the first in which the playwright allows viewers to see into a character's troubled mind. As Richard thinks about those he has murdered, his sentences begin to disintegrate. He shifts quickly between questions and answers, showing that his brain is leaping haphazardly from one thought to another.

THINKING OUT LOUD. Soliloquies appear most extensively in *Hamlet* and *Macbeth*. *Hamlet* contains eight soliloquies altogether—seven by the title character and one spoken by the usurper* Claudius. Hamlet's extensive use of soliloquy is the perfect expression of his character. He spends the play obsessively commenting on the actions of other characters and criticizing himself for not taking action himself. His speeches occupy critical turning points in the play, and most of them reveal the prince's reactions to the events that are taking place around him. In his first soliloquy, for example, he laments his father's death and his mother's hasty second marriage to Claudius. In his third he bitterly contrasts an actor's ability to express passion over an imaginary situation with his own unwillingness to take action in response to a real one.

Hamlet's fourth soliloquy is one of the most famous speeches in all of English literature, beginning with the immortal line, "To be, or not to be, that is the question" (III.i.55). Unlike Hamlet's other speeches, this one does not show the prince commenting on some specific occurrence. Instead it poses a general, philosophical question—whether continuing an unhappy life is preferable to ending it. Most people see this monologue as an indication that Hamlet is contemplating suicide. The speech, however, may not reflect the prince's actual thoughts, because it may not be a true soliloquy. It is spoken in the presence of another character—OPHELIA—and Hamlet's words may take on a different meaning based on whether he is aware of her presence. The prince may be expressing his inner confusion, or he may be pretending to have self-destructive thoughts in order to convince Ophelia (and Claudius and POLONIUS, who are listening in) that he is insane.

Many scholars consider Macbeth's soliloquies the greatest in all of Shakespeare's plays. Like Hamlet, Macbeth faces a moral crisis as he contemplates the murder of a king. His early monologues express his conflicting desires: his ambition for the crown and his reluctance to kill for it. He lets the audience share in his decision-making process as he balances the two alternatives in his mind. After the crime his soliloquies reveal the torments of a guilty conscience.

To modern audiences soliloquies may seem somewhat artificial, but they add to the overall sense of truth within a play by enabling characters

* **usurper** one who seizes power from a rightful ruler

See
color plate 3,
vol. 3.

to reveal their true selves. Shakespeare's use of soliloquy enables him to maintain two realities within a drama—the public images his characters present to each other and the private ideas they share only with the audience. (*See also* **Dramatic Techniques; Language.**)

SONGS IN SHAKESPEARE'S PLAYS

See *Music in Elizabethan Theater.*

SONGS INSPIRED BY SHAKESPEARE

See *Music Inspired by Shakespeare.*

SONNETS

* *sonnet* poem of 14 lines with a fixed pattern of meter and rhyme

In addition to his plays and major poems, Shakespeare wrote 154 sonnets* that deal with such subjects as love, loyalty, and the changes caused by time. Since their publication in 1609 the sonnets have been a source of intrigue to scholars trying to learn more about Shakespeare's life. Unlike the plays, in which the playwright speaks only through his characters, the sonnets often appear to many to be written in the poet's own voice. It is therefore tempting to read the 154-poem sequence as a description of events in Shakespeare's life.

In addition to the narrator there are two major figures in the sonnets, the poet's female lover and his male friend. Many critics have speculated about whether these two characters represent real people who were important in Shakespeare's life and have suggested possible identities for them. Aside from such historical guessing games, however, the sonnets are significant as works of literature that rank among Shakespeare's finest creations. Long after similar poems from the Elizabethan era have been forgotten, Shakespeare's continue to be read and treasured.

SOURCES AND HISTORY. In the early 1590s sonnet sequences—groups of sonnets that explored a theme, told a story, or dealt with related subjects—became popular with English poets. The Elizabethan sonneteers drew on a tradition that dated back to Petrarch, the creator of the form. Petrarch, an Italian poet of the 1300s, wrote more than 300 sonnets, mostly focusing on his tortured love for the idealized Laura. Love became a traditional topic for sonnet writers.

Elizabethan writers, such as Sir Thomas Wyatt, modified Petrarch's form. Italian sonnets consist of an eight-line section (an octave) followed by a six-line section (a sestet), with a shift in tone or thought following the break between them. The Elizabethan sonnet, sometimes called the Shakespearean sonnet, consists of three four-line sections

(quatrains) followed by a pair of rhyming lines (a couplet). Sir Philip SIDNEY launched the fashion for sonnet sequences among English poets with his *Astrophel and Stella*, published in 1591. Both this sequence and Samuel Daniel's *Delia* (1592) appear to have influenced Shakespeare's sonnets. Shakespeare also borrowed from the ancient Roman poet OVID, whose *Metamorphoses* developed the theme that a poet's praise conveys immortality.

No one knows the exact dates of Shakespeare's sonnets or the order in which he wrote them. They were first published in 1609, long after the fashion for sonnet sequences had waned. Most critics, however, believe that the majority of the poems were written between 1592 and 1598, when sonnet sequences were at the height of their popularity. The publisher of Shakespeare's sonnets, stationer Thomas Thorpe, may well have printed them without the poet's knowledge or cooperation. Elizabethan critic Francis Meres, in his *Palladis Tamia* (1598), made reference to sonnets that Shakespeare had circulated among his "private friends," and Thorpe may have obtained the manuscript from one of them.

Shakespeare's sonnets appear to be related and are usually considered a sequence. Thorpe organized them into two broad groups. Sonnets 1 through 126 are addressed to a young man of high birth who seems to be the poet's dear friend. Sonnets 127 through 152 are addressed to the poet's lover, a dark-haired woman whom scholars have called the DARK LADY. The final two sonnets, based on an ancient Greek saying about love, appear to stand apart from the rest and may be the work of another writer. Many later editors have objected to Thorpe's scheme and have attempted to arrange the sonnets in a different sequence, but most critics accept Thorpe's ordering of the sonnets as official.

THEMES. A major theme in the sonnets is the contrast between two types of love: the poet's passion for the Dark Lady and his affection for his male friend, often identified as the Fair Youth. He compares his relationship with the lady to a "sickly appetite" (Sonnet 147). His desire for her makes him an unwilling prisoner, even as his reason understands that she is unfaithful and hard-hearted. He contrasts these negative emotions with the purer and more wholesome love he feels for the Fair Youth. Sonnet 144, in particular, compares his "two loves," with the young man representing "comfort" and the Dark Lady "despair."

This poem is one of several that describe the intense pain the speaker feels when his friend and his lover become romantically involved with each other. He is hurt by this betrayal, but he tries to direct his anger entirely at the Dark Lady, doing his best to forgive the Fair Youth because he cannot bear the thought of losing his friendship. Many critics have commented on the intense emotion the poet displays in speaking of the young man, and some have speculated that Shakespeare and his male friend were involved in a real-life love affair. The passionate declarations of affection in the sonnets, however, do not necessarily indicate the poet's HOMOSEXUALITY. It was common in Elizabethan times for male friends to declare their devotion to each other without any suggestion that such feelings were sexual.

THE RIVAL POET

Sonnets 78 through 86 record a crisis between the narrator and his friend, who has been receiving poems in his honor from another poet. The narrator sadly admits that his friend deserves to be the subject of "a worthier pen" (Sonnet 79) and says in Sonnet 83 that even two poets cannot do him justice: "There lives more life in one of your fair eyes / Than both your poets can in praise devise." Various critics have proposed Christopher Marlowe, Samuel Daniel, George Chapman, and John Donne as candidates for the rival poet. But whether the rivalry was real, like the rival's identity, may never be known.

Sonnets

Another major theme in the sequence is mutability, or change, a subject that fascinated many Elizabethan writers. Change generally appears as a destructive force in the sonnets. The poet considers several ways to escape the clutches of "Devouring Time," as he calls it in Sonnet 19. In the first 17 sonnets he urges his young friend to marry and have children so that his beauty will be preserved in his descendants. Other poems, such as the famous Sonnet 18 ("Shall I compare thee to a summer's day?"), promise to immortalize the friend's beauty and virtue in words. In Sonnet 55 the narrator declares, "Not marble nor the gilded [monuments] / Of princes shall outlive this pow'rful rhyme," suggesting that by preserving his friend's memory in timeless verse, the poet may also gain immortality for himself. The narrator's fears about death and change intersect with his thoughts about love most vividly in Sonnet 116, which defines true love as eternal and unchanging, "an ever-fixed mark / That looks on tempests and is never shaken."

* *convention* established practice

Shakespeare's sonnets reflect the poetic conventions* established by Petrarch, but they also modify them in some ways. Instead of idealizing his female lover, the speaker comments on her bad qualities and bemoans his inability to escape from her spell. At the same time he praises his male friend's beauty, showing him in the same ideal light as Petrarch's Laura, and makes heroic efforts to explain away whatever faults appear in his friend's character. One of Shakespeare's most famous sonnets, Sonnet 130, mocks the conventional phrases used by Elizabethan sonneteers. Declaring "My mistress' eyes are nothing like the sun," the poet rejects the exaggerated praise other authors heap on their loves while at the same time swearing that his beloved is "as rare / As any she belied [lied about] with false compare."

INTERPRETING THE SONNETS. For nearly 200 years after their original publication, Shakespeare's sonnets received little attention. Later writers of sonnets, such as English poets Michael Drayton and possibly John Donne and John Milton in the 1600s, may have been inspired by the poems, but publishers and critics generally disregarded them. In 1793 editor George Steevens wrote that even an act of Parliament would not be enough to entice people to read them. The popularity of the sonnets first began to swell in the 1800s, around the time that readers were taking an increased interest in the personal lives of literary figures. Poet William Wordsworth called the sonnets the key with which "Shakespeare unlocked his heart."

People who read the sonnets as autobiography have proposed many identities for the friend and the Dark Lady. Speculation about the friend centers on the dedication of the 1609 volume, which mentions a "Mr. W. H." who appears to have either inspired the poems or given them to Thorpe. Leading candidates for the identity of W. H. are two of Shakespeare's literary patrons*, Henry Wriothsley, the earl of Southampton, and William Herbert, the earl of Pembroke. Researchers have proposed other identities for both figures, but it is impossible to prove that any of these theories is accurate—or even that the Fair Youth and the Dark Lady represent real people at all.

* *patron* supporter or financial sponsor of an artist or writer

Many 20th-century interpretations have focused on the form, language, and themes of the sonnets rather than on the author's voice. Douglas Bush, a modern Shakespearean scholar, has called the sonnets "an island of poetry surrounded by a barrier of icebergs and dense fog." The "icebergs" and "fog" are the elaborate theories put forth by those who seek the poet in his works. In the opinion of Bush and some other critics, the sonnets are simply great poetry, regardless of whether they were inspired by real events or were born entirely in the poet's creative imagination. (*See also* **Patronage of the Arts; Poetic Techniques; Poetry of Shakespeare; Shakespeare's Sources.**)

SPANISH ARMADA

The powerful fleet of warships known as the Spanish Armada consisted of 130 vessels. This engraving shows the fleet sailing toward England.

One of the most important battles in England's history took place in 1588, when King Philip II of Spain sent a fleet of ships, known as the Spanish Armada, to invade England. The immediate reason behind the attack was to stop England's raids on Spanish trading ships and territories, but Philip's larger goal was to restore the Roman Catholic Church in England. He believed that England, as a Protestant country, was a threat not only to Spain, but to all Catholic nations.

After almost two years of planning, the Spanish Armada left Lisbon, Portugal, in May 1588. The fleet consisted of about 130 ships, carrying perhaps 30,000 men. Only 40 of the vessels were actual battleships,

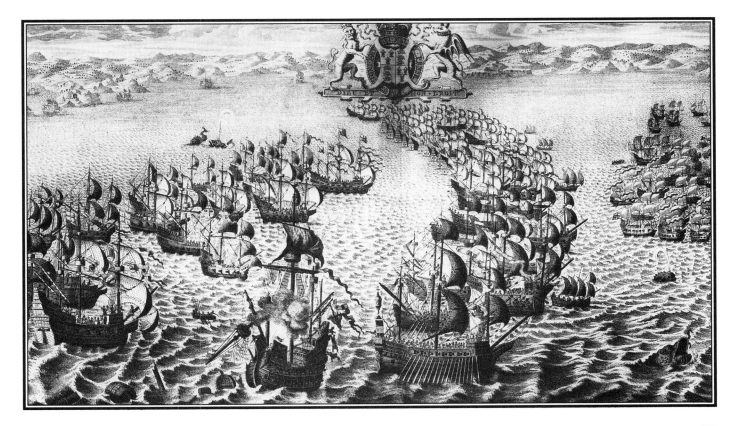

See
color plate 14,
vol. 1.

* *invincible* unable to be defeated

however, and all of the Spanish ships were slower than their English counterparts. Philip was nonetheless confident that his "invincible* armada" could defeat the English navy by boarding any ships that attacked. He hoped that with his ships occupying the British naval force, he would be able to attack the coast of England with a land force and overrun the nation.

The English fleet that sailed against the armada numbered nearly 200 ships. They carried fewer soldiers than the Spanish (between 16,000 and 17,000 men) but more weaponry, including more and heavier guns. When the Spanish Armada anchored off the coast of Calais, France, the English quickly took the advantage and maneuvered to the west of the armada. In the middle of the night, the English launched "fire ships" into the Spanish fleet. The British sailors lined up eight ships coated with pitch, steered them directly toward the enemy, set them on fire, and then escaped in small boats at the last minute.

The Spanish ships broke their formation, and the English blasted the scattered ships with cannon fire. Finally the winds changed, blowing what was left of the once-mighty Spanish Armada back to safety. Two thirds of the Spanish force had died in the battle, and many of the 80 ships that eventually returned to Spain were beyond repair. The defeat of the Spanish fleet was one of the most decisive victories in England's history and established the nation as the leading naval power in Europe for centuries to come. (*See also* **Ships; Warfare.**)

SPENSER, SIR EDMUND

ca. 1552–1599
Poet

* *pastoral* relating to the countryside; often used to draw a contrast between the innocence and serenity of rural life and the corruption and extravagance of court life
* *sonnet* poem of 14 lines with a fixed pattern of meter and rhyme
* *epic* long poem about the adventures of a hero
* *allegory* literary device in which characters, events, and settings represent abstract qualities and in which the author intends a different meaning to be read beneath the surface

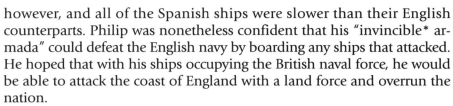

Sir Edmund Spenser is generally considered to be one of England's greatest poets. Born in London and educated at the University of Cambridge, he had a profound influence on the writers of his day. He first gained fame with the publication of *The Shepheardes Calendar* (1579), a collection of 12 pastoral* poems (one for each month of the year). The romantic episodes in this volume probably influenced Shakespeare's *A Midsummer Night's Dream.* Spenser was also an important figure in the development of the English sonnet*.

Spenser's greatest achievement, however, was *The Faerie Queene,* an epic* poem published between 1590 and 1596, that is considered to be one of the finest works in the English language. Its narrative of high adventure is also an allegory* about the glory of England. *The Faerie Queene* not only inspired many passages in Shakespeare's early plays and poems but also influenced such modern epics as J. R. R. Tolkien's *Lord of the Rings.* Spenser dedicated *The Faerie Queene* to "the most high, mighty and magnificent empress," Queen Elizabeth I.

Many scholars believe that Spenser penned one of the first literary references to Shakespeare. In *Colin Clouts Come Home Againe* (1595), the poet described one of his characters as a gentle shepherd whose imagination "does like himself heroically sound"—often taken to be a reference to Shakespeare's heroic-sounding surname. (*See also* **Friends and Contemporaries; Pastoralism; Playwrights and Poets.**)

SPIES

Spying—the gathering of secret information, especially about enemies—was an important task of the Elizabethan government. In fact England's intelligence agency, Her Majesty's Secret Service, was organized under Queen ELIZABETH I. During her rule the nation was involved in power struggles with France, Spain, and the Netherlands. In addition there were several conspiracies by Catholics who wished to assassinate the Protestant queen. Because of these dangers, access to reliable information about the crown's enemies was vital.

Elizabeth's foreign policy rested heavily on one man, Sir Francis Walsingham, the queen's secretary of state from 1573 until 1590. Before his appointment Walsingham had served his country in secret, obtaining information on the activities of foreign spies in London. An extremely clever man, he placed English agents in several foreign courts. Evidence suggests that one of his recruits may have been the playwright Christopher Marlowe. In addition to his talents in the field of espionage, Walsingham was highly respected for his diplomatic skills.

Walsingham was a strict Protestant who worked hard at detecting and stopping Catholic plots to kill Elizabeth. His activities helped frustrate an assassination scheme against Elizabeth by Catholic supporters of the imprisoned Mary, Queen of Scots. Walsingham's discovery of a letter of support from the Scottish queen to one of her treacherous supporters led to Mary's trial and execution. (*See also* **Diplomacy and Foreign Relations; Marlowe, Christopher.**)

SPORTS

See *Games, Pastimes, and Sports.*

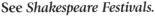

STRATFORD, ONTARIO, FESTIVAL

See *Shakespeare Festivals.*

STRATFORD-UPON-AVON

When William Shakespeare was born in 1564, his birthplace, Stratford-upon-Avon, was a small but prosperous market town with 1,500 to 2,000 inhabitants, mostly farmers and tradesmen. In the centuries since the playwright's death, Stratford has developed into a major center for the study and celebration of Shakespeare and his work.

HISTORY. Stratford rests on the banks of the Avon River in the county of Warwickshire in central England. Its name comes from the Anglo-Saxon words *straet* (street) and *ford* (river crossing), referring to an ancient road that led across the Avon at this site. By the early 1300s Stratford had become a local center for agriculture and trade.

During this period the town was governed by a religious organization called the Guild of the Holy Cross, which also operated local SCHOOLS and provided other public services. The order's guild hall, built in 1417, remains intact today. After England broke its ties with the Roman Catholic Church, the guild was abolished, and in 1553 King Edward VI created a new charter for Stratford. From that point on, the town was governed by an elected council, many of whose members were drawn from the former religious organization.

STRATFORD DURING SHAKESPEARE'S LIFE. The streets of Stratford were wide and straight, lined with thatch-roofed houses of stucco* and timber. Wealthier citizens typically had their own barns and gardens as well. Shakespeare grew up in the town's well-to-do northern section. His father was a local tradesman, dealing in leather goods and some agricultural crops, such as barley, which was used in Stratford's main industry, brewing. The town was especially lively on Thursday, the weekly market day.

The old guild hall had remained the seat of town government. The first floor housed the town council's meeting rooms, and the second floor was occupied by a grammar school that the playwright probably attended. The most important building in town, however, was the Church of the Holy Trinity, which still stands at the southern end of Stratford. The original church building dates from around 1200, although many sections have been added to the structure since that time.

During Shakespeare's childhood Stratford was subject to religious controversy. England had officially converted to Protestantism, but many of the town's residents refused to abandon the Catholic Church. The authorities who enforced the laws in Stratford, and were supposedly responsible for ensuring that all inhabitants attended Anglican* services regularly, tended to ignore such violations of the law. They focused more on secular* offenses, such as allowing household garbage to pile up too high in the streets.

Eventually, church officials began to notice that Stratford lagged behind its neighbors in rooting out Roman Catholic practices. In a nation where church and state were united, a failure to enforce the new Anglican faith was seen as disloyalty to the crown. Local religious officials came under suspicion and were forced to leave the town. The schoolmaster of Shakespeare's youth also left his position, retiring to Italy, where he became a Jesuit priest. By the mid-1580s Stratford had a new vicar*, and the town government actively ensured that citizens displayed Anglican loyalties and followed strict moral codes. The Church of England took hold in Stratford. Around this time the Shakespeare family experienced a decline in its fortunes and social status, possibly because of its strong Catholic sympathies. John Shakespeare, the playwright's father, was charged at least once with recusancy, or disloyalty to the Anglican Church.

William Shakespeare married at the age of 18 and raised a family in Stratford. After he began his career in the London theater, he maintained

* *stucco* building material made of cement, sand, and lime and used as a hard surface for exterior walls

* *Anglican* referring to the Church of England

* *secular* nonreligious; connected with everyday life

* *vicar* priest in the Church of England

his ties to his hometown, traveling back to Stratford at least once a year. As a successful actor, playwright, and businessman, he became one of the town's wealthiest landowners and most prominent citizens. He purchased a mansion known as New Place, which became his home when he retired from the theater. When he died in 1616 he was buried at the Church of the Holy Trinity, and within seven years the town had erected a monument in his honor. By 1630 Stratford was already known to visitors as Shakespeare's hometown.

THE GROWTH OF SHAKESPEARE INSTITUTIONS. The first major attempt to make Stratford a center of interest for lovers of Shakespeare came in 1769, when the great actor David Garrick organized the first SHAKESPEARE FESTIVAL there. In 1827 a group of producers attempted to recreate the success of Garrick's festival, but this second event was a financial failure.

See color plate 4, vol. 1.

The next major development in the emerging Shakespeare industry was the establishment of the Shakespeare Birthplace Trust in 1847. P. T. Barnum, a famous American entertainer (cofounder of the Barnum and Bailey Circus), had announced his plan to buy the house Shakespeare had grown up in and ship it to the United States. To preserve the playwright's childhood home, the newly established trust purchased the house for £3,000 and dedicated itself to preserving and maintaining the building. The organization now owns several other Stratford properties related to Shakespeare, including New Place. The trust also founded a library, housed in Stratford's Shakespeare Centre, that is devoted to the playwright. The collection includes not only manuscripts and printed editions of the playwright's works, but also a vast archive of press clippings, programs, and other theatrical documents.

Stratford held a grand festival in honor of Shakespeare's 300th birthday in 1864. The publicity generated by this event sparked a movement to establish a regular theater company to perform Shakespeare's plays in Stratford. The Shakespeare Memorial Theatre opened in 1879 and became the leading site for Shakespeare performances. The theater received a royal charter in 1925 and moved to its permanent home seven years later. In 1961 the facility changed its name to the Royal Shakespeare Theatre, home to the ROYAL SHAKESPEARE COMPANY (RSC). Many of England's leading actors and directors have been trained in the RSC, which remains well-respected in Stratford, London, and around the world.

In 1951 the University of Birmingham purchased a house in Stratford and established the Shakespeare Institute there. The goal of this organization is to assist the efforts of Shakespearean scholars and teachers from around the world. In 1963 the institute opened a second library at the university campus in Birmingham and began offering courses and degrees in Shakespearean studies. The organization has become a major sponsor of conferences and publications and a leading force in Shakespearean scholarship. (*See also* **Cities, Towns, and Villages; Markets and Fairs; Museums and Archives.**)

STRUCTURE OF
SHAKESPEARE'S PLAYS

See *Play Structure*.

SUPERNATURAL
PHENOMENA

Ghosts, fairies, witches, sorcerers, and other supernatural phenomena are central to the plots of four of Shakespeare's plays: *Hamlet*, *A Midsummer Night's Dream*, *Macbeth*, and *The Tempest*. The playwright often based his depiction of otherworldly occurrences on Elizabethan folklore, but he also drew on his imagination to create new versions of the supernatural.

In *Hamlet*, Shakespeare refers to several of the most common beliefs about ghosts. The apparition in the play, for example, returns from the dead because he has an important message to impart to the living and because he died before he was able to confess his sins. These were considered to be the two principal reasons that spirits roamed the earth. The ghost also appears between midnight and dawn, which was commonly thought to be the time that spirits walked among the living.

Another widely held belief about ghosts—that evil spirits could assume the likeness of a dead loved one—is a vital element in the play. Horatio warns Prince Hamlet that the apparition that resembles his father may actually be a devil that will "tempt [him] toward the flood . . . / Or to the dreadful summit of the cliff . . . / And there assume some other horri-

In Shakespeare's *The Tempest* the magician Prospero commands a legion of spirits. With their help he raises a powerful storm that causes a ship to be wrecked and the survivors cast ashore on his island home.

ble form" (I.iv.69–72). Later the prince delays taking revenge against his father's murderer because he wants to assure himself that the ghost is not an agent of Satan:

> The spirit that I have seen
> May be a [dev'l], and the [dev'l] hath power
> T' assume a pleasing shape, yea, and perhaps
> . . . .
> Abuses [deludes] me to damn me.
>
> (II.ii.598–603)

In *A Midsummer Night's Dream,* Shakespeare altered the popular Elizabethan view of fairies, which were believed to be evil creatures capable of causing illness and other human misfortune. The playwright's fairies are small, generally pleasant creatures who delight in playing harmless pranks on foolish humans. Shakespeare's depiction of fairies—also called elves, pixies, brownies, or little people—proved so influential that it replaced much of the traditional folklore.

Other supernatural phenomena featured in Shakespeare's plays include spirit conjuring, omens, and visions of GODS AND GODDESSES. In *Macbeth,* for example, the predictions of the three weyward (weird) sisters, or witches, trigger a chain of events that eventually lead to the downfall of the title character. In *The Tempest* the action begins with a storm that has been raised by Prospero, a powerful magician who is aided by the spirit Ariel. (*See also* **Fairies; Ghosts and Apparitions; Magic and Folklore; Witches and Evil Spirits.**)

See color plate 1, vol. 2.

SYMBOLISM AND ALLEGORY

In everyday language the word *symbol* refers to anything that represents or stands for something else. The character *$*, for example, signifies "dollars." In literature a symbol is usually a concrete image—such as an object, character, or place—that represents an abstract idea. One familiar example in Shakespeare's work is the Forest of ARDEN. This is the primary setting for *As You Like It,* and it serves as an escape from civilization, a fantasy world in which people can act out their true desires free from the restraints of society. An author's use of such images is known as symbolism.

A related literary device is allegory, in which all the various characters, events, and settings represent different abstract qualities. The interactions among these elements produce an extended symbolic meaning that can be quite distinct from the obvious, outward meaning of the plot. The morality plays* of the Middle Ages were Christian allegories in which the central character was surrounded by figures who personified virtue and vice. In this context the character's choice of good over evil signified the salvation of humankind.

* *morality play* religious dramatic work that teaches a moral lesson through the use of symbolic characters

SHAKESPEARE'S USE OF SYMBOLISM. Like most of the poets of his day, Shakespeare was a highly visual writer. Rather than state an idea

directly, he frequently chose to reveal it through a symbolic image. In *Macbeth*, for example, the witches show Macbeth three visions, or apparitions, that represent ideas related to the play's events. The first is an armed head, raising images of death and destruction. The second, a bloody child, hints at life born out of death. The third, a child wearing a crown and carrying a tree, suggests that royalty provides a connection between human life and the spiritual world that is visible in nature. This scene is ironic because Macbeth is blind to the symbolism of these images. He pays attention only to the literal meaning of what the apparitions say, while disregarding the implications of their physical shapes.

Shakespeare's symbols are not always obvious, and sometimes a single object has many levels of meaning. Gold, for example, can represent material wealth, but it can also symbolize spiritual worth. The meaning of any symbol depends on the context of the particular scene in which it appears. In *The Merchant of Venice*, Portia's suitors must choose from three caskets—gold, silver, and lead. If gold were being used in this instance as a symbol of true worth, the golden casket would be the obvious choice. As the play progresses, however, it becomes clear that the gold and silver chests are linked to superficial values such as greed and pride. The lead casket, which represents humility and a willingness to sacrifice, is the one that a successful suitor must choose. The poem sealed inside the gold chest, which observes that "All that glisters [glitters] is not gold" (II.vii.65), indicates that true value can be distinguished from wealth and showy outward appearances.

Abstract concepts, as well as physical objects, can function as symbols. In *Pericles* life and death appear in relation to the power of love. In the middle of the play, the title character believes that his wife, Thaisa, and his daughter, Marina, are dead and he falls into deep despair. Yet by the end of the play they have both been returned to him. Their symbolic rebirth represents the healing power of love and the restoration of the soul after deep grief.

SHAKESPEARE'S USE OF ALLEGORY. In an allegory many symbols are tied to one basic idea that drives the story. The epic* *The Faerie Queene*, by Elizabethan poet Edmund SPENSER, is an extended allegory in which each narrative centers on a knight who represents a specific virtue. All the knights serve the fairy queen, Gloriana, a symbol of greatness who is also an idealized image of Queen Elizabeth I.

The most obviously allegorical of Shakespeare's plays is *The Tempest*. The central character, PROSPERO, is a wizard who recognizes the potential of his magic to accomplish evil as well as good. His inner struggle is made visible by the interactions between his two servants, the sprite Ariel and the monster CALIBAN. These figures can be seen as representing two opposing sides of Prospero's character, his higher nature and his baser impulses. The enchanter himself can also be viewed as a symbol of the entire human race, like the central characters in morality plays. According to this interpretation his struggle is the same one that every human being must face between good and evil. Many readers also see a further allegory in *The Tempest*, which was one of the last plays Shakespeare wrote before

* *epic* long poem about the adventures of a hero

102

retiring from the theater. They interpret Prospero's magic as a symbol for the playwright's art and the entire play as a drama about the difficulty he had in ending his career.

Most scholars consider Shakespeare's poem "The PHOENIX AND TURTLE" to be an allegory about love. It describes the death of the phoenix and the turtledove, who willingly die in flames so that they can be united for eternity. In Greek mythology the phoenix is a bird that periodically destroys itself in flame and is reborn from its ashes. The Elizabethans viewed the phoenix as a symbol of immortality and the "turtle," or turtledove, as a symbol of constant love. By combining these two symbols, Shakespeare created an allegory about the unquenchable power of love. (*See also* **Imagery; Pageants and Morality Plays.**)

TAILORS

See *Craftworkers.*

TAMING OF THE SHREW, THE

The fact that Shakespeare's comedy *The Taming of the Shrew* is disturbing to many modern audiences may be one reason for its continued appeal. The "shrew" of the play's title is KATHARINA, a beautiful but foul-tempered woman who is "tamed" by PETRUCHIO, a man who has claimed that his only interest in her is in her money. This plot runs against modern notions of political correctness. Many viewers are uncomfortable seeing an assertive and strong-willed, if rather disagreeable, woman turned into a meek and dutiful wife by a crude, fortune-hunting husband. But right from their first scene together (perhaps the funniest in the play), there is clearly some attraction between the two, and their boisterous behavior and witty wordplay are as engaging today as they probably were for Shakespeare's audiences.

PLOT SUMMARY. The play is set primarily in the Italian city of Padua, initially at the home of Baptista, a gentleman with two daughters, Katharina (or Kate) and Bianca. Bianca is so beautiful and appears so sweet-tempered and obedient that several suitors are seeking her hand in marriage. Baptista, however, insists that Katharina must be married first. No men are interested in Katharina, despite her beauty, because she is so "curst and shrewd" (sharp-tongued and vicious). Kate behaves violently and uncontrollably in the play's early scenes, first tying up her sister in a jealous rage and striking her, then breaking a lute* over the head of her music teacher.

* *lute* stringed instrument

The only man willing to court Katharina is Petruchio, a stranger from Verona who announces boldly that he has come to Padua in search of a rich wife. He does not care about her appearance or her personality as long as she has money: "I come to wive it wealthily in Padua; / If wealthily, then happily in Padua," he declares (I.ii.75–76). He "woos" Katharina

The central character in *The Taming of the Shrew* is Katharina, a sharp-tempered woman (played here by Monica Dolan). In an early scene she ties up and slaps her younger sister, Bianca (Charlotte Randle), who is wooed by many suitors because of her beauty and apparent good nature.

* *tinker* mender of household goods

by engaging her in a battle of wits, behaves outrageously at their wedding, and takes her to his home, where he sets about "taming" her. He demands absolute obedience from his wife, declaring:

> I will be master of what is mine own.
> She is my goods, my chattels, she is my house,
> My household stuff, my field, my barn,
> My horse, my ox, my ass, my any thing.
>
> (III.ii.229–32)

Petruchio insists that Katharina agree with him on everything, even when he claims that the sun is the moon or that an old man is a pretty young woman. When she disobeys him, he deprives her of food, sleep, and clothing until she agrees to behave.

Meanwhile back in Padua the wealthy Lucentio decides to woo Bianca by changing places with his servant Tranio. In keeping with this plan Tranio presents himself to Baptista as Lucentio, a suitor for his daughter, and offers his "servant" as a tutor for Bianca. In this way Lucentio is able to court Bianca in person instead of simply asking her father for her hand. The same idea has occurred to Hortensio, another of Bianca's suitors, who disguises himself as a music tutor named Licio. When he observes the affection Bianca shows to the disguised Lucentio, however, he vows to leave her and marry a wealthy old widow instead. Tranio's assumed identity becomes a source of great comic confusion when Baptista insists on meeting Lucentio's father before allowing him to marry Bianca. Lucentio and Tranio quickly recruit an old man to play the role of Lucentio's father, unaware that Lucentio's real father, Vincentio, has arrived in Padua to visit his son. When Vincentio announces who he is, he is immediately arrested as an impostor. Confusion reigns until Lucentio reveals his true identity and announces that he and Bianca have just been married in secret.

The final scene takes place at Lucentio and Bianca's wedding feast. Petruchio arrives with Katharina and demonstrates for the crowd how well he has tamed her, even winning a contest with Lucentio and another recently married man over who has the most obedient wife. Kate then makes a long speech criticizing the two less obedient wives and preaching to them: "Thy husband is thy lord, thy life, thy keeper, / Thy head, thy sovereign" (V.ii.146–47). She even offers, as a token of her new sense of duty, to place her hands beneath her husband's foot.

The plot of Shakespeare's play takes place entirely within the context of a "frame story," presented during an induction (an introductory scene not related to the main plot). Set in England, the induction features a poor tinker* named Christopher Sly. Some noble huntsmen find Sly in a drunken stupor and decide to play a trick on him. They dress him up and pretend that he is a lord who has been insane for the past 15 years. Sly quickly becomes convinced that he is indeed a lord and agrees to watch a play put on by some traveling players—a play that turns out to be the main plot of *The Taming of the Shrew.* Shakespeare provides no closing scene to complete the story presented in this induction. There is another version of the text, however, called *The Taming of a* [not *the*] *Shrew,* which

seems to have been current at the same time as Shakespeare's play. In that version Sly wakes up at the end, finds himself a poor tinker again, and resolves to go home and tame his wife. Scholars are not sure whether this rendering of the *Shrew* material is a source for Shakespeare's comedy or a memorial reconstruction* of it.

SOURCES AND COMMENTARY. Shakespeare's play drew on an old tradition of wife taming in folklore and popular culture. According to scholar Lynda Boose, this tradition was based on historical fact. Some of the accepted techniques for controlling unruly women were extremely violent and brutal. One account, a possible source for Shakespeare's play, is a long ballad called "A Merry Jest of a Shrewd and Curst Wife Lapped in Morel's Skin for Her Good Behavior." The poem describes how a desperate husband beats, bloodies, and imprisons his untamed wife and finally wraps her in the salted skin of his dead horse Morel and locks her in the basement.

Shakespeare's play is much less physically violent than this source, since Petruchio never actually beats Katharina. He is, however, firm in his conviction that his wife is his property, a typical view of marriage in Renaissance England. Some modern scholars see the continuing popularity of the play as symptomatic of a secret desire on the part of modern men to subdue and control women. Penny Gay, for example, suggests that the play is appealing to men because it shows "the threat of a woman's revolt" being neutralized. By presenting this battle in a comic form, with "apparent good humour," *The Taming of the Shrew* "offers the audience the chance to revel in and reinforce their misogyny* while at the same time feeling good."

There is more to the play, however, than a desire to keep women in their place. It also contains two major themes drawn from literary sources. The first source is the *Metamorphoses,* by the ancient Roman poet OVID (translated into English by Arthur Golding in 1567). Ovid's long poem narrates a series of transformations, mainly of people who are changed into animals. Most of these apparent transformations, however, occur without any inner growth or change. *The Taming of the Shrew* contains several references to Ovid's work, particularly in the scene in which the disguised Lucentio gives a Latin lesson to Bianca (III.i). Even the name of Petruchio's dog, Troilus, comes from Ovid. The other literary influence is an Italian play, *I Suppositi,* by Ludovico Ariosto (translated into English by George Gascoigne, who called it *Supposes*). Ariosto's play provides the basis for the Bianca-Lucentio plot. As its title suggests, this work centers on the theme of assumed, or "supposed," identities.

Shakespeare joins the two major themes he found in these sources—confused identities and apparent transformations—into a single thread that runs throughout the play. Most of the "metamorphoses" that take place in the play, therefore, turn out to be mere illusions. Tranio poses as Lucentio, Lucentio as a Latin instructor, Hortensio as a music teacher, a traveler as Vincentio, and Bianca as a dutiful daughter, but all of these "supposes" are exposed as mere appearances in the end. Real changes occur only in Kate and Petruchio, who are transformed into a loving couple,

* ***memorial reconstruction*** version of a play reconstructed from the memory of an actor without benefit of a script

* ***misogyny*** distrust or hatred of women

with Petruchio apparently taking his traditional place as master and Katharina apparently accepting the role of a dutiful wife. Their marriage shows more promise of happiness than the other two that occur at the same time. As Petruchio observes in his final line: "Come Kate, we'll to bed. / We three are married, but you two are sped [finished]" (V.ii.184–85). The transformation of Christopher Sly in the induction is less clear. Shakespeare's version, which leaves Sly's story unfinished, creates the impression that a permanent transformation has taken place. The version in *The Taming of a Shrew,* however, exposes it as just one more illusion.

PERFORMANCE HISTORY. Since its first appearance in the early 1590s, *The Taming of the Shrew* has provoked strong audience reactions. As early as 1611 John Fletcher (a playwright who sometimes worked with Shakespeare) had produced a sequel called *The Woman's Prize, or The Tamer Tamed,* in which a strong-minded second wife succeeds in taming Petruchio. Fletcher explains in his epilogue that he has tried to encourage "true equality" and "mutual love" by teaching husbands that they "should not reign as Tyrants o'er their wives." Fletcher may have been making obvious what some interpreters have inferred from Shakespeare's text. But the original, and adaptations based on it, have remained much more popular than Fletcher's play.

During the late 1600s and early 1700s Shakespeare's play was seen only in adaptations, which usually preserved the main features of the Kate-Petruchio story but dropped the subplots. Around 1667 John Lacy wrote a popular adaptation called *Sauny the Scot.* Lacy's adaptation was replaced around 1754 by David Garrick's version, *Catherine and Petruchio,* which dominated the dramatic scene until the middle of the 1800s. Shakespeare's original play returned to the stage in 1844. The first American production of the relatively full play, produced by Augustin Daly in 1887, ran for more than 120 performances, and many other productions followed.

Modern directors have varied greatly in deciding what to do with Christopher Sly and the induction. Some omit the induction altogether, others keep Sly on stage to the end, and still others have added the epilogue from *The Taming of a Shrew.* A much bigger problem has been how to deal with the play's apparently antifeminist plot. Productions in the 1800s often encouraged domination fantasies by having either Kate or Petruchio carry a whip. A 1908 production took a different approach, having Margaret Anglin perform Kate's final speech as a joke secretly shared by husband and wife. Anglin's interpretation remained fashionable throughout the 1900s. The first "talking" film version of a Shakespeare play was a 1929 film of *The Taming of the Shrew* starring Mary Pickford and Douglas Fairbanks. Pickford ended her final speech with a large wink to the ladies, making it clear that Kate's submission to Petruchio was only an act.

Other productions have played the story straight. Franco Zeffirelli's 1966 film, starring Elizabeth Taylor and Richard Burton, did the same, but the actors were so much their famous selves that it was impossible to

THE WOMAN IS SMARTER

The Taming of the Shrew presents an intelligent, strong-willed woman whose even more stubborn husband insists on putting her in her place. In most of Shakespeare's later comedies, however, the women control the action. Perhaps the best contrast to *The Taming of the Shrew* is *The Merry Wives of Windsor,* which features a cast of bumbling men continually outwitted by clever women. The contrast between these two plays shows Shakespeare's willingness to examine important issues, such as male-female relations, from many different and often conflicting viewpoints.

see Taylor as a truly tamed wife. The BBC television version (1981) shows a truly tamed Kate in a "happy" ending. A more recent movie, *Ten Things I Hate About You* (1999), a very free adaptation of the play, depicts the Katharina character as more educated than tamed. A stage production by the Washington Shakespeare Company (1998) featured an all-female cast, but aside from providing more roles for women it did nothing to transform Shakespeare's plot into a feminist text. The audience quickly adjusted to the women simply as actors, much as Elizabethan audiences must have adjusted to boy actors playing women's roles, and Katharina delivered her final speech with simple sincerity. When asked how she managed this scene, the actor playing Kate replied without irony that she believed every word.

In 1948 Cole Porter wrote a musical adaptation of *Shrew* called *Kiss Me, Kate*, which was successfully revived in 1999. It included such well-known songs as "Brush Up Your Shakespeare," "Too Darn Hot," and "Why Can't You Behave?" Porter's adaptation distanced the play from "reality" by adopting Shakespeare's own device and making the plot of *The Taming of the Shrew* a play-within-a-play. Instead of using the Christopher Sly story, he presented his main characters as actors performing a musical version of Shakespeare's play. It is tempting to imagine that Shakespeare's framing narrative was intended to have the same effect, but his induction is simply too fragile a story to support such a fantasy. The main plot, centering on Katharina and Petruchio, sticks in the audience's mind, while Sly's story is of so little interest that many productions leave it out altogether. Today's audiences must accept *The Taming of the Shrew* as it is: unashamedly sexist, yet so engaging that they cannot help becoming entangled in it. (*See also* **Feminist Interpretations; Gender and Sexuality; Literature and Drama; Shakespeare on Screen; Shakespeare's Sources; Shakespeare's Works, Adaptations of.**)

TEACHING SHAKESPEARE

Millions of students around the world study Shakespeare. In classrooms from grade school through graduate school, thousands upon thousands of teachers instruct their students in the playwright's works. Their teaching methods may include explanation, discussion, attendance at performances, and various ways of encouraging students to enact scenes from the texts.

SHAKESPEARE'S JOURNEY TO THE CLASSROOM. Although Shakespeare's plays and poems were widely seen and read in his own day, no one in the 1500s and 1600s would have thought to teach Shakespeare, or any other contemporary author, in school. Only classical* authors appeared in the curriculum, along with a few medieval* writers. Over the years, however, Shakespeare has enjoyed a growing popularity among the reading public. Many respected authors, such as John Milton (1608–1674), Alexander Pope (1688–1744), and Samuel Johnson (1709–1784), praised his works. Others published Shakespeare's plays

* *classical* in the tradition of ancient Greece and Rome
* *medieval* referring to the Middle Ages, a period roughly between A.D. 500 and 1500

* *rhetoric* art of speaking or writing
  effectively

and verse in elaborate editions, performed his works, celebrated his birthday, and commemorated his Stratford birthplace.

In the early 1800s passages from Shakespeare began to appear in school texts teaching elements of rhetoric*. At first students saw only brief quotations from the plays, such as Mark Antony's oration over the corpse of Julius Caesar or Henry V's famous speech to his troops on Saint Crispin's Day. Teachers did not ask students to savor such speeches for their own meaning or for their significance within the play. Rather, they used the speeches as examples of effective rhetoric. Gradually, however, interest expanded to include the full texts of Shakespeare's plays. One reason for the increased attention lay in the increasing frequency of stage productions in many American cities, combined with the steady decline of Latin authors and language at the heart of the school curriculum. Another factor was that the texts of the plays were becoming more widely available.

By the mid-1800s school editions of selected Shakespeare plays were being published. Students were increasingly asked to study not only Shakespeare's rhetorical style and his plots but also the motivations of his characters. In the early 1900s the value of Shakespeare as a school subject was largely taken for granted. Teachers experimented with teaching methods that emphasized, variously, Shakespeare's vocabulary and interpretation of passages, how his scenes are constructed and presented in theaters, and how students might benefit from their own speaking and acting of Shakespeare.

During the Great Depression of the 1930s, some educators argued that Shakespeare was inappropriate for middle and high school students. They found his LANGUAGE overly complex, sometimes dull, and sometimes obscene. They also considered some of his ideas racist (such as his portrayal of the Jewish moneylender SHYLOCK) or undemocratic (such as his positive portrayal of kings and his often satirical depiction of lower-class characters). Others argued, however, that Shakespeare wrote mainly in the common idiom of his day, a form of expression that remains lively and expressive to modern readers. Students' attention was increasingly directed to the study of Shakespeare's POETIC TECHNIQUE—to patterns of words, images, and actions in the plays. Shakespeare was seen as a tolerant and modest author who spoke for all of humanity.

During the last third of the 20th century, the majority of Shakespeare teachers continued to ask students for close reading of the texts, character analysis, and traditional summaries of action and theme. At the same time, however, many began exploring the ambiguities in Shakespeare's language, the differences between Elizabethan and modern society, and the various ways in which Shakespeare can be performed. Now many teachers encourage students to read Shakespeare in a variety of textual forms; to see Shakespeare's plays on stage, film, and television; to perform Shakespeare themselves in a wide range of acting styles; and to discuss or write about Shakespeare in a number of new instructional environments.

CURRENT METHODS FOR TEACHING SHAKESPEARE. Teachers usually begin their Shakespeare studies by selecting one or more of the plays to teach. Among the most accessible texts for middle school students are *A Midsummer Night's Dream* and *Romeo and Juliet.* Younger students are normally not asked to read an entire work but instead to read selected passages, view or listen to performances, and engage in classroom activities. Plays often recommended for high school students are *Henry IV, Part 1; Hamlet;* and *Measure for Measure.* Play selection is sometimes dictated by high school anthologies.

See color plate 2, vol. 2.

To cover a Shakespeare play adequately in the classroom usually requires at least four weeks. Because some students expect Shakespeare to be boring or difficult, teachers may choose to begin with classroom activities before starting the reading. Such activities may include viewing the video of a recent film production, such as *Romeo and Juliet* or *Shakespeare in Love,* and learning to speak aloud memorized phrases—Shakespearean nuggets, images, insults, or brief exchanges—in appropriate rhythms and tones. In the early stages of Shakespeare study, students can learn simultaneously to speak Shakespeare's lines with feeling and to read them with understanding. It is generally best for students to avoid prolonged reading before learning to speak lines aloud, since Shakespeare remains appealing largely because his speeches are so expressive.

See color plate 3, vol. 2.

Shakespeare's language is powerful, emotional, and pleasing partly because it is highly rhythmical. This crucial fact may be demonstrated through unison clapping or marching on the beats or through choral chanting (which works even for prose passages). Shakespeare's lines are also filled with images that appeal not just to sight and hearing but to all the senses. Teachers can readily demonstrate this by helping students explore the implications of word patterns and paraphrase the thoughts and feelings of different characters.

To encourage student progress toward speaking and eventually enacting Shakespeare, teachers may have students stand in circles and pass the words of key passages from person to person—first one word at a time, then one phrase, then one line, then one sentence, then a given character's entire speech. Student groups may then distribute character parts for sections of scenes, beginning with brief segments and progressing to longer ones, and eventually presenting entire scenes as a group—first to group members and then to the entire class, preferably in memorized form. Enabling students to explore performance possibilities on their own can make the material more engaging. Teachers can also use such classroom exercises to demonstrate the amazing range of possibilities for staging a single scene. They may also ask students to compare two different film versions of the same play, such as *Romeo and Juliet, Henry V,* or *Hamlet.*

Students understand Shakespeare better when teachers explain his sentence structures and use of figurative language. Students can build their confidence by translating Shakespearean passages into their own words, either alone or in groups. They can also increase their understanding of Shakespeare by writing study questions and answers or personal essays about their responses to characters, situations, and themes. Other useful writing exercises include journal writing that describes the unexpressed thoughts of characters, speculations about how audiences might

respond to particular speeches and actions, and letters addressed to characters, to Shakespeare, and to each other about their responses.

Once students are involved with the material, teachers may assign more ambitious projects. Classroom discussion and student writings can be expanded to include historical background or interpretive issues. Students may also engage in full-scale performances of scenes or even entire acts. The most important task for the teacher, however, is to capture the students' interest through activities that demonstrate the accessibility, emotional power, and relevance of Shakespeare today. (*See also* **Literature Inspired by Shakespeare; Shakespeare on Screen; Shakespeare's Works, Changing Views.**)

TELEVISION

During Shakespeare's lifetime private performances of his plays were limited to the royal court and to the homes of powerful aristocrats. In the 20th century television brought Shakespeare's plays into the dwellings of ordinary people. Some modern audiences view Shakespeare's works as "high culture," inappropriate for the "popular" medium of television. But the plays were written as popular culture 400 years ago, and today's mass media are making them available to the general public once again. Thanks to the powerful combination of Shakespeare's words and television's visual impact, the playwright's works are reaching a wider audience than ever before.

ISSUES IN TELEVISING SHAKESPEARE

Television offers special opportunities for drama beyond what is possible in the theater. The camera provides close-up shots that give the viewer a sense of immediacy and intimacy, a feeling of being present as the action unfolds rather than watching it from afar. Television can also capture some of the energy of a live performance, and in fact all telecasts during the first 20 years of television were presented live. Now that television also has the technology to capture live shows on tape, performances can be edited to increase their effectiveness.

MONEY FACTORS. Shakespeare's works first appeared on television in 1937, when the British Broadcasting Corporation (BBC) produced scenes from 12 of the plays. Since World War II, when the BBC resumed broadcasting after an interruption in service, television plays—including Shakespeare's—have been a regular feature of the network's programming. Today the BBC is the leading producer of televised Shakespeare not only because of its commitment to drama but also because it is publicly funded. It can broadcast whatever it believes is worth seeing, without worrying about finding advertisers to pay for the programming. In addition the plays it shows can be presented without commercial interruptions, making these television productions more like the uninterrupted performances seen in theaters.

Most television, however, is commercial, and money concerns have had a major impact on the history of Shakespearean drama on television. In the 1950s, when the medium was relatively new, sponsors of America's three commercial channels wanted to host serious drama. There were many showcases for television plays in those days, among them the "Hallmark Hall of Fame," the "Kraft Theater," "Westinghouse Studio One," "Philco Playhouse," and the "Dupont Show of the Month." As early as 1949 Shakespeare's works were featured in these series. But America's corporate sponsors eventually abandoned the playwright, leaving the Public Broadcasting Service (PBS) to pick up the slack. Shakespeare telecasts had become "specials" rather than regular features.

Not even the BBC has escaped the effect of commercial interests. In the 1970s, when the BBC began producing Shakespeare's complete works for television, the corporate coproducers from the United States insisted on a very traditional production style. At a time when unusual interpretations and modern-dress productions were popular, the BBC versions were limited to period costumes of the Renaissance, Middle Ages, and ancient Rome. Rather than trying to make televised Shakespeare exciting and imaginative, the sponsors insisted on a safe, traditional, and "educational" interpretation.

TIME FACTORS. In the United States, commercial programming is carved into 30- and 60-minute blocks, then subdivided into units of 7 or 8 minutes to run between commercials. As raw material for television, Shakespeare's plays do not naturally fit this structure. Using the standard approximation that it takes an hour to perform 1,000 lines of verse, only one Shakespeare play, *The Comedy of Errors*, runs under 2 hours uncut. Twenty-one plays run 2 to 3 hours; 13 more run up to 3½ hours, with *Richard III* and *Hamlet* running even longer. Therefore, Shakespeare has to be trimmed to fit the blocks and subdivided so that commercials for antacids and automobile tires can alternate with Hamlet's soliloquies.

Before cable television and videotape recorders, three hours of television was considered an entire evening's viewing. As a result networks usually cut Shakespeare's plays to run between one and two hours. Such cuts are in keeping with the traditions of the stage, where Shakespeare's longest plays are seldom performed at full length. The same is true of Shakespearean films, which typically replace Shakespeare's elaborate descriptions with visual images. Nonetheless, Shakespeare's shortest well-known tragedies—*Macbeth* and *Julius Caesar*—are among the most frequently televised plays in the United States and Britain, in large part because they require less cutting than others. Other popular plays for television are *Twelfth Night*, often considered Shakespeare's finest comedy, and *Hamlet*, which makes up for its excessive length with its compelling main character.

Another way of dealing with the length of Shakespeare's plays is to convert them into a series of episodes. Miniseries take advantage of television's ability to bring the audience back week after week. In 1960 the BBC produced a 15-part serial drama, *The Age of Kings*, based on the playwright's English history plays. In 60-minute segments, it presented cut versions of Shakespeare's eight major histories in chronological order, from *Richard II* through *Richard III*. This program, which involved 30 weeks of rehearsal and recording, was a tremendous hit with critics and audiences alike. The enthusiastic response led to another award-winning BBC serial drama in 1963, *The Spread of the Eagle*. This series presented three of the Shakespearean tragedies that are based on Roman history—*Coriolanus, Julius Caesar,* and *Antony and Cleopatra*—in nine 50-minute segments.

Returning to English history, the next year the BBC recorded the ROYAL SHAKESPEARE COMPANY's (RSC's) latest version to date of Shakespeare's first history tetralogy*: *Henry VI, Parts 1, 2,* and *3,* and *Richard III*. These performances were condensed into a sequence of three 3-hour programs called "The Wars of the Roses." The BBC adapted the RSC production to the needs of television by recording extra scenes, converting some of the battle scenes from the stage play into action drama. The added camera work, combined with an already experienced stage cast, brought the BBC and Shakespeare another televised hit on both sides of the Atlantic.

MEDIUM AND MESSAGE. Critic Alice Griffin praised these RSC/BBC productions in *Shakespeare Quarterly,* saying, "truth to the script was [the] first consideration, and . . . techniques of the medium were employed in the best interest of the play, never as an end in themselves." Her comments highlight another crucial issue in televising Shakespeare. She speaks as a lover of Shakespeare who believes the television producer's job is to show the plays to their best advantage. Television professionals, by contrast, tend to believe that Shakespeare's works should be adapted to their needs. The question of whether the camera should serve the interests of the text or vice versa has a major impact on these productions. Televising Shakespeare has always involved a balance of power between the visual and the verbal.

As a performance medium, television lives between the worlds of theater and film. Television resembles film in its use of the camera to select and shape the action. As in film the television director may record several "takes" of each scene and then edit them to shape the final product. Like stage productions, however, many television series use a simple studio setting to represent diverse localities—for example, the home or workplace of the main characters. As onstage, the setting may be as realistic or as stylized* as the director and designer choose to make it. Yet building elaborate sets or filming on location can distract from Shakespeare's characters and action as often as it adds to them. Shakespeare created his characters for the Elizabethan stage, which featured simple sets, and many television productions have allowed these characters to function in their original environment, the theater.

Because an effective Shakespearean production depends on strong performances and direction, many fine televised renderings are based on stage versions of the plays. When a performance has already been rehearsed for the stage and ripened during a long theater run, all the producer needs to add is camera rehearsal and shooting time. Recording

* ***tetralogy*** four-part series of literary or dramatic works

* ***stylized*** constructed according to a specific, obviously artificial style

exceptionally successful stage productions for television also guarantees a high-quality production, since better theater usually makes for better television. This blending of stage and screen also captures the spirit of live performance.

PRODUCTION STYLES

Shakespearean productions have gone through cycles of abstraction and realism. The GLOBE THEATER's open stage called for a very spare approach to staging. But with the development of new technology, such as photography, audiences' tastes changed. By the mid-1800s theaters favored realistic "box" sets, with three walls, a ceiling, and an authentically furnished interior, into which the audience peered through an invisible "fourth wall." Film productions allowed for an even higher degree of realism that theaters could not hope to match, so stage settings and concepts gradually grew more abstract until Shakespeare was once again appearing on a bare stage. Television has inherited these varied approaches to Shakespeare and has explored them all by turns.

STAGE TO SCREEN. Some of the freshest and most exciting Shakespearean performances on television have been versions of stage productions, such as those of the Royal Shakespeare Company. For instance, the RSC produced a modern-dress, musical *Comedy of Errors* in 1976 that became a colossal hit and ran for 18 months in Stratford and London. A live performance at the Royal Shakespeare Theater was taped for television, and separately taped close-up scenes were added later. The television audience that saw this production in April of 1978 shared the laughter and excitement of the bustling crowd in the theater. This *Comedy of Errors* provided the "best of both worlds." The production included just enough shots of the live audience to keep television viewers aware of the theater setting, while the BBC cameras effectively translated the lively farce* and richly characterized performances onto the small screen.

Britain's Thames Television also televised two long-running and successful RSC stage productions, *Antony and Cleopatra* (1972) and *Macbeth* (1976). Rather than take the camera to the theater, Thames remounted and recorded the productions in a studio, with outstanding results. The designers of the televised *Antony and Cleopatra* abandoned the stage production's complicated hydraulic set and replaced it with an open space similar to the staging that was probably used in Shakespeare's time. This spare, delicate set created a scene through the use of props and lighting—for example, using layers of sheer draperies and a pile of pillows to suggest the luxury of Cleopatra's court. The designers focused on costumes rather than sets, enabling the camera to capture the essential details even in close-up shots. With this simple but powerful design, supported by superior camera work, the play's characters became the focus of the action—vividly standing out against the spare scenery instead of having to compete for attention with a lavish backdrop.

The *Macbeth* presentation achieved equal success with an even more spare design. The television designers preserved the effective starkness of

A FEW REWRITES

Adapting Shakespeare's plays for television presents special challenges. The power of Shakespeare's drama is verbal, but the power of the television camera is visual. When the British Broadcasting Corporation began recording Shakespeare's plays for television in 1978, the staff sometimes joked, "If only we could get the author in for a few rewrites." They felt sure that if Shakespeare had understood the needs and potential of television, he would have written differently for the new medium than he had for the stage.

* *farce* light dramatic composition that features broad satiric comedy, improbable situations, stereotyped characters, and exaggerated physical action

the stage set—a circle of wooden boxes in a black-outlined circle on a small stage. Combined with black-and-white costumes and a strong use of light and shadow to define space, this bare set complemented the intense portrayals by Ian McKellen and Judi Dench. These two productions, both available on videotape, reveal Shakespeare's plays as they were originally written, for talented actors and their audiences.

A similarly successful restaging for television was seen in the United States when PBS's *Great Performances* series taped the 1976 American Conservatory Theater production of *The Taming of the Shrew*. This production, influenced by the Italian tradition of commedia dell'arte*, was set on a simple platform stage that PBS re-created in the studio before a live audience. The spare staging, brisk pace, and physical humor transferred easily to the camera. As in the RSC productions, the camera complemented the bold style of the stage performance, giving it extra power rather than changing it. All these televised Shakespeare productions share a willingness to let Shakespeare's text take the lead, capturing on camera what is already strong and clear. Three of these four productions minimized the scenery, giving the visual focus to costumes and powerful acting. This approach is one of the most effective ways to make Shakespeare's plays compelling for the small screen.

MADE FOR TV. Television's potential for realism has not been neglected, however. Studio productions of Shakespeare can be grand affairs, with large budgets, sets, and casts. The BBC production of *A Midsummer Night's Dream* (1958) tapped into the theatrical traditions of the 1800s by including a group of ballet dancers. Directed by Joan Kemp-Welch for Rediffusion in 1964, this *Midsummer Night's Dream* featured Felix Mendelssohn's famous incidental music*, more ballet-dancing fairies, gauze flats* for the trees, and famous British comedian Benny Hill as Bottom. The forest scenes in this production had trees that looked like Victorian* props with 1960s hairdos. The BBC has also taken Shakespeare on location to Britain's medieval and Renaissance CASTLES, filming the same play at Scotney Castle in Kent (1971) and *Twelfth Night* at Castle Howard (1974).

In the mid-1970s the BBC undertook its most ambitious Shakespeare project ever. Cedric Messina, an experienced producer who had already worked on eight BBC Shakespeare productions, proposed presenting all 37 of Shakespeare's plays as 2½-hour programs using well-known actors. The BBC and several American cosponsors agreed to finance the venture. The early performances in this series, produced by Messina, were fairly conventional*. When Jonathan Miller took over the project, he began to explore its potential more fully, but by that time the series had too much momentum and too uneven a reputation for him to take too daring an approach. Nonetheless, the "Shakespeare Plays" series ended up with a remarkably broad range of production styles.

The directors of these productions experimented with different visual approaches. For instance, *Hamlet*—which starred Derek Jacobi, just back from a two-year stage run of the play, as the Danish prince—had a stylized open setting. Several of the productions in the series used realistic

* **commedia dell'arte** improvisational comedy that began in Italy during the Middle Ages and featured stock characters such as a boastful captain, pairs of lovers, and bumbling servants

* **incidental music** instrumental music written to accompany a play
* **flat** stage backdrop composed of flat pieces of painted wood or cloth
* **Victorian** referring to the reign of Victoria, queen of England from 1837 to 1901

* **conventional** following established practice

settings to advantage. The studio became a medieval castle for *Richard II*, a stately home for Olivia in *Twelfth Night*, and an English village in *The Merry Wives of Windsor*. Interior settings for this series were generally superb, but exteriors proved more challenging, as they usually do on television. The first season, 1978–1979, included the first-ever BBC production of *Henry VIII*, filmed on location at Leeds Castle, and an *As You Like It* filmed on the grounds of Glamis Castle in Scotland. These productions were visually beautiful—sometimes almost overpowering—but were also quite expensive. Because of budget concerns, the other 35 plays were recorded in the studio.

See color plate 8, vol. 3.

Miller and director Elijah Moshinsky both drew on art history in creating their set designs. The work of 17th-century Dutch painter Jan Vermeer provided inspiration for the set of *All's Well That Ends Well* and that of 18th-century French painter Antoine Watteau for *Love's Labor's Lost*. Settings for the comedies were generally well defined, reinforcing comedy's focus on the social world. By contrast the tragedies, which focus on an individual's actions and choices, often featured more abstract settings. Miller used a planked platform and curtains as a set for *King Lear*, while Rodney Bennett set *Hamlet* in an open studio space with shortened walls.

The history plays again became serial dramas within the "Shakespeare Plays" series. Both David Giles, who directed the second tetralogy, and Jane Howell, who directed the first, used the same actors in leading roles throughout the sequence of plays. Howell's tetralogy did not disguise the television studio but used a set that looked like a combined playground and fortress, which showed the increasingly destructive effects of war. She cast the same actors in comparable roles throughout the series. For instance, the actor who played the pious Henry VI reappeared as a priest. Howell also kept the battles varied and violent, climaxing in a tower of mangled corpses at the end of *Richard III*, a graphic statement about the consequences of war and ambition. This *Richard III* was the first (and perhaps only) televised production to run four full hours, because Miller had parted from Messina's plan to make all the performances the same length.

As many people had expected, the seldom-televised plays, such as *Measure for Measure*, *All's Well That Ends Well*, and *Henry VIII*, became the critics' favorites. Many disliked the first productions in the series. Some disapproved of the less conventional productions, others of the familiar styles. American critics objected to the fact that all the actors were British, continuing a long-standing battle over the "ownership" of Shakespeare.

APPROACHES FOR THE 21ST CENTURY. The BBC series may have seized the last possible moment that a project such as this could have been produced on television. The increasing popularity of videotapes and cable channels has changed the very nature of the medium. Once ruled by a few commercial channels and the BBC, television now is far more specialized—although it does not seem likely there will soon be an all-Shakespeare channel. Although Shakespeare seems to have largely lost his place on American television, in Britain the BBC continues its dedication to televising plays. Audiences continue to experience Shakespeare in the theater and on film, but for many there is no better place to feel the power of Shakespeare than in their own homes. The BBC's projects have demonstrated that Shakespeare's great stories, great characters, and great language can be great television as well. (*See also* **Directors and Shakespeare; Plays: The Histories; Settings; Shakespeare on Screen; Wars of the Roses.**)

TEMPEST, THE

* *classical* in the tradition of ancient Greece and Rome

One of the late romances, *The Tempest* is generally believed to be the last play Shakespeare wrote without a collaborator. It highlights many of the same themes found in his other late works, among them time, remembrance, loss, and restoration. The central character, the magician PROSPERO, displays an obsession with temporal concerns, repeatedly asking what time it is. Prospero's emphasis is due in part to Shakespeare's decision to follow the classical* practice of restricting the action to the two or three hours occupied by an actual performance (a tradition he had followed in only one other play, *The Comedy of Errors*). But the magician's sense of haste may also stem from his conviction that he has only a short while to carry out a long-cherished plan: to reform his ancient enemies and regain his rightful authority.

PLOT SYNOPSIS. *The Tempest* is set on an uncharted island whose location appears to be somewhere between the west coast of Italy and the north coast of Africa. The title of the play refers to a ferocious storm that occurs in the opening scene. The storm causes a shipwreck, and all the passengers are cast ashore on Prospero's island, among them several Italian noblemen: King Alonso of Naples; his son, Ferdinand; his brother, Sebastian; the old counselor Gonzalo; and Prospero's brother, Antonio, who is the duke of Milan. Also shipwrecked are two of their servants, the jester Trinculo and the drunken butler Stephano.

In the second scene Prospero reveals to his daughter, MIRANDA, that the storm was an illusion conjured by his magic. To explain why he raised the storm, Prospero tells Miranda how they arrived on the island, 12 years before the play's events. The theme of remembrance resounds as the magician explains that his scheming brother deposed* him from his position as duke of Milan. With Alonso's help Antonio usurped Prospero's title and sent him and Miranda to sea in a leaky boat. Although in Milan they were presumed dead, the castaways landed on a distant island inhabited by two mysterious creatures. The first, CALIBAN, was the orphaned son of a previous inhabitant, the witch Sycorax, who had been exiled to the island from Algiers. The other, Ariel, was an "airy spirit" who had been confined within a pine tree by Sycorax until he was released by Prospero's magic.

Twelve years later, having learned that his enemies will be sailing nearby, Prospero has seized the opportunity to confront them. For the

* *depose* to remove from high office, often by force

remainder of the play, the shipwrecked party is scattered around the island. By happy chance Ferdinand meets Miranda, and the two fall in love. Meanwhile Antonio and Sebastian plot to assassinate Alonso, and Trinculo and Stephano conspire with Caliban to murder Prospero and take over the island. As Prospero ponders these developments, it seems possible that his anger will overcome any impulse he has for reconciliation*, but at Ariel's urging he eventually chooses forgiveness. With his own magic and Ariel's aid, Prospero foils the two conspiracies, then reveals himself to the Italian nobles as the banished duke. The play ends peacefully, with Prospero's dukedom restored, Ferdinand and Miranda engaged, and on the surface at least all the parties reconciled.

* *reconciliation* act of bringing together again in friendship

Throughout the play Prospero controls events through his powerful charms, which come partly from the books he has brought from Milan and partly from Ariel's supernatural powers. Ariel raises the storm that opens the play, enacts the magician's commands, sings and plays music to enchant the shipwrecked Europeans, and keeps Prospero informed about events on the island. Prospero also uses magic directly to subdue his enemies, as when Ferdinand raises a sword against Miranda's father only to have his arm paralyzed in midair. The most common use of enchantment in the play, however, relates to the creation of spectacles that thrill or disturb the island's onlookers. Antonio, Sebastian, and Alonso are terrified into a helpless stupor when they encounter Ariel in the shape of a giant harpy*. Ferdinand and Miranda, by contrast, are delightfully entertained by a masque presented by the goddesses Iris, Ceres, and Juno. But Prospero's magic has limitations. As he learns from Caliban's conspiracy against him and his own brother's persistent hostility, it cannot change the human heart.

* *harpy* creature from Greek mythology that is part woman and part bird

SOURCES. The events of *The Tempest* were probably inspired by published accounts of strange magicians, supernatural apparitions, wild

In the final scene of *The Tempest*, Prospero's rightful title, duke of Milan, is restored. He does not punish his monstrous servant Caliban for plotting against his life, however, saying "This thing of darkness I acknowledge mine."

monsters, and abandoned princesses. Specific sources include the works of the ancient Roman poets Virgil and Ovid and essays by the 16th-century French essayist Michel de Montaigne (translated into English by John Florio). Shakespeare also seems to have been influenced by historical events. In 1610, when he probably began working on the play, the daughter of King James I was about to marry a foreign ruler in a dynastic alliance between Protestant England and Germany. This event is paralleled in *The Tempest* by the marriage of Alonso's daughter, Claribel, to the king of Tunis. The Italian nobles are on their way home from this wedding when they are shipwrecked on Prospero's island.

In 1610 reports were circulating in London about a ship bound for Virginia that had been wrecked on the coast of uninhabited Bermuda. Miraculously, all of the passengers survived the shipwreck and lived for nearly a year on Bermuda's abundant natural food and drink. The English colonists salvaged the remnants of their vessel and constructed two smaller boats that successfully transported them to Virginia. From there the story of their dramatic survival reached England. Prospero's island may be based on these reports, but unlike Bermuda, it is inhabited by one other human. Caliban, who is described in the play's cast list as a "savage and deformed slave," may be based in part on Shakespeare's image of an American Indian. He shows the exiled duke and his daughter the island's springs and edible resources but is later enslaved for a sexual attack on Miranda.

COMMENTARY. References to America, along with Miranda's exclamation "O brave new world" (V.i.183), have led many critics to identify *The Tempest* as Shakespeare's "New World" play. They see the drama as representing the relations of power and race in lands subject to European colonialism. More recent critics have pointed out, however, that colonialism was not limited to the New World. It also flourished in such "Old World" sites as Ireland, where English colonies caused bitter conflict, and in Africa, where several European nations built outposts and sold the natives into slavery.

The Tempest was a favorite with the English Romantic* poets of the early to mid-1800s, who saw Prospero's magic island as a place where nature prevailed. The Romantics began a trend, which continues to the present day, of identifying Prospero, the magician who creates spectacular illusions, with Shakespeare the dramatist. Just as Prospero abandons his "art" and returns to the ordinary world of Milan, Shakespeare, they assumed, saw *The Tempest* as his last major dramatic effort. In fact the playwright seems to have retired to his home in Stratford-upon-Avon about two years after the play's debut in late 1610 or early 1611. Many Romantic critics saw Shakespeare and Prospero as equally skillful interpreters of human nature—wise men who understood both the world and the evil within the human heart and relied on reason to steer a civilized course.

Such critics perceived Caliban, in contrast, as the embodiment of savagery, a subhuman creature who needed to be tamed and educated. After Charles Darwin proposed his theory of evolution in 1859, Caliban was often identified with the "missing link"—the half-man, half-beast

* **Romantic** referring to a school of thought, prominent in the 1800s, that emphasized the importance of emotion in art

connection between humans' animal ancestors and their enlightened modern selves. Prospero's major challenge, as these critics saw it, was to prod this creature forward, to educate him in the ways of European civilization, to help him "evolve." In stage productions of the 1800s and early 1900s, Caliban was frequently portrayed as hairy and apelike. English actor Frank Benson prepared for the role by watching monkeys at the zoo.

Prospero's attempts to teach Caliban language, manners, and morals were sometimes seen as akin to what poet Rudyard Kipling called the "white man's burden" of civilizing colonized peoples during the height of the British empire. In the late 1900s, when many of these colonized cultures began to reject the label of inferiority imposed by their foreign conquerors, Caliban's status likewise changed in critics' eyes. When he said, "The red-plague rid you for learning me your language!" (I.ii.364–65), Caliban became the symbol of anticolonial sentiment in plays, poetry, and political writings from the Caribbean islands, Latin America, and Africa. His defiant speeches to Prospero were read by many as the demands of enslaved peoples for independence and the right to define their own identities.

Alongside these interpretations modern scholars have seen troubling environmental issues in the play. From the native Caliban, Prospero learns where to find the natural resources of his island home, including fresh water, food, and firewood. The ecology of "this bare island" is preserved only because Prospero returns to Milan at the end of the play (it is not clear whether Caliban accompanies his master).

Like other forms of human invention and technology, Prospero's magic contains the potential for vast destruction as well as for remarkable benefit. How it will be used depends, as Prospero learns, on human choice. In due course Prospero learns that "the rarer action is / In virtue than in vengeance" (V.i.27–28), and he chooses to drown his magic books rather than be tempted further by their potential for abuse. The ethical issues in *The Tempest* are so ambiguous that the play will always be open to differing interpretations, both in critical writings and on the stage.

STAGE HISTORY. Until the 1700s, when editors began to examine Shakespeare's sources closely, performances of *The Tempest* seem to have overlooked the play's New World connections. Instead it was viewed as the triumph of enlightened civilization (represented by Prospero) over human greed and brutality (personified in his brother, Antonio, and the savage Caliban).

At first *The Tempest* was probably performed as it appears in the FIRST FOLIO of 1623 (where it is the opening work). Although the play enjoyed early success in this form, most productions in the late 1600s used a substantially revised version of the script developed by John Dryden and William Davenant. This text, subtitled *The Enchanted Island*, added several new characters, including a sister for Miranda and a noble young man whom Prospero has hidden on the island, and multiple love affairs result. These romances are parodied in a subplot in which Trinculo (spelled

THE COMMEDIA DELL'ARTE

Shakespeare may have taken some of his ideas for *The Tempest* from popular Italian tragicomedies of the 1500s. Plays such as *Lost Island* center on a benevolent magician, who traditionally carries a book and a staff. This "magus" controls good and evil spirits and keeps them imprisoned in a cave, as Prospero does with Caliban. He uses his magic to restore friendship between enemies and unite young lovers in marriage.

Many of these plays include details found in *The Tempest,* such as a shipwreck in the first scene, an unsuccessful plot in which a native of the island and some castaways attempt to steal the magician's book, and a magical feast that rises from the ground and then disappears.

* **allegory** literary device in which characters, events, and settings represent abstract qualities and in which the author intends a different meaning to be read beneath the surface

* **mulatto** person of mixed African and European ancestry

Trincalo in the new version) and Stephano pursue Caliban's sister, Sycorax (his mother's name in Shakespeare's play). Nearly all productions of *The Tempest* in English theaters used this adaptation, often with extravagant musical embellishments, until 1838. That year the prominent English actor-manager William Charles Macready restored Shakespeare's original text to the stage.

Many modern productions of *The Tempest* reflect the tendency to read the play as an allegory* for European colonialism. During the late 1900s Prospero was often portrayed as an insecure, sometimes tyrannical colonizer who brutally subdues the island's natives. To reinforce this interpretation, Caliban and Ariel were often played by actors of African or Caribbean ancestry. After reading an analysis of interpersonal relations in the French colony of Madagascar, English director Jonathan Miller cast Prospero as an abusive colonial governor, Ariel as a mulatto* house servant, and Caliban as a darker field slave. The natives expressed defiance throughout the performance, which ended with Caliban raising his fist as all the Europeans left the island.

SCREEN HISTORY. There have been several television versions of *The Tempest*, which have generally followed Shakespeare's text closely. Among them are the 1960 "Hallmark Hall of Fame" production, the 1979 BBC/Time-Life version, and the Bard rendering (part of a series of educational videos) of the 1980s. Most were taped on a bare stage with minimal scenery and props. They tend to be moving photographs of stage productions rather than cinematic interpretations of Shakespeare's drama.

The most prominent film versions of the play were directed by Derek Jarman (*The Tempest*, 1980) and Peter Greenaway (*Prospero's Books*, 1991). Jarman emphasized power relations by having a tyrannical Prospero abuse his servants and explored the play's sexual tensions by making Miranda sexually aware and casting Stephano and Trinculo as openly gay. Greenaway's film presented Shakespeare's text as Prospero's fantasy. The magician, played by Sir John Gielgud, conceives all the roles and writes the actors' lines in the only blank book in his extensive library. The rest of his books, 24 volumes in all, contain obscure lore of medicine, magic, geography, architecture, and other topics that might have been in the library of Michelangelo or Leonardo da Vinci. Greenaway also filmed his islanders naked, in contrast to the lavish, formal costumes of the Europeans, exaggerating the opposition between nature and nurture (upbringing) in Shakespeare's text.

The Tempest has also inspired such adaptations as the science fiction classic *Forbidden Planet* (1956). In this film Prospero is transformed to Professor Morbius, a space explorer marooned on a distant planet. The movie reflects the influence of Freudian* psychology on interpretations of *The Tempest*, turning Caliban into the representation of Morbius's id, the part of the mind from which the sex drive and other physical urges spring. Paul Mazursky's film version of *The Tempest* (1982) moves the play's characters to modern-day Manhattan and an abandoned Greek island. This film also takes a Freudian approach, emphasizing the danger of incest* between

* **Freudian** based on the theories of Sigmund Freud, a doctor in Vienna during the late 1800s and early 1900s who developed the practice of modern psychotherapy

* **incest** sexual relationship between family members

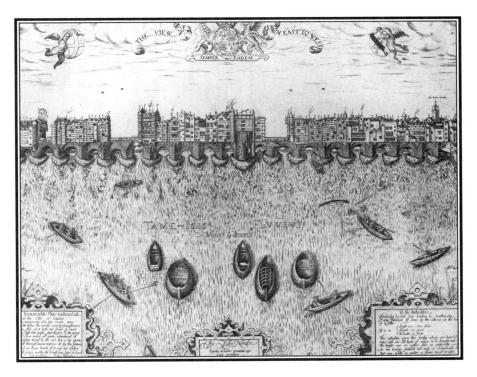

Miranda and her father. (*See also* **Actors, Shakespearean; Directors and Shakespeare; Magic and Folklore; Plays: The Romances; Playwrights and Poets; Settings; Shakespeare's Plays, Adaptations of; Shakespeare's Sources; Television.**)

THAMES, THE RIVER

Because London's streets were narrow, crowded, noisy, and dirty, the easiest way to go from place to place was on the river. For this reason the River Thames served as London's main highway for many centuries. The river is more than 200 miles long, from its source at Thames Head to the place where it flows out to sea, a sandbank known as the Nore. The river follows a path through rolling lowlands, and it figures in many of the lovely rural settings that appear in the literature about the English countryside.

During Shakespeare's time the GLOBE and other theaters were located in Bankside, a suburb on the south bank of the Thames. Stairs cut into the riverbanks led to the water, where boatmen waited in rowboats. The equivalent of modern taxicab drivers, they charged a fee to transport customers upstream, downstream, or across the river. They prided themselves on effectively managing the tidal currents of the Thames, announcing which way they were headed by shouting, "Westward ho!" (upstream) or "Eastward ho!" (downstream). Some of the more daring boatmen became famous for the skill with which they maneuvered in and around the swiftly running waters that flowed beneath the arches of London Bridge.

Small boats sailed constantly up and down the Thames, carrying passengers from place to place about the city. Skilled boatmen learned to navigate the swift currents that flowed under the arches of London Bridge.

See
color plate 12,
vol. 1.

Although Londoners spent much time on the river, they avoided drinking from it. As a tidal river the Thames is salty, at least in the London area. Furthermore, in Shakespeare's time much of the waste generated by the city's inhabitants flowed into the river. Consequently, most people imported their drinking water from wells or springs outside the city. (*See also* **London; Transportation and Travel.**)

THEATER

See *Elizabethan Theaters; Performances; Shakespearean Theater: 17th Century; Shakespearean Theater: 18th Century; Shakespearean Theater: 19th Century; Shakespearean Theater: 20th Century.*

THEMES IN SHAKESPEARE'S PLAYS

See *Disguises; Dreams; Fate and Fortune; Friendship; Ghosts and Apparitions; Gods and Goddesses; Humor in Shakespeare's Plays; Love; Loyalty; Madness; Magic and Folklore; Medievalism; Morality and Ethics; Nature; Philosophy; Revenge and Forgiveness; Supernatural Phenomena; Topical References; Warfare; Weather and the Seasons.*

THEOLOGY

See *Astronomy and Cosmology; Philosophy; Religion.*

TIMON OF ATHENS

* *steward* person who manages another person's household or estate

A fable-like play, *Timon of Athens* is about a bitter and angry man who has lavished gifts on his friends only to have them abandon him in his time of need. Long regarded as a minor work, the play has finally attracted some overdue attention from scholars and directors.

At the opening of the play Timon is shown to be a generous nobleman who showers his friends with gifts and feasts, ignoring the warnings of his steward* about the amount of money he is spending. When his fortune is nearly gone, Timon seeks aid from his friends, but they refuse him. In response he immediately turns from excessive generosity to excessive rage. Cursing Athens and all its inhabitants, he retreats to a cave to live as a hermit, calling himself Misanthropos (Greek for "hater of mankind"). He rails against the world and all of humanity, mocking everyone who appears at his cave, from his former servant to the Athenian senators who come to beg for aid to avert an attack by the banished army captain Alcibiades. To Alcibiades himself Timon gives gold, which he has

In this scene from *Timon of Athens,* two Athenian senators plead with Timon to help save the city from destruction. Timon, who has become a bitter and disappointed man, refuses to supply the aid they seek.

* **misanthropic** marked by hatred or distrust of humankind

* **morality play** religious dramatic work that teaches a moral lesson through the use of symbolic characters

* **misanthropy** hatred of humanity

discovered buried in his cave. The captain conquers the city, but eventually agrees to spare its inhabitants. Later a soldier discovers Timon's grave, marked with the epitaph "Here lie I, Timon, who, alive, all living men did hate" (V.iv.72).

Shakespeare took this story from Sir Thomas North's 1579 translation of PLUTARCH'S LIVES. He probably wrote the play late in his career, between the other tragedies and the romances, and he may have collaborated on it with Thomas Middleton. The story of Timon's descent into misanthropic* fury lacks most of the usual dynamics of a drama, although it somewhat resembles the morality plays* of the Middle Ages. The FIRST FOLIO version of the play contains several plot inconsistencies and other textual problems. For these reasons, scholars have long regarded *Timon* as fundamentally flawed. Modern interpreters, however, consider it "an almost finished play" and admire its examination of the intellectual traditions of misanthropy* and pessimism. The corrupt Athens that Shakespeare depicts in this play resembles LONDON during the early years of the reign of King JAMES I, a ruler who ran up enormous debts of his own with extravagant gift giving.

Titania

In the theater *Timon of Athens* has been produced more often in the past 50 years than in the preceding 200. The play's recent popularity is due partly to overexposure of the better-known plays and partly to the eagerness of today's Shakespeare festivals to perform every play in the canon*. But the drama is also increasingly relevant to the modern world. Timon's "strange times, that weep with laughing, not with weeping" (IV.iii.486) resemble the modern world in many ways, and his own disillusionment with a morally bankrupt society seems increasingly pertinent. Modern viewers frequently relate to Timon's powerful expressions of despair, particularly when he says, "My long sickness / Of health and living now begins to mend, / And nothing brings me all things" (V.i.186–88).

Major presentations of this once rarely staged play include a production at the Bouffes-du Nord in Paris, directed by Peter Brook (1973), and a performance as Timon by James Earl Jones at the Yale Repertory Theater (1980). The ROYAL SHAKESPEARE COMPANY also produced the play in 1980, with Richard Pascoe as Timon. The Stratford Festival in Ontario, Canada, presented Brian Bedford as Timon in a 1991 production that was set in the Jazz Age 1920s. The National Actors Theatre successfully brought this production to New York for a Broadway run two years later. (*See also* **History in Shakespeare's Plays: Ancient Greece and Rome; Shakespeare's Sources.**)

TITANIA

Titania is the queen of the FAIRIES in Shakespeare's romantic comedy *A Midsummer Night's Dream.* Her brief, spell-induced love affair with a simpleminded weaver named Nick Bottom emphasizes the main theme of the play: the blindness and folly of love.

The play's subplot involving Titania centers on her decision to take custody of a "little changeling boy," a human child raised by fairies. Her refusal to give up the boy causes conflict with OBERON, her husband, who wants the child for an attendant. Their dispute causes foul weather throughout the realm, demonstrating how closely the fairies are connected to nature. To punish Titania's defiance, Oberon casts a spell to make her fall in love with the first creature she sees. Awakened by Bottom, she immediately becomes infatuated with him. Adding to Titania's humiliation is the fact that PUCK, a mischievous fairy, has replaced the weaver's human head with that of a donkey. The enchanted queen lavishes praise and affection on Bottom, telling him, "Thou art as wise as thou art beautiful" (III.i.148) and offering to kiss his "fair large ears" (IV.i.4). Eventually Oberon releases her from the spell. After recovering from her shock she reunites with her husband and helps him bless the marriages of three pairs of mortal lovers.

In many productions Titania and Oberon are played by the same actors who assume the roles of Theseus, the duke of Athens, and Hippolyta, the queen of the Amazons, who is betrothed to Theseus. Double-casting these roles highlights some similarities in the relationships between the two male leaders and their female counterparts. Hippolyta has become engaged to Theseus only after he has defeated her in battle, and Titania undergoes a similar defeat by falling victim to Oberon's prank. Feminist scholars in particular have noted that both Theseus and Oberon reinforce their power by controlling the women in their lives. (*See also* **Feminist Interpretations; Nature; Supernatural Phenomena.**)

TITUS ANDRONICUS

Titus Andronicus is Shakespeare's bloodiest play. This photograph from the 1981 Royal Shakespeare Company production of the play shows Titus (played by Patrick Stewart) moments before he stabs Tamora to death.

Written around 1593, *Titus Andronicus* is one of Shakespeare's earliest plays and his first tragedy. The action is gruesome and horrifying, with violent characters who mutilate themselves and others for honor, power, and revenge. Although modern critics consider the play one of Shakespeare's lesser works, it was extremely popular with Elizabethan audiences.

PLOT SUMMARY. Titus Andronicus, a general, returns to Rome after successfully battling the Goths. He declines an offer to be emperor because he believes that the rightful heir is Saturninus. The emperor's jealous brother, Bassianus, abducts Titus's daughter, Lavinia, while the corrupt Saturninus marries Tamora, the queen of the Goths. Earlier Titus had provoked Tamora's wrath by executing one of her sons. In revenge Tamora's lover, Aaron the Moor, enlists two of the queen's other sons to kill Bassianus and rape Lavinia. To prevent her from identifying her attackers, they cut off her hands and tongue. Then they frame Titus's sons Martius and Quintus so that they will be blamed for their brother's murder.

In a plea for mercy toward his sons, Titus cuts off his own hand, but he soon learns that the young men have been executed anyway. When Titus discovers the identity of his daughter's rapists, he murders them and cooks them into pies, which he serves to Saturninus and Tamora. In the bloody finale he kills Lavinia to end her dishonor, then slays Tamora before he himself is fatally stabbed by Saturninus. Order is finally restored to Rome when Titus's son Lucius kills Saturninus and is immediately proclaimed emperor.

SOURCES. Scholars have yet to identify any direct source for *Titus Andronicus,* though many believe it was based on an older play that is now lost. Shakespeare adapted some incidents, such as the rape of Lavinia, from writings by the Roman poet OVID. The violent tone of the play shows the influence of the Roman playwright Seneca, and some incidents appear to have been borrowed from Elizabethan playwrights Christopher Marlowe and Thomas Kyd, contemporaries of Shakespeare who were popular at the time.

COMMENTARY. *Titus Andronicus* foreshadows several of Shakespeare's later, more developed characters and themes. Titus resembles Othello in his stubborn honor and his gullibility. Aaron, a Moor who delights in his own villainy, may be an early version of IAGO, the man who causes Othello's

125

downfall. In addition the play begins with a dispute over the succession to the throne, a theme that is explored throughout Shakespeare's history plays and in some of his later tragedies.

PERFORMANCE HISTORY. Despite its early popularity *Titus Andronicus* was held in low regard and was rarely performed in the 1700s and 1800s. In the 1850s a British revival featured the African American actor Ira Aldridge as Aaron. A 1955 production starring Laurence Oliver generated some interest in the play, but it remains one of the least performed of Shakespeare's works. Several television and movie versions have been made, including *Titus* (1999), a feature film by Julie Taymor that stars Anthony Hopkins as Titus and Jessica Lange as Tamora. (*See also* **Plays: The Tragedies.**)

TOPICAL REFERENCES

Shakespeare's plays and poems are filled with references to Elizabethan celebrities, scandals, and fads. Most of these allusions are veiled, however, because playwrights were sometimes punished for commenting too boldly on issues of the day. Modern readers of the words often find these references confusing, and performers of the plays may have difficulty presenting them in a way that their audiences will understand.

Scholars have found dozens of topical references in *Love's Labor's Lost*. The character Holofernes, for example, is widely believed to be a parody of Gabriel Harvey, a scholar who was notorious for using pretentious language. Elizabethan theatergoers may have recognized Harvey's wordy style in Holofernes's description of a deer that was killed during a hunt: "The deer was (as you know) *sanguis*, in blood, ripe as the pomewater [type of apple], who now hangeth like a jewel in the ear of *caelo*, the sky, the welkin, the heaven" (IV.ii.3–6). Shakespeare also ridicules the fad of pretending to be depressed, which was popular among members of the royal court. When Don Armado asks Moth, "Boy, what sign is it when a man of great spirit grows melancholy?" his simpleminded page answers, "A great sign, sir, that he will look sad" (I.ii.1–3).

In *Hamlet*, Shakespeare includes a topical reference to children's acting companies, which were so popular that they threatened the livelihood of adult performers. Rosencrantz tells the prince that established theater troupes are losing business to "children, little eyases [hawks], that cry out on the top of question, and are most tyrannically clapp'd for't" (II.ii.339–41).

Topical references have helped scholars determine when Shakespeare wrote some of his plays. In the prologue of *Henry V*, for example, the Chorus* speaks about the expected triumphant return of the earl of Essex, who had embarked on a mission to crush an Irish rebellion in March of 1599. Essex returned in defeat five months later. For that reason scholars infer that this prologue must have been written during the months when the earl was away and before his defeat was known.

* *Chorus* character in Elizabethan drama who recites the prologue and epilogue and sometimes comments on the action

TOURNAMENTS

* *lance* weapon with a long wooden shaft
   and a sharp metal tip

Jousting was a sport that dated back
to the Middle Ages. In 1510 King
Henry VIII jousted before his queen,
Catherine of Aragon, in honor of the
birth of their son, Henry (who did not
survive to adulthood).

Many Elizabethan sports, such as jousting and archery, were related to the serious business of WARFARE. Tournaments, which dated from the Middle Ages, began as organized events that provided opportunities for soldiers to test their combat skills against each other in a controlled situation.

Jousting tournaments were open only to men of the upper classes. They gave the rich the opportunity to show off their armor, clothes, and well-groomed horses. During the Middle Ages tournaments had involved melees, mock battles between two large groups on horseback. By the late 1500s, however, most tournaments were limited to one-on-one jousting. Two men mounted on horseback, each carrying a lance* with a blunted end, charged toward each other, and each attempted to knock the other off his horse. Both men were dressed in armor and carried shields for protection. Another jousting event was tilting, in which a rider charged toward a series of small metal rings suspended in the air and attempted to skewer them with his lance. Noblemen trained for jousting matches by practicing with a quintain, a shield mounted on a post. This target was attached to a revolving bar. If the jouster failed to hit the target in just the right spot, the bar swung around and knocked him off his horse.

Archery was another popular tournament sport. Unlike jousting, archery was open to commoners as well as noblemen. In fact Elizabethan law required all healthy men under 60 to practice shooting a bow, which—in spite of the development of gunpowder—remained the most important battle weapon. Because men could be called into battle at any time, it was crucial for all able-bodied males to know how to use a bow and arrow. The English were known and feared throughout Europe for their skill with the bow. During tournaments archers fired their arrows at targets mounted on bales of hay, known as butts.

During Shakespeare's lifetime the popularity of tournaments as a form of entertainment had begun to decline. Queen Elizabeth allowed them at court because she loved the lavish display of gleaming armor, blaring trumpets, and prancing horses. But her successor, King JAMES I, hated military displays, and during his reign tournaments died out almost completely. (*See also* **Arms and Armor; Games, Pastimes, and Sports.**)

TOWER OF LONDON

The Tower of London is a famous fortress that is the setting of several scenes in Shakespeare's history plays. The Tower is actually not a single structure but a cluster of fortified buildings enclosed within a protective wall. It has played a famous role in history as the site at which traitors were imprisoned and in many cases executed. Its bloody past made it a natural choice as the backdrop for political struggles in several of the histories, most notably *Richard III*. The role played by the Tower of London in Shakespeare's plays has helped spread its notorious reputation.

HISTORY OF THE TOWER. William the Conqueror, who became ruler of England in 1066, began the construction of what would eventually become the Tower of London. The fortifications he devised were originally designed to control access to the city's port on the THAMES River. The oldest of the structures in the complex, the White Tower, was begun around 1078. Its name comes from the color of the limestone used in its construction, which was imported from King William's hometown of Caen in Normandy, France.

The White Tower was built within the old city wall that had been erected by the Romans, but by the 1100s the fortifications had expanded beyond that boundary. The Tower complex eventually became a coordinated group of buildings, centering on the White Tower and covering 18 acres of land. The whole area is encircled by a wall and has only one land entrance, located on the southeast side of the complex. During Shakespeare's time, however, most people entered the area through a gate leading from the Thames into the Tower's moat, which was drained in 1843. This water entrance was known as the Traitor's Gate because prisoners accused of crimes against the state came into the Tower through it.

Over the years the Tower of London has served a variety of purposes. It was a royal residence until the 1600s, and it has also been used as a storage place for weapons, a public records office, a royal mint*, and even a zoo where exotic animals were kept for the pleasure of the royal court. (The building in which the animals were once housed is known as the Lion Tower.) It is best known, however, as a place of imprisonment and execution for enemies of the state. A long list of famous English subjects have spent time in the Tower, and many lost their lives there. Among these victims have been Sir Thomas More, Anne Boleyn (second wife of King Henry VIII), and Lady Jane Grey, who ruled England for 19 days before being imprisoned and executed by Queen ELIZABETH I. As a princess,

* **mint** to make coins by shaping and stamping metal; also the place where coins are made

Elizabeth herself spent a short time in the Tower when her sister, Queen Mary I, suspected her of plotting to seize the throne. The Tower was the scene of political executions as recently as World War I, when several enemy spies were put to death there.

Today the Tower is one of the most popular tourist sites in London, hosting some 3 million visitors each year. Among its main attractions are the British crown jewels and the official guides known as yeoman-warders, or beefeaters, in their colorful Tudor* uniforms. One Tower official is in charge of maintaining the flocks of ravens that inhabit the grounds. According to a legend dating from the time of King Charles II (reigned 1660–1685), if the ravens ever leave, both the Tower of London and the British kingdom will fall. To ensure that such a calamity never occurs, the wings of the Tower ravens are regularly clipped.

THE TOWER IN SHAKESPEARE'S PLAYS. Five of Shakespeare's history plays feature scenes set in the Tower. The earliest play to feature the Tower is *Henry VI, Part 1,* in which two noblemen argue over who will control the fortress. Later in the same play Edmund Mortimer, the earl of March, dies of old age while imprisoned there for having rebelled against Henry IV. The fourth act of *Henry VI, Part 2,* includes a scene in which Lord Scales, the Tower's commander, helps expel rebels from London.

Later references to the Tower of London are much more sinister. The Shakespearean character most associated with the Tower is King Richard III, portrayed as a ruthless opportunist who unhesitatingly murders his political opponents to gain and hold on to the throne. Many of these killings occur in the Tower. In *Henry VI, Part 3,* Richard (who is not yet king) assassinates King Henry while he is imprisoned in the Tower. In *Richard III,* Richard's brother the duke of Clarence is thrown into the Tower for treason. This arrest, ordered by King Edward IV, has been secretly arranged by Richard, who later hires two men to slay Clarence in his cell. *Richard III* also refers to the killing of Richard's nephews, the prince of Wales and the duke of York, who have been imprisoned in the fortress. Although this act occurs offstage, the text makes it clear that Richard is responsible for the deaths of his young rivals.

Shakespeare's final reference to the Tower occurs in *Richard II,* which was written later than the other histories but deals with events that took place earlier. The king loses his throne and is sentenced to death while a prisoner in the Tower—although his actual death takes place in Pomfret Castle to the north. (*See also* **Crime and Punishment; History in Shakespeare's Plays: England; Plays: The Histories.**)

* **Tudor** referring to the dynasty that ruled England from 1485 to 1603

TRADE

English trade and industry advanced dramatically during Shakespeare's time. In the early 1500s the country was a largely undeveloped agricultural nation, lacking the wealth and naval power to conduct much trade with other countries. This situation began to change when ELIZABETH I came to the throne in 1558. The population boomed.

Many immigrants, fleeing the persecution of Protestants on the European continent, came to the British Isles with their skills, enthusiasm, and energy. The production of wool cloth, long a staple of the English economy, improved in quality and increased in variety. Trade between England and the continent became more active and more profitable. The nation's lively commercial culture—brimming with shops, markets, and dazzling fairs—became more vital than ever. As England's wealth and power grew, its merchants and seamen ventured far and wide on the open seas.

BUILDING BLOCKS OF TRADE

In the years before Elizabeth became queen, England had about 3 million people, of whom only 200,000 or so lived in towns and cities. The rest of the population was scattered throughout the countryside, on open land and in villages of 200 to 500 residents. A typical village had a self-contained economy. Between the farms and the local bakery, brewery, and smithy (blacksmith's shop), the residents could fulfill all of their basic needs.

During the 1500s the English economy began to change. AGRICULTURE became more specialized, with farmers focusing on the crops and animals that were easiest to raise in their regions. At the same time, manufacturing, which was concentrated in the cities and towns, increased in importance. By the time of Elizabeth's death, one-fifth of England's 5 million inhabitants lived in towns and cities. The surge in urban population created a two-way trade, as food and raw materials flowed from the countryside to the towns and manufactured goods proceeded in the other direction.

RAW MATERIALS. English farmers grew a variety of grains and vegetables, including wheat, barley, hops*, and cabbage. They also produced meats and dairy foods such as butter and cheese. Coastal villages provided fish, a staple of the English diet. The most valuable agricultural product, however, was wool. When Elizabeth began her reign, her kingdom included more than 10 million sheep, whose wool was the anchor of the economy and England's only major export.

The countryside also produced raw materials for the nation's small but growing industries. Timber was in great demand for shipbuilding and home heating, and it also fed the blast furnaces of the young metalworking and glassblowing industries. A wood shortage soon resulted, and many people saw coal as the best alternative. Coal mining, centered on the city of Newcastle in the northeast, began a steady growth. Meanwhile other mining enterprises produced stone, lead, tin, iron, and more.

MANUFACTURED GOODS. Elizabethan England had no real industry in the modern sense—no large factories, costly machinery, or mass production—but the English were able to manufacture most of the goods they needed. Their largest industry was the production of woolen cloth. Much of England's cloth was still made by individuals who sold their finished products directly to customers. Merchants known as clothiers sometimes

hops berries used in the brewing of beer

NEW WORLDS OF TRADE

English men and women of Shakespeare's time were exposed to a stunning variety of exotic foods and goods. These strange and exciting products came from distant parts of the world that English ships had only reached within the past few years or decades. Spices, silks, and fine woods came from Asia, while Africa provided such luxuries as ivory and coffee. The exotic products imported from the Americas included corn, tomatoes, potatoes, and—most profitably of all—tobacco. By the early 1600s smoke shops were everywhere in London, and King James himself wrote an angry pamphlet against the new habit.

During the reign of Elizabeth I, international trade expanded. Busy seaport towns on Britain's east coast traded with northern Europe, while cities in the southwest traded with Ireland, Spain, Portugal, and France. Britain exported cloth and imported dyes, wine, salt, and spices.

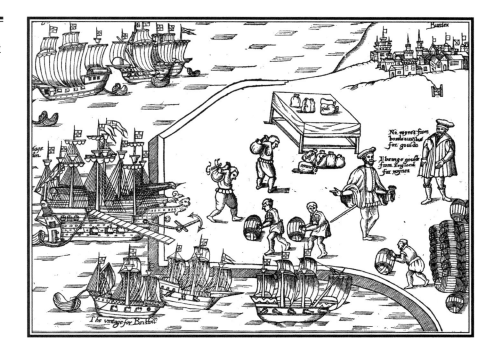

organized this process on a larger scale, distributing wool to several manufacturers and selling large quantities of finished goods, mostly in the LONDON market. England was best known for its rough, inexpensive woolens, but it also produced linen and canvas from locally grown flax and hemp. Protestant immigrants from European countries brought new techniques for producing finer fabrics, more colorful dyes, and even silk garments.

Large-scale organization was also becoming common in the metalworking and glassblowing industries. The vast majority of English manufacturing took place on a small scale in villages and towns throughout the country, however. Independent shoemakers, blacksmiths, leather workers, brewers, and other CRAFTWORKERS plied their trades in small workshops, supplying their local areas with finished goods. Most craftsmen were assisted by apprentices, young men who served without pay for seven years to earn the right to sell their skills in the open market. The apprenticeship system, along with many other aspects of manufacturing, was regulated by the guild* for each craft.

* **guild** association of craft and trade workers that set standards for and represented the interests of its members

TRANSPORTING WARES. As England's urban population grew, the locations of production and manufacturing centers moved farther apart. For this reason the transportation of raw materials and finished goods became increasingly important. The most common and basic form of transport was by road. Pack animals and wagons carried goods along a network of highways and byways that radiated out from London, linking farms and villages to towns and cities. The quality of the roads was very inconsistent. Many were far too poorly built and maintained to sustain the increasing traffic, and most were totally blocked by snow during the winters.

For bulk goods such as grain and coal, water transport was easier and more efficient. Small, sturdy SHIPS navigated the English coastline and the rivers that linked many cities to the sea. Larger vessels braved the English Channel, the North Sea, and the Baltic Sea to trade with northern Europe. Fishing fleets traveled as far as Newfoundland, off the coast of North America, and oceangoing ships opened trade with the newly established colonies in North America and the wealthy merchant cities of the Mediterranean.

TRADING IN ENGLAND AND ABROAD

Trade was both a business and a pleasure for the English. It thrived in every area, from the great city of London to the smallest farming communities. Traveling vendors, or peddlers, brought goods to remote farms, and villagers journeyed to nearby towns and cities to visit shops, markets, and fairs. Increasingly, these markets made luxury goods from other countries available to English consumers.

BUYING AND SELLING WITHIN ENGLAND. In isolated farming communities everyone looked forward to visits from traveling vendors. These men and their pack animals brought a wide variety of manufactured goods, from farm tools and cooking utensils to silks and other luxury items. Some of these vendors were not completely honest about the quality of their wares. The peddler Autolycus, in Shakespeare's *The Winter's Tale,* boasts that he has managed to trick the local peasants into buying "trumpery."

Country dwellers also traveled to the shops in urban areas. Craftworkers in villages and towns commonly displayed wares in the front sections of their shops that had been built in the workshops at the back. Often the shop owners lived in rooms above or behind their stores. In the larger towns and cities, many shopkeepers earned their livings entirely by selling goods they had purchased elsewhere. Competing with the shops were vendors at temporary street stalls, lobbing cries of "What d'ye lack?" at the passersby.

The greatest concentration of shops was in London, where the nation's first shopping mall, the Royal Exchange, opened in 1571. Its gate opened onto a courtyard surrounded on three sides by brick buildings four stories high. About 100 shops sold everything from books to armor, and covered walkways offered still more space for meeting and trading. The mall stayed open in the evenings, lighted by hundreds of candles. A second such mall, called the New Exchange, opened on the other end of town in 1609.

Most towns of any respectable size held markets once a week. Market day was a busy and lively event, with people coming from all the surrounding areas to buy and sell at the temporary booths, tables, and tents. Less frequent but far more elaborate were the grand fairs that occurred once or twice a year in well-populated areas. Fairs were huge, sprawling festivals that lasted days, weeks, or even months. Vendors sold anything that people might need—and many things they did not know they

wanted. Buyers and sellers haggled fiercely, while other visitors passed the time eating, drinking, admiring exotic wares, and enjoying the spectacles of musicians, jugglers, and freak shows. Lovers walked the lanes, children ran underfoot, and pickpockets slipped through the crowd. Meanwhile constables and clergymen tried their best to maintain law, order, and morality.

INTERNATIONAL TRADE. Trade with other countries began on a modest scale during Elizabeth's reign. Some ports on England's east coast, such as Hull and Newcastle, traded with northern Europe. Southwestern cities such as Bristol and Exeter traded with Ireland, France, Spain, and Portugal. London traded with all of these nations, controlling more of England's trade in exports and imports than all of the other English ports combined.

London's domination of international trade was due in part to its profitable ties with the Dutch city of Antwerp, the chief financial center of western Europe. An organization called the Fellowship of the Merchant Adventurers, which held a monopoly* on exports of English cloth, operated out of both London and Antwerp. The trade between these two cities helped distribute English cloth throughout Europe, while bringing such goods as dyes, salt, wine, and spices into England. In 1564, however, the Merchant Adventurers left Antwerp because of worsening political relations with the Netherlands. Because London had relied on the Antwerp trade, this development limited England's ability to expand its commercial empire.

For the next 40 years Spain and Portugal dominated international commerce, thanks to their control of trade routes to Asia and their access to gold and silver mines in the Americas. When the power of Spain and Portugal diminished in the 1580s, the English, Dutch, and French moved in, establishing their own trade networks and North American colonies.

Queen Elizabeth granted charters to several new trading companies in the late 1500s. The Muscovy Company did business in Russia while exploring for a safe northern sea route to the Far East. The East India Company sent its ships to the Orient by the long route, bringing back valuable goods such as spices. Meanwhile the Levant Company traded with Mediterranean nations from Italy and Greece to Egypt and Syria. International trade opened up new markets for exports and new sources of imported goods, and it eventually became the lifeblood of the British empire.

Antonio, the title character in *The Merchant of Venice,* is the best example in Shakespeare's plays of a merchant involved in international trade. When his friend Bassanio asks him to take out a loan on his behalf, Antonio is confident he will be able to pay it, because he presently has "an argosy bound to Tripolis, another to the Indies . . . a third at Mexico, a fourth for England" (I.iii.18–20). He expects the profits from these voyages to pay his debt before it comes due, but all four of his ships fail to return by the required date. Antonio's sudden reversal of fortune illustrates the high risks involved in trading ventures. (*See also* **Banking and**

* *monopoly* exclusive right to engage in a particular type of business

Commerce; Cities, Towns, and Villages; Coins and Currency; Country Life; Exploration; Guilds; Transportation and Travel; Work.)

See *Plays: The Tragedies.*

Shakespeare's works have been translated into at least 70 languages. Published translations of Shakespeare include the complete works, individual plays, and a variety of selections from the plays and poems. The playwright's words have spread around the globe and have become an important part of the cultures of many different nations. The translation process involves not only converting English into other languages but also converting words and ideas of the late 1500s to the languages of later times.

THE TRANSLATOR'S TASK. In general the word *translation* is defined as the replacement of a text in one language (the source language) with an equivalent text in another language (the target language). The difficulty lies in determining what can be considered "equivalent." With densely structured literary works such as Shakespeare's, this question is always complicated. Moreover, languages and literary styles evolve continuously, with the result that the gap between source and target is ever widening. For this reason, in most major languages there are numerous translations of Shakespeare to choose from, with none being considered so perfect that they may not be challenged, updated, and replaced by others.

All translations are approximations of the author's original meaning and style. The various approximations that have arisen over time represent not only a variety of possible responses to particular texts but also the diversity of readers and audiences that individual translators have been trying to reach. In some respects translations have an advantage over the original Elizabethan English, which is not completely understandable to many of those who speak modern English. Some attempts have been made to "translate" Shakespeare into contemporary English, but these efforts have usually failed because they distort the author's distinctive style.

EARLY TRANSLATIONS OF SHAKESPEARE. Shakespeare's plays first appeared in Europe around 1600, when English actors toured the continent performing them. These garbled versions of the texts did not survive long. It was not until 1729, when the French author Voltaire introduced his works into France, that Shakespeare became well known in continental Europe. Voltaire was somewhat critical of the playwright and of his more devoted French admirers, but he was nevertheless one of the first writers to offer a French translation of a Shakespearean speech. He presented two

* *classical* in the tradition of ancient Greece and Rome

French-language versions of Hamlet's famous "To be, or not to be" soliloquy, converted into alexandrines, the rhymed 12-syllable verse lines that were the standard poetic meter of French drama. One of his translations was very literal, the other a *belle infidèle* (unfaithful beauty). By contrasting the two, he demonstrated that a faithful word-for-word translation does not best capture the spirit of the original.

The first play to be translated in its entirety was *Julius Caesar*, translated into German in 1741. The translator, Caspar Wilhelm von Borck, converted even the prose passages into elegant alexandrines. Early translations of the collected plays, however, tended to be entirely in prose and were concerned with the story and subject matter rather than with the playwright's poetic language. In France, Pierre-Antoine de la Place included ten Shakespeare dramas in a collection of English plays (1746), but their language, for all its elegance, sounded more like a paraphrase of Shakespeare's text than a translation of his poetry. La Place's work was replaced in 1776 by Pierre Le Tourneur's more refined translation of the complete works. (Le Tourneur was one of the enthusiastic admirers of Shakespeare who provoked Voltaire's harsh criticism.)

German poet Christoph Martin Wieland translated 24 of Shakespeare's plays, mostly into prose, with only *A Midsummer Night's Dream* in verse. His goal was to preserve the texts as Shakespeare had written them, along with all the violations of classical* principles that Alexander Pope had criticized in his English-language edition. Wieland also added some mistakes of his own, not surprisingly, considering the fact that adequate dictionaries were yet to be compiled. Eventually, Wieland's versions were corrected and added to by Johann Joachim Eschenburg, whose German edition of the complete plays (1775–1777) nearly coincided with Le Tourneur's French one.

Although these translations were designed to be read rather than performed, they provided raw material for some spectacular adaptations in the theater. In Germany, for instance, Friedrich Ludwig Schröder reshaped the prose translations of Wieland and Eschenburg for his groundbreaking productions in Hamburg, beginning in 1776. At the same time, prose translations of Shakespeare had a great influence on young German dramatists of the Sturm und Drang (storm and stress) movement, among them the young Johann Wolfgang von Goethe. Reading Shakespeare's works in prose encouraged these writers to defy classical rules and to produce powerful plays of their own, taking Shakespeare's natural genius as their model.

* *Romanticism* school of thought, prominent in the 1800s, that emphasized the importance of emotion in art

ROMANTIC TRANSLATIONS. A new approach came during the period of Romanticism*. Critics such as August Wilhelm von Schlegel in Germany and Samuel Taylor COLERIDGE in England recognized and justified the independence of Shakespeare's art from that of ancient drama and poetry. They described Shakespeare's works as "organic," as poems and plays in which all details are interconnected and are thus less important individually than the experience being described.

Schlegel applied this view to his verse translations of 17 Shakespeare plays, including all the histories (1798–1810). Recognizing that artistic

Translations of Shakespeare

form is a distinctive carrier of meaning, he paid sensitive attention to both. Because blank verse* was being established at that time as the primary medium for serious German drama, Schlegel was able to adopt the same form that had originally been used by Shakespeare. He eventually abandoned his project, but Ludwig Tieck took it up and had it completed by 1833. Once it was finished, the "Schlegel-Tieck" translation achieved a privileged status that enthroned Shakespeare as the "third German classic," alongside Goethe and Friedrich von Schiller. Nearly all future German translations reproduced Shakespeare's blank-verse meter and highlighted his significant switches between verse and prose.

The Schlegel-Tieck Shakespeare did not go unchallenged, however. Even before it was completed there were several proposed alternatives. Between 1818 and 1829 Johann Heinrich Voss—known for his translations of the works of the ancient Greek poet Homer—and his sons countered the smooth beauty of Schlegel's translation with a rougher style. They considered their work closer to Shakespeare's complex language structure, suggestive shadings of meaning, and irregularities of verse. Other translators preferred to be guided by the style of German popular poetry or tried to do justice to Shakespeare's spirit rather than to his words.

With the help of Shakespeare's followers in France and Germany, as well as Le Tourneur's prose and Schlegel's "organic poetry," the playwright's work was introduced into the rest of Europe. In some countries he had already made an impression during the late 1700s. *Hamlet,* for instance, had been translated and adapted into Russian, Danish, Dutch, Portuguese, Polish, and Spanish. More or less complete editions of Shakespeare in translation began to multiply after 1800. In France prose translations remained common throughout the 1800s, although some authors continued to attempt renderings that turned Shakespeare's iambic pentameter* into alexandrine verse. Prose translations also predominated in Italy and Spain. Verse translations were generally favored in Germanic (German-related) languages such as Dutch and Danish; in Slavic (Russian-related) languages such as Russian, Polish, and Czech; and even in languages as distant from English as Hungarian and Finnish.

MODERN TRANSLATIONS. In the 1900s Shakespeare's fame spread beyond Europe. Spanish and Portuguese translations made their way into Latin America. In the former colonies of Great Britain, such as India, the original English versions were imported along with the British educational system. Even so, prose and verse translations appeared in the various native languages of India, particularly Hindi, Bengali, and Urdu. Despite some fundamental differences between the traditions of classic Indian (Sanskrit) drama and Western drama, translators were intent on forging connections between them, particularly in the tragicomedies, or romances.

Outside the Indo-European region translators struggled, with varying success, with the problems posed by literary traditions and language systems that were fundamentally different from English, among them some that were not even using a phonetic* alphabet. Since around 1900, translations have appeared in Chinese, Japanese, and Korean. Former European

PEOPLE

Plate 1

The reign of Queen Elizabeth I has been referred to as England's Golden Age. Elizabeth was both a strong ruler and a great supporter of the arts. Although she was the official patron of the Queen's Men acting company, she also favored Shakespeare's company, the Chamberlain's Men. Their frequent performances at court may have helped attract the attention of Elizabeth's successor, James I, who adopted the company as his own King's Men.

Plate 2

Ellen Terry was one of England's leading Shakespearean actresses in the late 1800s. After playing Ophelia in Henry Irving's 1878 production of *Hamlet*, the two were inseparable. She played the leads in all of his productions, several of which were in the United States. Toward the end of her career, which spanned more than 50 years, Terry delivered a series of lectures on Shakespeare. She is shown here as Lady Macbeth in an oil painting by American artist John Singer Sargent (1889).

Plate 3

Sir Herbert Beerbohm Tree, shown here in the role of Hamlet, was one of the notable actor-managers of the late 1800s. As manager of the Haymarket in London, he frequently altered the texts of Shakespeare's plays to expand his own roles at the expense of others. His productions were extraordinarily lavish, with elaborate and expensive sets.

Plate 4

There are no known portraits of Shakespeare painted during his lifetime. Since the playwright's death, many artists have attempted to capture his image. Only one portrait of Shakespeare, the engraving created for the title page of the 1623 First Folio, is considered an authentic likeness. This image of the dramatist as a young man was based on an oil painting by an unknown artist and is a typical example of the way most artists have presented him.

Plate 5

William Charles Macready was one of England's greatest Shakespearean actors in the mid-1800s. He was popular with audiences in the United States as well. His appearance as Macbeth in 1849, however, met with disaster. Supporters of a rival actor staged a protest outside the Astor Place Opera House, leading to riots in which 23 people were killed.

Plate 6
Considered by many to be the greatest actor of the 1900s, Sir Laurence Olivier played numerous Shakespearean roles, from Hamlet to Sir Toby Belch in *Twelfth Night*. He also directed Shakespearean productions on stage and screen, including three films he produced himself: *Henry V* (1944), *Hamlet* (1948), and *Richard III* (1954). Olivier, shown here as King Lear, commonly played the leading roles in his own productions.

Plate 7
Nathan Field, the son of a Puritan minister fiercely opposed to the theater, gained fame as an actor and a playwright. As a student at St. Paul's Grammar School, Field was a child actor in the Children of the Chapel. Although few boy actors from the children's companies went on to careers in the theater as adults, Field was a notable exception. When the children's company broke up, Field joined Lady Elizabeth's Men, and later the King's Men, sharing the lead roles with Richard Burbage.

Plate 8

British director Jonathan Miller is one of many modern directors who have favored an original approach to Shakespeare. He is particularly well known for his work on the British Broadcasting Company series that adapted all 37 of Shakespeare's plays for television in the 1980s. His productions presented the plays in a wide range of visual styles, from the traditional to the highly abstract. Miller has also directed Shakespeare on the stage, including a notable *Merchant of Venice* (1970) with Laurence Olivier as Shylock.

Plate 9

Born in the same year as Shakespeare, Christopher Marlowe was England's leading dramatist until his early death in 1593. His private life was as dramatic as his works. He served as a soldier in the Netherlands but was deported for minting counterfeit coins. Scholars believe that he later worked as a spy for Queen Elizabeth. His death in a tavern brawl may have been a fellow spy's attempt to silence him. This portrait by an unknown artist dates from 1585.

Plate 10
Born Henriette-Rosine Bernard, the French actress Sarah Bernhardt was one of the legendary performers of the late 1800s. Her immense stage presence and her exquisite, bell-like voice earned her the nickname "The Divine Sarah." Her Shakespearean roles included Cordelia in *King Lear* and Desdemona in *Othello*. In 1899 she appeared as Hamlet in both Paris and London. Artist Alphonse Mucha created this poster to promote the French production.

Plate 11
Twentieth-century actor Alec Guinness was known for his ability to immerse himself completely into his roles. One admiring critic observed that Guinness "had no face," because he altered his appearance and manner so perfectly to fit each character. He is shown here, at the Chichester Festival in 1984, in the role of Shylock, the Jewish moneylender in *The Merchant of Venice*.

Plate 12
Richard Burbage was the leading actor in Shakespeare's company, the King's Men. He was the son of James Burbage, who built the Theatre—the first English play-house—and also converted an old monastery into the Blackfriars theater. After his death, James Burbage left his two theaters to his sons, who tore down the Theater and reassembled it in a new location as the Globe. The Globe and the Blackfriars became the summer and winter homes of the King's Men.

Plate 13
Henry Irving was the actor-manager of the Lyceum Theater from 1878 to 1902. One of his specialties as an actor was playing villains, especially demons such as Mephistopheles in Goethe's *Faust.* Irving's business manager, Bram Stoker, may have had his boss's talent for playing villains in mind when he created the character of Dracula. He even asked Irving to play the part of Dracula in a stage version of his novel, but Irving refused be-cause he found Stoker's play "dreadful."

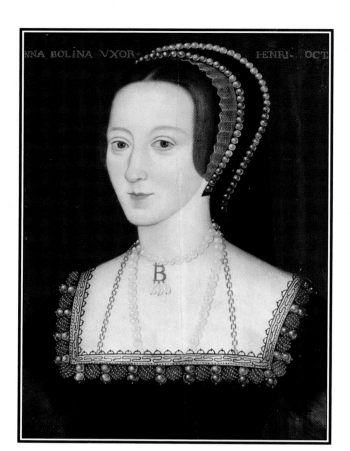

Plate 14

Queen Elizabeth's mother, Anne Boleyn, was the second wife of King Henry VIII. In order to marry her, the king dissolved his marriage to his first wife, Catherine of Aragon--angering many of his subjects. When Anne failed to give him the son he wanted, Henry had her executed on charges of adultery, incest, and treason. At her execution she made a short speech, saying, "by the law I am judged to die, and therefore I will say nothing against it."

Plate 15

Among the leading Shakespearean actors of the late 1700s were John Philip Kemble, his brother Charles, and their sister, Sarah Siddons. Siddons has been described as England's greatest tragic actress. Her performance as Lady Macbeth was widely acknowledged as a masterpiece, inspiring one viewer to insist that he "smelt blood" during the sleepwalking scene. This oil painting by artist Thomas Beach captures Siddons in her greatest role, opposite her brother John's Macbeth.

colonies in the Middle East and Africa debated about whether adopting the works of a European cultural hero would strengthen or weaken the new identities of emerging nations. Messages in Shakespeare's works, however, were found to be significant to these nations, and now at least some of the plays are available in Arabic, Hebrew, and Swahili. Wherever native theatrical traditions, such as Kabuki theater in Japan, were alive, performances of Shakespeare drew on and merged with them. The results of this blending eventually made their way back to Europe.

In 20th-century Europe new Shakespeare translations were mostly stage oriented. Translators stripped the Romantic elements from the poetry of the earlier German editions of Shakespeare and restored "indelicate" language that had been suppressed in previous translations. Rudolf Flatter, in the early 1950s, made an effort to include in his target text the nonverbal, theatrical elements of the original works: patterns of language, irregularities of meter, even punctuation. Hans Rothe, in his broadly modernized and restructured versions (1963–1964), successfully—if controversially—added to the plays' stage effects. Others, such as Maik Hamburger and Heiner Müller, emphasized the elements that related to body movements and gestures, influenced perhaps by similar elements in the dramatic works of Bertolt Brecht.

This focus on the plays' theatrical potential probably also accounts for the fact that prose translations in France have been largely replaced by verse translations, such as those of Yves Bonnefoy (1957), who continually revised his text for later stage productions. Verse translations have also become more popular in Italy and Spain. It is not unusual now for translations to be commissioned for specific occasions, inspired by the ideas of directors, and shaped and tested in the rehearsal process. For this reason the end product is frequently a joint creation of translator, director, and cast.

Translations of the complete works, intended for the bookshelf, seem less inventive than translations of single plays, even those that exist only for the duration of a single production. Some creators of performance translations, however, have produced impressive publications of their accumulated work. Furthermore, because English has become a more widely understood language than it used to be, Shakespeare often appears today in bilingual editions. The 16th-century text exists alongside a translated version, providing readers with the benefits of both.

PROBLEMS OF TRANSLATION. No translation can do full justice to the complex texture of the original. Something will always be lost. Preserving the strict meaning of the words means sacrificing the treatment of verse and rhyme and vice versa. Making the texts more readable often means making them less speakable, and presenting them in terms familiar to modern readers strips away the sense of them as products of another era and culture. A literal translation of a figure of speech, a pun, or an ambiguous* phrase can easily lose its point in the target language, and the only way to restore it is to substitute words with different meanings. Another problem is Shakespeare's repeated use of certain words in a text. The word *honest*, for example, appears about 100 times in *Othello*,

* *ambiguous* unclear; able to be interpreted in more than one way

in various forms. The magic of such repetitions may be reduced or lost when there is no equivalent word in the target language that covers a similar range of meanings ("reliable," "decent," "faithful," "chaste," and so on)

Every translation depends on an intensive analysis of the original. The quality of the translation depends not only on which elements of the source are stressed—literal accuracy, poetic language, rhyme and meter, and so on—but also on the order and consistency with which these elements are stressed. Every reading of a text reflects the interpreter's personal ideas and tastes, and every proposed version of that text is colored by the resources available within the target language and culture, as well as by the talent of the translator. The sheer number of translations available is itself a revealing indication of the lasting richness of Shakespeare's works. (*See also* **Language; Poetic Technique; Prose Technique.**)

TRANSPORTATION AND TRAVEL

Transportation during Shakespeare's lifetime was difficult, slow, and expensive. Most of England's roads were little more than dirt paths that turned to mud when it rained. Because England is an island nation, travel to foreign lands was even more difficult. Despite these hardships travel was common. Farmers and merchants regularly transported their goods to markets, and wealthy young men traveled to France, Italy, Germany, and other parts of the world to complete their education.

MODES OF TRANSPORTATION

The basic types of transportation available to Shakespeare and his contemporaries had not changed for hundreds of years. Overland travel was usually undertaken on foot or on horseback, and water traffic was conducted on vessels propelled either by the wind or by oarsmen. Some changes were occurring, however. Wagons were beginning to replace packhorses for transporting goods, and wealthy Elizabethans traveled in carriages.

ON FOOT. Walking was a popular way to make short journeys because it enabled travelers to take shortcuts that were unavailable to horseback riders. It was not only the poor who depended on walking to get them from place to place. University students typically walked several miles each day to their classes, and acting companies journeyed from town to town on foot, carrying their costumes and other baggage aboard a cart. Even merchants and peddlers walked from town to town, although they usually traveled together in large groups in order to protect themselves from bandits.

IN THE SADDLE. Horseback was the most common form of travel. All but the poorest rural inhabitants owned at least one horse. Although most city dwellers did not need a horse, they could rent one for a day or

more for a small sum. One of the least expensive arrangements for a long trip, however, was to buy a horse at the beginning of a journey and sell it at the end. Wealthy travelers typically provided a mount for every member of their party, including their servants.

Because English saddles were small and hard, horseback was often an uncomfortable mode of transportation. When women traveled on horseback they customarily rode sidesaddle. In some cases they rode on a pillion, a cushion placed behind the man's saddle. For extra comfort, harnesses were equipped with a little board that served as a footrest for traveling noblewomen. In exceptional cases a noblewoman or a sick person might be carried on a stretcherlike device, called a litter, supported between two horses.

THE EXPRESSWAY. The fastest way to travel on land was by the post relay system, which consisted of stations located every ten miles along major roads. At post stations riders could exchange tired horses for well-rested ones. This system was established in the early 1500s to carry official messages throughout the land. When not fully occupied with official business, however, postmasters often rented their horses to ordinary travelers.

HORSEPOWER. Many horses in England were accustomed to carrying more goods than people. Farmers, millers, and other rural workers relied on sturdy packhorses to transport their products to market. While not swift or elegant, a packhorse was hardy enough to withstand long journeys and surefooted enough to make its way across difficult terrain. A string of heavily loaded packhorses tied nose-to-tail was a common sight on rural roads. Men called carriers accompanied the packhorses and were responsible for ensuring their safe arrival.

WHEELED VEHICLES. There were two basic types of wheeled vehicles available to the Elizabethan traveler: the cart and the coach. Carts had two wheels and were pulled by horses or oxen. Farmers and merchants used carts to transport their goods to market towns. These lumbering, creaking vehicles also carried passengers, though only the poorest travelers relied on such slow and uncomfortable transportation.

Coaches provided a new form of conveyance available only to the wealthy. These four-wheeled vehicles often featured elaborately carved roofs and open sides that were covered by heavy curtains. Wealthy city dwellers traveled in smaller coaches, called caroches, designed for London's narrow streets. Despite their luxurious appearance, coaches provided an uncomfortable ride. Because these carriages lacked springs or other forms of suspension, passengers were jolted and shaken as they passed along England's poorly maintained roads.

ON THE WATER. Traveling by water was often faster and more comfortable than going overland. In London most people preferred to avoid the city's narrow, crowded, and filthy streets by using boats on the Thames. Along the riverbanks, boatmen waited to take customers upstream, downstream, or across the river.

Because there were no passenger ships, overseas travelers usually booked passage on cargo ships. The seas were dangerous even for commercial vessels, so most ships were fitted with cannons to defend against pirates. In addition to the dangers posed by violence and shipwrecks, sea travelers had to endure other hardships. Food and water often spoiled on extended voyages, and living in the cramped and dirty quarters of an Elizabethan ship for several months could result in illness.

TRAVEL EXPERIENCES

Despite the difficulties of travel, many Elizabethans journeyed from home for business purposes. A small number of people, mostly university graduates, were known to take extended trips as a way of completing their education.

ON THE ROAD IN ENGLAND. Travel within England was almost solely business related. Carts, wagons, packhorses, and pedestrians carried goods to market towns and to London. Given the generally wretched state of the roads, it is somewhat surprising that goods actually reached their destinations. According to law each community was responsible for maintaining its own roads. This was usually accomplished through forced labor, with members of the community required to spend a certain number of days each year on road repair. The law was never properly enforced, however, and most of England's roads remained little more than paths beaten through the forests and fields. Wheeled vehicles dug ruts in the roads that worsened their condition, especially after heavy rains. Domestic journeys were made even more hazardous by bandits who preyed on travelers. Certain stretches of road were notorious for the number of ruffians who waited for victims to appear. Highway robbery was punishable by death, but this did little to stop determined thieves.

In addition to wheeled vehicles, a wealthy Elizabethan might ride in a litter, such as the one shown here, slung between two steady and reliable horses. Usually reserved for delicate ladies and invalids, horse litters were believed to be more comfortable than other types of coaches.

One positive aspect of domestic travel was the quality of English inns. Most towns had at least one establishment where travelers could rent a room and receive a hot meal for a reasonable fee. Larger towns and cities typically boasted a dozen or more inns of varying quality that catered to different classes of travelers. Some were little more than alehouses that offered a hard bed for the night. Others provided fine food, comfortable rooms, and even private dining arrangements suitable for nobles. Guests at most inns dined in a common room with other travelers and shared rooms, although private accommodations were usually available for an additional sum.

OVERSEAS TRAVEL. Business travel was not exclusively local. English merchants traded in lands as distant as India and Russia, and English investment companies established colonies in Asia and America. The dangers of such travel were as great as the potential rewards. Few reliable maps existed at the time, even for places that were relatively well traveled. Many profit-seeking expeditions set out specifically to find riches or trade in new, unexplored lands whose existence might be no more than a rumor. Those who ventured to faraway lands literally wagered their lives on the success of such enterprises.

Travel for pleasure and for the sheer enjoyment of sightseeing was a new pastime during the Elizabethan age, but one that captured the imagination of many Englishmen. By Shakespeare's day it had become common for young noblemen attending a university to take the "grand tour" of important cities in Europe. Tutors usually accompanied their students on such tours to keep them safe and ensure that they focused on the educational aspects of the journey. A typical itinerary included France, Italy, Germany, and Holland, although some foreign travelers went as far afield as Asia Minor (modern Turkey) or even India. Italy was the most popular destination because it offered the opportunity to see the ruins of ancient Rome. Spain and Portugal were typically off-limits to Englishmen because of the unfriendly relations between those countries and England.

In Europe travel was typically on horseback. Since maps were rare, travelers usually hired local guides to show them the way. Public coaches were common in France, Germany, Holland, and Poland. Although they were no more comfortable than English coaches, they offered an alternative to the expense of horseback travel as well as an opportunity to meet and talk with the local people. Inns in Europe, particularly those in Poland and northern Germany, were typically less attractive than their counterparts in England. French inns by contrast were noted for their luxury and expense.

The merits of foreign travel were much debated in England. Some Englishmen, including Sir Francis Bacon, felt that travel improved a person and broadened his horizons. Others felt that those who journeyed abroad returned to England with dangerous new ideas and corrupted morals. Puritans especially feared that young travelers would fall prey to wicked influences abroad and return as Catholics, or even worse, atheists*. The Elizabethan curiosity about other people and places, however, was hard to discourage. Within a few generations of Shakespeare's death, explorers,

* *atheist* person who denies the existence of God

settlers, and merchants would carry English culture to virtually every part of the globe. (*See also* **Exploration; Navigation.**)

TRAVELING PLAYERS

See *Acting Companies, Elizabethan; Acting Profession.*

TROILUS AND CRESSIDA

* *ambiguity* quality of being unclear or able to be interpreted in more than one way

For nearly 400 years critics saw *Troilus and Cressida* as a difficult, confusing, and rather distasteful play. There is no definite record of any performance of it in England before 1907. Today, however, this complex work is widely appreciated by both critics and directors. Like the other "problem plays," *All's Well That Ends Well* and *Measure for Measure*, it combines the elements of comedy with a dark and pessimistic atmosphere that seems more suited to tragedy. This ambiguity* appeals more to modern viewers than to the audiences of past centuries.

SOURCES, PLOT, AND CHARACTERS. The plot of *Troilus and Cressida* is based on the Trojan War, a ten-year conflict between the armies of Greece and Troy, first narrated by the ancient Greek poet Homer in his *Iliad*. Shakespeare's sources probably included George Chapman's English translation of the *Iliad*, published in 1598, and the poem *Troylus and Criseyde*, by the medieval* English poet Geoffrey Chaucer.

* *medieval* referring to the Middle Ages, a period roughly between A.D. 500 and 1500

The play opens seven years into the war. The Trojan prince Troilus falls in love with Cressida, the daughter of Calchas, a Trojan priest who has joined the ranks of the enemy. Cressida's uncle Pandarus arranges for the lovers to meet in secret, but their time together is short. As part of a prisoner exchange, Cressida is forced to join her father in the Greek camp. There she takes Diomedes, a Greek warrior, as her lover. Meanwhile Troilus's brother Hector has challenged the Greeks to one-on-one combat with any warrior of their choice. Achilles, their best fighter, at first refuses to fight, but when Hector kills Achilles' best friend, Patroclus, Achilles takes Hector prisoner and stands by while his thugs slaughter him. Troilus, who has visited the Greek camp during a truce and learned of Cressida's unfaithfulness, ends the play in despair at the loss of his lover and his brother. Thus the play's two plots—love and war—both end in disaster.

Scholars have found this plot hard to classify. Various early printings of Shakespeare's works list *Troilus and Cressida* as a comedy, a tragedy, even a history. It can probably best be described as falling under the genre* of comical satire, a literary form coined by Ben JONSON in 1598. Modern audiences appreciate the play as a satire* with some bitingly funny passages directed at the idealized heroes of ancient Greece and Rome.

* *genre* literary form

* *satire* literary work ridiculing human wickedness and foolishness

Troilus and Cressida presents these worthies on stage, at first, with apparent respect. Then as the play progresses, however, they appear all too human—weak, foolish, or corrupt. The Greek warrior Ulysses delivers a

This engraving shows Troilus and Cressida reunited with the help of Pandarus, Cressida's uncle. Because of Pandarus's role as messenger between the two lovers, Elizabethan audiences would have associated his name with the word *pander,* or pimp.

* *illicit* forbidden; unlawful

great speech on the importance of order in the universe (I.iii.75–137), but this sentiment appears less noble when the speaker is revealed as adept at manipulating others with trickery. Agamemnon, the Greek commander, also sounds impressive, but his speeches contain nothing but stale, meaningless phrases. Achilles, the foremost Greek warrior, and his henchmen murder his Trojan rival, an unarmed prisoner. Paris, whose affair with the beautiful Greek queen Helen started the war, will not leave her bed to fight on her behalf: "I would fain [eagerly] have arm'd today, but my Nell would not have it so" (III.i.136–37). Helen herself is a beautiful but brainless chorus girl whose refrain is "This love will undo us all" (III.i.110–11). Perhaps the wisest character in the play—Troilus's sister, Cassandra, who is gifted with prophecy—is invariably dismissed by her relatives as a raving madwoman.

COMMENTARY. Shakespeare attacks not only the ancient heroes as individuals but also the values they represent. Hector, for instance, defends the war in the Trojan council as "a cause that hath no mean dependance / Upon our joint and several dignities" (II.ii.192–93). His willingness to prolong a seven-year war solely to avoid the embarrassment of a dishonorable retreat is a sign of the fatal, foolish pride that will cause his and his nation's downfall. *Troilus and Cressida* offers a moral lesson for present-day leaders involved in prolonged, unjustifiable wars.

The love between Troilus and Cressida is as doomed as the Trojans' battle against Greece. In many ways their story is similar to that of Romeo and Juliet, with Pandarus assuming the roles of go-between and priest that might have been played by Juliet's nurse and Friar Lawrence, respectively. The difference between the two stories lies in the motivations of the characters. Juliet yields her love to Romeo only when he proves his honorable intentions by making her his wife. The relationship Pandarus arranges between Troilus and Cressida is quite different—an illicit* affair, never named as such but plainly assumed to be so by all. So Troilus's shock at Cressida's "betrayal"—"This is, and is not, Cressid!" (V.ii.146)— may prompt members of the audience to wonder what commitment he made to her that requires her to remain faithful to him. As the only woman in an army camp, Cressida needs a protector. Taking one may be construed as a necessary act of self-preservation, notwithstanding the guilt she feels as she surrenders the love token Troilus has given her to Diomedes.

In the past most critics agreed with Ulysses' judgment of Cressida's "wanton spirits" that offer "sluttish spoils of opportunity" (IV.v.62). In context, however, Ulysses' remark seems like a petty show of resentment, since Cressida has put off his request for a kiss with the demand that he "beg" for it. Four Greek soldiers have already kissed her without asking permission. Her rejection of Ulysses is the first opportunity she has had to assert her independence.

The play appears at a glance to center around two stereotypes: the faithful Troilus and the faithless Cressida. A closer examination, however, reveals traits in both characters that contradict the stereotypes. When Troilus encounters Aeneas in Pandarus's house, he urges Aeneas to say

143

soliloquy monologue in which a character reveals his or her private thoughts

"We met by chance, you did not find me here" (IV.ii.71). He sees his relationship with Cressida as a social embarrassment. Cressida, by contrast, bitterly regrets her parting from Troilus. Her final soliloquy*—"Ah, poor our sex!" (V.ii.109)—sums up the conflict at the heart of her character. Most actresses portray Cressida as a sympathetic character, and modern critics are generally inclined to take her part.

PERFORMANCE HISTORY. *Troilus and Cressida* appeared very seldom on the stage until the 20th century. Some scholars believe it was performed during Shakespeare's lifetime at the Inns of Court, but no record of such a performance exists. It was probably staged in Dublin in the mid-1600s, and John Dryden wrote an adaptation of the script in 1679. After that the next known production occurred in Germany in 1898.

Troilus and Cressida began to gain in popularity during the period between the two World Wars, and since 1945 it has been staged often. A notable television production, directed by Jonathan Miller, appeared on BBC-TV in 1982. Many directors focus on the minor character Thersites, a "deformed and scurrilous Grecian" who comments sarcastically on the actions of the main characters. A 1968 production by the Royal Shakespeare Company, under the direction of John Barton, printed one of Thersites' lines on the program: "Lechery, lechery, still wars and lechery" (V.ii.194–95). It is tempting to see this statement as a neat summary of the spirit of the play, but such a view is not necessarily justified. Shakespeare examines love and war without veiling them in idealistic illusions, but at the same time he does not dismiss lightly the emotional anguish of the title characters. As critic Benedict Nightingale wrote in reference to the Barton production, *Troilus and Cressida* is "only too lucid"; that is to say, its significance to modern-day society is all too clear.

TWELFTH NIGHT

Written around 1600, *Twelfth Night* is one of Shakespeare's so-called middle comedies. Like other comedies from the middle of the playwright's career, it focuses on a clever and appealing heroine who challenges the traditional views of women in Elizabethan England. The humor in the play centers on a combination of absurd situations and witty wordplay. At the same time, the drama has a serious side that hints at the pessimism of Shakespeare's late comedies (sometimes known as the problem plays).

SOURCES AND PLOT. The plot of *Twelfth Night* is taken from the story "Of Apolonius and Silla," published in 1581 by Barnabe Riche. Riche's narrative, in turn, was based on the anonymous Italian play *Gli'Ingannati,* published in 1537. The story has many of the elements of traditional Italian comedy: mistaken identity, a woman dressed as a man, and a tangled knot of love relationships among the main characters.

The central character of the play is Viola, who finds herself stranded in the country of Illyria after a shipwreck in which, she believes, her twin

See color plate 4, vol. 2.

* *steward* person who manages another person's household or estate

FAITHFUL ANTONIO

Shakespeare adds to the plot confusion in *Twelfth Night* with the character of Antonio, the sea captain who rescues Sebastian from drowning. He insists on accompanying Sebastian into Illyria, even though he is wanted by the authorities there, and on lending his new friend money. He later sees Sir Andrew fighting with Viola, tries to protect her, and is arrested. When he asks her to pay his ransom and she claims not to know him, he bitterly curses "Sebastian's" ingratitude. Critics have pointed to the character of Antonio as an example of absolute loyalty—much like the title character in *The Merchant of Venice*, who has the same first name.

brother, Sebastian, has been drowned. To protect herself from danger she disguises herself as a boy, assuming the name Cesario. She enters into the service of Duke Orsino and soon falls in love with him. Orsino, however, is in love with a noblewoman named Olivia, who has repeatedly rejected him, claiming that she cannot marry because she is still in mourning for her own brother. When the duke decides to make his new servant the bearer of his messages of love, Olivia immediately falls in love with Cesario.

Meanwhile Olivia's uncle, Sir Toby Belch, has been disturbing the household by drinking and carousing all night with his friends, Fabian and Sir Andrew Aguecheek. Olivia's steward*, MALVOLIO, criticizes their rowdy behavior and threatens to throw them out. Annoyed by his superior attitude, they agree to an elaborate prank that has been conceived by Maria, Olivia's serving woman. Maria forges a letter that convinces Malvolio that Olivia is in love with him. The steward then behaves so strangely that he is locked up as a madman.

Sir Andrew, who wishes to marry Olivia, is offended by her favors to Cesario. Sir Toby persuades him to challenge the young messenger to a duel, but he accidentally attacks not Viola but her twin brother, Sebastian—who has surfaced in Illyria after being rescued from the shipwreck. Olivia breaks up the fight and then, thinking Sebastian is Cesario, asks him to marry her. Confused by her offer but enchanted by her beauty, Sebastian accepts. When Viola later appears at Olivia's house, still in her male disguise, Olivia bewilders both her and Orsino by calling her "husband." The confusion is cleared up when Sebastian appears. Viola reveals her true identity, and the duke promises to marry her. Fabian explains the trick that was played on Malvolio, and Olivia releases him from his cell. He exits the stage with a vow to "be revenged on the whole pack of you" (V.i.378). Rather than end the play on this sour note, however, Shakespeare concludes the drama with a song performed by Feste, Olivia's jester.

COMMENTARY. The play's title refers to January 5, the eve of the Feast of Epiphany (January 6), which concludes 12 days of Christmas festivities. Twelfth Night is both a feast, then, and an end to feasting. The dual nature of its title influences the mood of the entire play, beginning with Orsino's opening speech: "If music be the food of love, play on, / Give me excess of it; that surfeiting, / The appetite may sicken, and so die" (I.i.1–3). This passage expresses the idea that "surfeit," or overindulgence, leads to dissatisfaction. After a prolonged season of feasting, a return to the routines of daily life may be a welcome change.

A pivotal scene occurs in Act II. Returning home drunk after a night of holiday merrymaking, Sir Toby and Sir Andrew are confronted by the stern Malvolio, who wants to put a stop to their noisy celebration. This scene reveals the conflict between excessive merriment, represented by Sir Toby, and harsh discipline, represented by Malvolio. Sir Toby may be seen as the die-hard party-goer who wants the festivities to continue while everyone else is ready to go to bed: "Come, come, I'll go burn [heat] some sack [sherry], 'tis too late to go to bed now" (II.iii.190–92). He presides

Twelfth Night

The hard-drinking, fun-loving Sir Toby Belch is one of the most memorable characters in *Twelfth Night*. In this scene Olivia puts a halt to the duel between Sir Toby and Sebastian.

* **blank verse** unrhymed verse, usually in iambic pentameter—lines of poetry consisting of ten syllables, or five metrical feet, with emphasis placed on every other syllable

* **puritanical** referring to the strict Protestant faction and characterized by rigid morality

over the festive spirit of *Twelfth Night* like the Lord of Misrule, a figure who traditionally served as master of ceremonies at Christmas celebrations in the English countryside.

Like most of the play's characters, however, Sir Toby has a tragic side as well. His last name, Belch, suggests a comic stereotype such as those created by Ben JONSON, but as Sir Toby he is also a knight and a gentleman. Sir Toby is an example of a typical unemployed knight. During the Middle Ages knights were employed to defend castles, but by Shakespeare's day they had become largely unnecessary, and their rowdy behavior was seen as an annoyance. Sir Toby has no possessions of value except his title, and he realizes that his position as a freeloader in his niece's house is shaky. At one point he remarks that he is "now so far in offense with my niece that I cannot pursue with any safety this sport" (IV.ii.69–71). That is, he dares not carry his joke on Malvolio any further. His fondness for drink is also extreme: when he appears before Olivia in Act I, Scene v, staggering, belching, and slurring his speech, she remarks that he is only "half drunk." There may be a note of self-disgust in Sir Toby's remark "I hate a drunken rogue" (V.i.201).

The half-serious nature of this play is most clearly revealed in the prank against Malvolio. In the first half of the play, he appears as a self-important bureaucrat, "a kind of puritan" (II.iii.140) who wishes to squelch all enjoyment (as suggested by his name, which means "ill will" in Latin). The audience is inclined to sympathize with Sir Toby's remark, "Dost thou think because thou art virtuous there shall be no more cakes and ale?" (II.iii.114–16). But the punishment Toby and Maria carry out against Malvolio—locking him in a dark cell and taunting him about his "madness"—is so severe that the audience may begin to feel uncomfortable. As Sir Toby grows less appealing, Malvolio appears more so, and his lines in prison display a noble side the audience has not previously seen. His final speech—which is delivered in blank verse*, associated with noble and educated characters—shows him to be a victim who has suffered "notorious wrong." The copy of the FIRST FOLIO in the Windsor Castle Library contains a marginal note, possibly written by King Charles I, labeling the play "Malvolio: a Tragedy."

Even the minor characters in this play show a dual nature. Maria is often played as young and appealing, but she can also be viewed as a calculating older woman who sees Sir Toby as her last chance to improve her station. According to this interpretation the jest she plans with Sir Toby and Sir Andrew is a way of winning favor with two people of higher rank. Her reward is a marriage that raises her social standing: at the end of the play, Maria becomes Lady Belch.

Feste, as his name suggests, is an entertainer who represents the "festivity" of the play, but he also shows a calculating and grasping nature. He sings only after receiving a tip and never converses with anyone without asking for money. Like Sir Toby, Feste suggests a fairly recent change in England's social structure: servants, idealized in the character of Adam in *As You Like It*, were being replaced by a service industry. Feste is not a loyal follower but an independent spirit who pursues his personal goals first. His "festive" nature is naturally at odds with Malvolio's "puritanical*"

one, and when given a chance, he does not hesitate to taunt Malvolio mercilessly. This humorous but hardheaded character closes the play with a song that centers on the refrain "For the rain it raineth every day" (V.i.192). This phrase provides a reminder that when the celebration of Twelfth Night is over, the party-goers must return to the "every day" world in which rain continues to fall.

PERFORMANCE HISTORY. *Twelfth Night* has been popular on stage for most of its history. It may have been written as an entertainment for a specific Twelfth Night celebration, perhaps in 1601, when an Italian duke named Orsino visited the court of Queen Elizabeth. There is no clear evidence of such a performance, but it is clear that the play was written before 1602. In February of that year a law student saw the play performed at Middle Temple Hall at one of the Inns of Court and reviewed it favorably in his diary. Seldom performed during the early 1700s, *Twelfth Night* regained favor around 1740, and since then it has remained one of the most popular Shakespearean comedies, more frequently staged today than any other.

There has, however, been a major shift in the play's production style since the late 1960s. Directors used to treat *Twelfth Night* primarily as a farce*. Sir Toby was played as an amusing buffoon, with actors taking full advantage of his last name. Malvolio was simply an object of ridicule, and his downfall was greeted with catcalls. The PROMPT BOOK for Ada Neilson's 1878 production has a revealing stage direction in Act II, Scene iii: "All laugh and keep it up as long as possible." This remark, which anticipates the present-day use of "canned laughter," shows how *Twelfth Night* was viewed as a machine for generating laughs. In general, directors tended to ignore the darker, more serious side of the play.

This attitude began to change during the 1960s. Jan Kott, in his influential *Shakespeare Our Contemporary* (1966), placed *Twelfth Night* in a chapter titled "Shakespeare's Bitter Arcadia*." The first production to take full advantage of this new view was directed by John Barton for the ROYAL SHAKESPEARE COMPANY (RSC) in 1969. He treated the characters with sympathy and understanding rather than as caricatures. Barton was influenced by the works of Russian playwright Anton Chekhov, which inspire sympathy for even the least likable characters. *Twelfth Night* contains a very Chekhovian moment when the normally ridiculous Sir Andrew observes, "I was ador'd once too" (II.iii.181).

Since Barton's production most directors have attempted to analyze the main characters and present them with a degree of psychological depth. In 1974 the RSC program quoted psychiatrist and philosopher R. D. Laing on the problems of role-playing. Some modern productions stress the ambiguities of the romantic relationships in this play, such as whether Olivia can be said to love Cesario when she willingly accepts the identical Sebastian as a substitute. Directors and scholars alike have also speculated about Orsino's affection for Viola, whom he has never seen as a woman, and about the overall gender confusion surrounding the role of Viola. It is a mistake, however, to focus exclusively on the "dark" side of *Twelfth Night*. The central point of the drama lies in its balance of laughter

* *farce* light dramatic composition that features broad satiric comedy, improbable situations, stereotyped characters, and exaggerated physical action

* *Arcadia* region of ancient Greece that is often used as a setting for pastoral poetry in praise of the virtues of a simple life

147

and seriousness. The best productions aim for an atmosphere of romance coupled with realism—a comedy, but with a touch of sadness.

There have been several film and television versions of *Twelfth Night.* One of the best was directed by Trevor Nunn (1997) and offers a polished and sophisticated reading in tune with the two-sided nature of the play. The setting is autumn, with the gardeners of the great house raking leaves. The season provides a metaphor for the mood of the play. The holiday atmosphere, represented by summertime, is drawing to a close, and the cold—but not always unpleasant—reality of winter is on its way. (*See also* **Festivals and Holidays; Fools, Clowns, and Jesters; Gender and Sexuality; Humor in Shakespeare's Plays; Love; Plays: The Comedies.**)

TWO GENTLEMEN OF VERONA, THE

* *convention* established practice

* *protagonist* central character in a dramatic or literary work

* *smitten* romantically attracted

Shakespeare's *The Two Gentlemen of Verona* is one of his earliest comedies, written sometime between 1590 and 1595. It depicts two young Italian aristocrats, Valentine and Proteus, whose friendship becomes strained when they fall in love with the same woman. Frequently criticized as crude and simplistic, the play tends to mock the conventions* of Elizabethan romantic comedy. In writing it Shakespeare drew from a wide range of comedic styles and sources and began developing his own style of comedy. In the process, he produced characters who are memorable in spite of their obvious flaws.

PLOT SUMMARY. As the action begins the two protagonists* are discussing Valentine's departure from Verona for the court of the duke of Milan. Valentine teases Proteus for staying behind to pursue the love of Julia. Valentine's witty servant, Speed, delivers a love letter from Proteus to Julia, but she scornfully tears it up, pretending not to care for its sender. Almost immediately, however, she laments over the torn pieces and admits that she loves Proteus. She sends him a love letter in return, but after he receives it the young man's delight turns to dismay when his father orders him to leave Verona and join Valentine at court.

Meanwhile in Milan, Valentine has fallen in love with the duke's daughter, Silvia. She has asked him to write a poem for her to give to the object of her affections, but when he presents his verses, she promptly returns them to him. Speed tries to explain to Valentine that Silvia loves him, but Valentine remains confused. Back in Verona, Proteus and Julia exchange rings and part tearfully. Proteus's clownish servant, Launce, is sad to leave his family and complains that his dog, Crab, shows no emotion at all over the parting. When Proteus arrives in Milan he meets Valentine and Silvia. Valentine confides that he plans to run away with Silvia before her father can marry her to another suitor, Thurio. Proteus, who has become smitten* with Silvia, decides to reveal the lovers' flight to the duke. Meanwhile Julia misses Proteus and decides to disguise herself as a male servant and travel to Milan to seek him.

After learning of Valentine's intention to elope with Silvia, the duke catches the young lover as he is attempting to carry out his plan. He banishes

Valentine from Milan but does not expose Proteus's betrayal. Proteus helps his friend leave, but as Valentine and Speed flee they are captured by bandits in a forest. When the robbers learn that Valentine is a gentleman, they elect him as their leader.

Thurio grows annoyed as Silvia continues to pine for Valentine. Proteus slyly volunteers to talk with Silvia, promising to praise Thurio and criticize Valentine. Instead, however, he confesses his love for her. Silvia rejects him angrily and reminds him of the woman he has left behind. Proteus claims that she has died, not knowing that Julia has arrived in Milan and is nearby, listening sorrowfully to their conversation. Silvia resolves to run away and find Valentine, taking the chaste* knight Sir Eglamour with her as a protector. Launce informs Proteus that Silvia has refused the dog he sent her as a present, but he then confesses that the fine breed Proteus gave him was stolen and that he replaced it with Crab, who greeted Silvia by urinating on her gown. Proteus fires Launce in disgust and hires a new servant, who turns out to be Julia in disguise. He asks her to deliver a ring to Silvia, and she sadly observes in an aside that it is the ring she had given him in Verona.

Silvia and Eglamour flee Milan. The duke pursues them, along with Thurio, Proteus, and Julia. In the forest the bandits capture Silvia, but Proteus and Julia free her. When Silvia continues to refuse Proteus's love, he attempts to rape her. Valentine emerges from his hiding place to stop Proteus's brutality. Proteus feels grief and remorse for his behavior. With a rush of emotion Valentine forgives him, even offering to surrender Silvia to him. Julia faints, and when she revives she abandons her disguise. Proteus realizes that he truly loves Julia. Valentine then threatens to fight Thurio for Silvia's hand, and Thurio abandons his claim to her. Everyone returns to Milan to celebrate the reunion of the two couples.

SOURCES. The two love stories in *The Two Gentlemen of Verona* were based on two distinct sources. Proteus's betrayal of Julia came from an episode in the Spanish romance* *Diana Enamorada,* by Jorge de Montemayor. Montemayor's original version was first published in 1542, but Shakespeare probably drew more from an English translation by Bartholomew Yong that appeared in manuscript form around 1582. A play called *The History of Felix and Philomela,* based on the same story, was performed for the royal court in 1585. This play, written by an unknown author, may have been Shakespeare's immediate source.

The other major plotline in Shakespeare's play, concerning a friend who falls in love with his best friend's fiancée, comes from the immensely popular *Decameron,* a collection of tales by the Italian poet Giovanni Boccaccio. Many English versions of this story existed, including a chapter in Sir Thomas Elyot's *The Governour,* published in 1531. Several lines in Shakespeare's play resemble those of Elyot, including Valentine's offer to give his beloved to Proteus.

COMMENTARY. In the past, scholars often argued that Shakespeare could not have written a work as crude and confusing as *The Two Gentlemen of Verona.* Most modern critics, however, believe that the play is authentic,

* *chaste* sexually pure

* *romance* story of love and adventure, the forerunner of the modern novel

TWO MINDS ON VERONA

Critics have long struggled with divided opinions about *The Two Gentlemen of Verona.* In 1765 Samuel Johnson admitted that the play was "not very successful," but he praised its many "lines or passages which, singly considered, are eminently beautiful." William Hazlitt, writing in 1817, was also torn. He called the play "little more than the first outlines of a comedy loosely sketched in," but he enjoyed its "passages of high poetical spirit, and of inimitable [unique] quaintness of humour, which are undoubtedly Shakespeare's."

* **medieval** referring to the Middle Ages, a period roughly between A.D. 500 and 1500

* **commedia dell'arte** improvisational comedy that began in Italy during the Middle Ages and featured stock characters such as a boastful captain, pairs of lovers, and bumbling servants

* **genre** literary form

In *The Two Gentlemen of Verona,* Shakespeare drew on the medieval tradition of "friendship literature"— that of companionship between men, sometimes interrupted by romance, but usually restored. This photograph, from a 1981 Royal Shakespeare Company production of the play, shows the two friends, Proteus (Peter Land) and Valentine (Peter Chelsom).

pointing especially to the skill with which the author combined existing literary traditions.

The plot borrows from a variety of medieval* traditions. Its overall structure reflects the Italian commedia dell'arte*, which plays on the comical interactions of familiar character types. The two servants— Launce, the bumbling clown, and Speed, the quick-witted jester—are typical stock characters of this genre*, as is the disappointed lover who disguises herself as a young servant. The beautiful lady pursued by three suitors—the chosen lover, the jealous rival, and the cowardly nobleman—was also a common plot element in the commedia. Many of these figures were also typical of romance narratives, in which the hero travels widely, faces danger, and is eventually reunited with his loved ones. The plot also reflects the influence of friendship literature, which revolved around the devotion between two male companions. Characters in these medieval genres are larger than life in their virtues, vices, and passions.

The play also shows the influence of Shakespeare's contemporaries, particularly John Lyly, a popular Elizabethan playwright who had a strong impact on Shakespeare's early works. For example, the play's symmetrical structure—featuring two male friends, two virtuous ladies, and two servants—is typical of Lyly's work. So is the play's witty language, with its frequent use of puns and other wordplay. Shakespeare was if anything more skillful in his use of language than Lyly, and the comic monologues of Launce accurately mimic the speech of the English lower classes.

Even as Shakespeare drew on traditional styles of comedy, he also exaggerated and mocked them. Valentine is an especially ridiculous hero. He praises his beloved in conventional, exaggerated terms, but in reality he is immature and ignorant. He foolishly boasts to Proteus of his plan to elope with Silvia, but when the duke catches him he is unable to invent a way out of the situation. The plot involving the bandits in the forest, who choose him as their honorable leader, parodies a convention of the romance tradition. Valentine's most absurd moment comes when he offers to give Silvia to Proteus, who has just tried to rape her. Silvia makes no protest, for she herself is little more than a plot device. The most intelligent character in the play is Speed, and the most admirable is probably Julia, who is both courageous and faithful—although her decision to accept Proteus's love after he has betrayed her seems difficult to accept. Julia is a crudely drawn example of the charming heroines who would appear in Shakespeare's later plays, women who often assume male disguises and take control of the action.

PERFORMANCE HISTORY. The play's unlikely plot, weak characters, and bizarre sense of morality have limited its appeal to actors and directors. *The Two Gentlemen of Verona* was probably acted during Shakespeare's lifetime, but no record exists of particular performances. The first known production was staged by actor-manager David Garrick in 1762. Like most of the few other directors who produced the play during the 1700s and 1800s, Garrick used an adapted version of the text. The script alterations typically added material for Launce and Speed, the strongest and most popular characters, but nearly all of the adaptions were financial and artistic failures. The one exception was an operatic version produced by Frederick Reynolds in 1821, with music by Henry Bishop.

The number of performances increased in the 1900s, and a few productions—such as Joseph Papp's musical version in 1971 and a New York production that included a team of jugglers—were moderately successful. The play was made into a German film in 1963, and the British Broadcasting Corporation produced it for television in 1983. (*See also* **Plays: The Comedies; Plays: The Romances; Shakespeare's Sources.**)

TWO NOBLE KINSMEN, THE

Written around 1613, *The Two Noble Kinsmen* is one of Shakespeare's last dramatic works. The play was created in collaboration with John Fletcher, who became the leading playwright of the KING'S MEN after William Shakespeare retired.

The play opens with three queens interrupting the marriage of Theseus, the duke of Athens. They ask him to attack King Creon of Thebes, who has slain their husbands in battle and refused to bury the corpses. Theseus agrees to help and during the ensuing battle captures Arcite and Palamon, two noble kinsmen of Thebes. While looking out their prison window, both men see and fall in love with Emilia, a noblewoman, and argue over who will claim her. Arcite is later released from jail and banished from Theseus's kingdom. Instead of leaving, however, he disguises himself and enters a wrestling and running competition to gain Emilia's attention. Meanwhile the jailer's daughter falls in love with Palamon and helps him escape to the nearby woods. There he meets Arcite, and the two agree to duel for Emilia's love. Theseus interrupts the duel and declares that the winner will marry Emilia and the loser will be put to death. After losing the duel Palamon is about to be executed when news arrives that Arcite has been crushed under a horse. The play ends with the dying Arcite giving Emilia to Palamon as a gesture of his steadfast friendship.

Scholars disagree about how much of the play Shakespeare wrote, but most concur that he is responsible for the first and last acts as well as part of the third. Critics have faulted the play (especially those parts written by Fletcher) for its mediocre verse and the weak motivations of its characters. Because of its uneven quality, the play is rarely produced. (*See also* **Plays: The Romances; Playwrights and Poets.**)

UR-HAMLET

Most scholars believe that Shakespeare's *Hamlet* (written around 1600) was based on an earlier, now lost, play referred to as the *Ur-Hamlet*, or "original Hamlet." Several references indicate that a tragedy containing elements very similar to those in Shakespeare's *Hamlet* was performed in England before 1600. In 1589, for example, the critic Thomas Nash complained about the poor quality of plays based on the Roman dramatist Seneca, calling them "whole Hamlets, I should say

handfuls of tragical speeches." In this statement Nashe appears to have been referring to the playwright Thomas Kyd, whose *Spanish Tragedy* was one of the earliest English revenge tragedies. Because of this remark some scholars believe that Kyd was also the author of the *Ur-Hamlet*. Another early mention of a play whose hero was named Hamlet dates from 1594. Apparently Shakespeare's acting company, the Chamberlain's Men, staged the play in that year in collaboration with a company called the Admiral's Men.

Scholars have attempted to reconstruct the *Ur-Hamlet* based on what they knew about its sources and the works that borrowed from it. A tale by the French poet François de Belleforest, for instance, is widely believed to be the source for the *Ur-Hamlet*. Belleforest's story includes Hamlet's delayed revenge on the uncle who has killed his father and married his mother, his murder of a spy, and his exile to England. Scholars have also examined *Der Bestrafte Bruder-Mord,* a German version of *Hamlet,* for clues to the content of the *Ur-Hamlet*. The German play includes details that are not found in Shakespeare's *Hamlet* but are present in Belleforest's story. Many scholars have concluded that these elements were taken from the *Ur-Hamlet*. (*See also* **Shakespeare's Sources.**)

VAGABONDS, BEGGARS, AND ROGUES

The number of poor and rootless people in England grew dramatically during the 1500s. Many factors contributed to this increase. During the 1530s King Henry VIII closed all the Catholic monasteries that had once provided relief for the poor. Then in the mid-1500s, changes in English AGRICULTURE drove many small farmers off the lands their families had worked for generations. Those who could not support themselves became vagabonds—homeless, unemployed people who wandered from place to place. Some of these poor nomads died of starvation, disease, or exposure. Others scraped out a meager living by either begging or stealing.

Vagabonds in Shakespeare's day were a mixed lot: unemployed laborers, farmers who had lost their land, soldiers returning from overseas campaigns, and others who simply had no taste for hard work. Some had chosen a wandering lifestyle; others had been forced into it. Many vagabonds earned money as traveling entertainers, singing, juggling, putting on plays, or even running small circuses with performing animals. These bands of roving entertainers, who often supplemented their income by theft, helped give legitimate actors a bad reputation in Elizabethan England.

People who were unable to hold a job because of some physical disability were given licenses to beg for a living. Although they were considered a drain on society, they were in no danger of being jailed for their actions. Less fortunate were the insane, sometimes known as "Bedlam beggars" (after Bethlehem Hospital, the insane asylum in London). Shakespeare drew a pitiful picture of such a beggar in *King Lear*. Edgar, disguised as the madman Poor Tom, laments that he is "whipt from tithing to tithing, and punish'd and imprison'd" (III.iv.134–35). A "tithing" was a territorial division, and it was common for those who were caught begging to be whipped and run off to the next town, where they would become someone else's problem.

Another class of vagabond was the rogue, who made a living by preying on others. Most rogues limited themselves to minor crimes, such as picking pockets, stealing purses, cheating at cards or dice, or engaging in scams such as attempting to pass for a licensed beggar by pretending to be injured or insane. Some of these petty criminals were unfortunate people who had turned to crime as a last resort. More dangerous were the highwaymen who prowled the roads robbing travelers and occasionally murdering them as well. English law dealt harshly with all criminals who used force or violence, and even pickpockets were routinely sentenced to hang for their crimes. Swindlers who merely used trickery against their victims usually escaped with much lighter sentences.

The number of vagabonds in England declined after 1597, when the government passed a comprehensive Poor Law that taxed the rich to help the poor. This law was so effective that it remained unaltered until the late 1900s. (*See also* **Poverty and Wealth.**)

VENUS AND ADONIS

* *plague* highly contagious and often fatal disease; also called the Black Death

The narrative poem *Venus and Adonis* was probably Shakespeare's first printed work, although it was probably not his first composition. Published in 1593, it was most likely written between the summer of 1592 and the spring of 1593, when London's theaters were closed due to an outbreak of plague*. The poem is based on a story from the *Metamorphoses,* a collection of tales by the ancient Roman poet OVID that was very popular with Elizabethan readers.

Venus and Adonis is notable for its reversal of the traditional roles of male and female lovers. In Shakespeare's poem, Venus, the goddess of love, is the pursuer, who aggressively tries to seduce an unwilling Adonis by stressing the physical delights of lovemaking. Adonis, the handsome young hunter, has a much more spiritual view of love and considers Venus's obsession with its physical side to be nothing more than lust. Throughout the poem the goddess does all she can to win Adonis, including seizing him from the back of his horse and showering him with unwanted kisses. Adonis escapes her clutches in order to follow his true love, hunting, but he dies when the boar he is pursuing mortally wounds him.

Venus and Adonis is considered an immature work, lacking the character development and keen insight into human nature that mark Shakespeare's later poems and plays. Nevertheless, it displays the young poet's gift for language, and its examination of conflicting views of love hints at a major theme in some of his mature creations. The poem was extremely popular in its day, going through nine printings during Shakespeare's lifetime—although some critics spoke disapprovingly of its frank sexual references. (*See also* **Playwrights and Poets; Poetry of Shakespeare; Shakespeare's Sources.**)

Vice, The

VICE, THE

* *morality play* religious dramatic work that teaches a moral lesson through the use of symbolic characters
* *protagonist* central character in a dramatic or literary work

In the morality plays* of the Middle Ages, the Vice is a stock character who tempts characters to commit acts that will lead to their downfall. His chief goal is to lead the protagonist* into pursuing sensual pleasures, such as sex and drunkenness. Vice is traditionally presented as an immoral but amusing jester who entertains the audience through bawdy jokes, witty puns, and slapstick humor. He mocks the misfortunes of other characters and delights in his own wickedness. In his efforts to corrupt his targets, he deceives them with laughter, tears, and appeals to friendship, tricks that most of the characters in the play see through but Vice's victims usually fail to recognize.

Several Shakespearean characters resemble the Vice. For example, many of the dramatist's FOOLS boldly mock the actions and motivations of others in the manner characteristic of the Vice. The most memorable Vice figure in Shakespeare's plays is Sir John FALSTAFF, who first appears as a companion of Prince Hal in *Henry IV, Part 1*. Falstaff is a braggart, thief, and drunkard who encourages Hal to indulge in a life of drinking and carousing. But in a reversal of the typical relationship between Vice and the hero, Hal continually outwits Falstaff and resists the temptation to follow him into irresponsible behavior. Several of Shakespeare's villains, most notably Richard III and IAGO, resemble the Vice in the pleasure they seem to take in their evil deeds. (*See also* **Characters in Shakespeare's Plays; Medievalism; Morality and Ethics; Pageants and Morality Plays.**)

WAR OF THE THEATERS

* *parody* literary composition in which an author's work is imitated for the purpose of humor or ridicule

The War of the Theaters involved the playwrights Ben Jonson, John Marston, and Thomas Dekker and lasted from 1599 to 1602. During that time these dramatists wrote a series of dueling plays that exchanged vicious parodies* and insults. Historians are unsure whether the conflict arose from rivalries among the playwrights or from competition between the theater companies for which they wrote. Some historians assert that the entire quarrel was staged to generate publicity and sell more tickets.

The battle began in 1599, when John Marston and Thomas Dekker wrote *Histriomastix*, which included a foolish character meant to resemble Ben Jonson. Insulted, Jonson struck back with *Every Man Out of His Humour*, in which he mocked Marston's pretentious use of language. Shortly thereafter, Jonson learned that Marston and Dekker were planning to attack him again in an upcoming play. He quickly wrote a new work called *The Poetaster*, in which he presented Marston as an inferior poet and Dekker as a plagiarist. In one of the most famous scenes in the play, Jonson's character forces Marston's character to vomit his pompous vocabulary.

Some scholars believe that the War of the Theaters was part of a larger conflict between CHILDREN'S COMPANIES, which performed for an elite audience in expensive indoor playhouses, and adult companies, which performed in open theaters for large audiences composed of people from all walks of life. Shakespeare refers to this rivalry in *Hamlet* when Rosencrantz

speaks of "an aery [nest] of children . . . These are now the fashion, and so berattle [satirize] the common stages" (II.ii.339–42). Whatever the source of the conflict, the playwrights involved seem to have eventually reconciled. In 1605 Jonson and Marston even collaborated on a play, *Eastward Ho!* (*See also* **Elizabethan Theaters; Playwrights and Poets.**)

WARFARE

England's military history was a major source of material for Shakespeare's plays. Elizabethans loved stage violence, and battle scenes provided many opportunities for bloodshed. Such drama also appealed to the audience's sense of patriotism, particularly when it depicted England's past military triumphs. Some of the clashes Shakespeare staged, however, were less glorious, such as the WARS OF THE ROSES, which tore the nation apart for 30 years. Although these conflicts had ended more than 100 years before Shakespeare transformed them into drama, they still had the power to remind the English of a very troubled period in their society's not-so-distant past.

ENGLISH WARFARE

Shakespeare's England in general was a nation at peace. During the reigns of ELIZABETH I and JAMES I, there were no military conflicts within the nation's borders. England did, however, send soldiers to aid its allies in continental Europe, with battles in such locations as the Netherlands, a Protestant nation that Catholic Spain claimed as part of its territory.

During the 1500s there were major changes in English military practices, from the way soldiers were hired to the way battle was conducted. The most significant development was the increasing dependence on firearms, which reduced the importance of archers and cavalry (horsemen) and increased that of infantrymen (foot soldiers).

THE NATIONAL DEFENSE. England differed from most European countries in that it did not have a standing army—a large, permanent force that guarded towns and fortresses during peacetime. Surrounded by water, the island had to rely on its navy as a first line of defense. England had a long history as a seafaring nation, and with its defeat of the SPANISH ARMADA in 1588 it became the unquestioned ruler of the seas. English ships were smaller and more maneuverable than the warships of other nations. This gave them an advantage in conflicts with the Spanish, who often attempted to pull alongside an enemy ship and send aboard a force of soldiers armed with swords and pistols. The English by contrast fought primarily with cannons mounted on and below the decks. The only way to aim these cannons was to position the entire ship advantageously, a feat requiring great navigational skill. English sailors of the 1500s were highly capable at maneuvering ships in almost any kind of weather, and only when the wind died down completely were they left helpless.

If an invading force ever succeeded in reaching England's shores, it would have to confront the nation's militia. Every household with an annual income of more than £1,000 was required to stock a certain quantity of weapons, armor, and horses for military service. In addition every able-bodied man between the ages of 16 and 60 years could be called up to defend his country in a crisis. To maintain their battle skills Englishmen were required to attend a muster every four years. All men of fighting age in a particular shire, or county, gathered to receive basic military training. Unfortunately, some had difficulty following even the simplest orders. The more skilled soldiers belonged to trained bands that drilled more often than strictly required. Although they were not professional soldiers, these trained bands were provided with weapons by the shire. They worked at their regular trades during peacetime and were called up for duty only in emergencies.

For overseas conflicts England relied on mercenaries, professional soldiers who could be hired to work for money. Few of these soldiers were volunteers, since only those who were truly desperate would risk their lives for such miserable pay as the army offered. A character in Shakespeare's *Pericles* notes that he may lose his leg in combat and "have not money enough in the end to buy him a wooden one" (IV.vi.172–73). Most mercenaries were forced, or pressed, into service by local authorities.

Many of Shakespeare's plays, especially the English histories, feature battle scenes. In *Richard III* the playwright depicts the defeat of King Richard at the battle of Bosworth Field.

Among those who were recruited many succeeded in avoiding military service by bribing the recruiters to let them go.

In general the pressed infantrymen were poor soldiers. In *Henry IV, Part 2*, for example, Shakespeare depicts a ragged group of would-be warriors with such names as Mouldy, Wart, and Feeble. When times were hard criminals might be taken from jails and forced to serve in the military. Captured VAGABONDS frequently met a similar fate. Even a crowded church service on Easter Sunday could provide soldiers. The church would be surrounded by a "press gang," a group of officials who held the entire congregation hostage until they had pressed the required number of healthy men into service. Press gangs were also known to snatch men right off the streets if necessary and take them away.

OFFICERS. The basic unit in the Elizabethan army was the company, a group of 100 to 200 men under the command of a captain. The captain was responsible for all aspects of his soldiers' lives, from their pay (which was sent first to him) to their clothing and food (which he paid for out of their salaries). It was also the captain's responsibility to recruit new soldiers to replace those who died or deserted. He was assisted by a lieutenant, who carried out some of his duties, and by several lower-ranking officers. An ensign bearer carried the flag, two sergeants were responsible for training the men, two drummers led the troops into battle, one surgeon treated the wounded, and several corporals maintained the company's equipment.

The captain's position provided many opportunities for corruption. If he lost a soldier, he could continue to draw a paycheck for the missing man until he reported the loss to his superiors. Some captains went so far as to send their men into danger on purpose so that they could collect the pay of those who died. To prevent such abuses the army sometimes conducted surprise inspections, but a clever captain could quickly replace his missing men with soldiers borrowed from another company. Shakespeare's FALSTAFF is a classic example of a corrupt army captain. He allows his recruits to "buy out their services," then replaces them with ragged beggars and thieves. He also refuses to buy clothing for them because "they'll find linen enough on every hedge" where it has been left out to dry (*Henry IV, Part 1*, IV.ii.47–48).

During Queen Elizabeth's reign a new army unit was established. Called a regiment, it was in fact a group consisting of several companies under the direction of a single colonel. Colonels in turn reported to generals, who were appointed directly by the monarch for a particular campaign. Generals were always chosen from the ranks of the aristocracy. A general was under the direct command of the sovereign and the Privy Council*, which made the major decisions about how to conduct a campaign.

* *Privy Council* body of advisers serving an English monarch

THE ART OF WARFARE. Until Shakespeare's day the most important weapon in England was the longbow. First developed in the Middle Ages, this weapon could be up to six feet in length and required great strength and skill to use. Most nations preferred crossbows, which were easier to fire but had a shorter range. The powerful longbow gave the English a

major advantage in battle. In fact the nation relied so heavily on its archers that all men under 60 were required by law to learn how to fire a bow.

Although bows and arrows were still the primary missile weapon of the English army, they had certain disadvantages. In bad weather bowstrings tended to loosen and feathers fell off the arrow shafts. More importantly a bowman could not kill someone in armor except at extremely short range. For these reasons firearms began to increase in importance. Although they were heavier than bows and were not particularly accurate, they required much less skill and strength to fire. The three basic firearms in use were the musket, the caliver, and the pistol. The musket was a large gun, about five and a half feet long, and so heavy that it had to be propped on a special stick for firing. The caliver was about three feet long and could be fired from the shoulder. The pistol, though larger than its modern American counterpart, was small enough to be worn at the waist and fired from horseback. The Elizabethan pistol posed another danger: it frequently backfired and injured the user.

For close-up combat a variety of weapons existed. The sword was the weapon of choice for the upper classes. Only gentlemen were allowed to carry swords, so wearing a blade was a way to advertise one's social rank. The art of fighting with a sword, called fencing, required years of study to master. A swordsman could wear a small shield, called a buckler, on his free arm, or he could use his spare hand to carry a dagger. For the lower classes the most common weapons were the pike, a spear up to 20 feet long, and the bill, a spike-headed ax with a 6-foot handle.

Horses were used in battle only by the upper classes. Warhorses had to be exceptionally strong, for they frequently carried a rider in heavy armor, not to mention his saddle and other gear. They also had to be carefully trained to deal with the excitement, noise, and danger of the battlefield. Meanwhile the horse's rider required extensive training to be able to maneuver his large animal on a crowded battlefield while using his hands to wield a sword. Members of the upper classes practiced their mounted combat skills by participating in TOURNAMENTS during peacetime.

WAR ON STAGE

In the Prologue to *Henry V,* Shakespeare expresses his fear that the Elizabethan stage is too small to stage a war, and he begs his audience to let its "imaginary forces" supply the battle scenes with all their bloody splendor. Shakespeare's own imagination, however, provided spectacular images of warfare on the stage. Many of Shakespeare's plays, especially the histories, feature battle scenes, and many others refer to war and warriors.

THE ROLE OF WAR. War, or the threat of war, is a constant presence in Shakespeare's history plays. News arrives of battles lost or won; threats of rebellion force military leaders and rulers to spring into action; exiles return, armed and dangerous. War plays such a primary role in the histories that in the prologue to *Henry VIII,* his only battle-free history, Shakespeare warns his audience that those who have come to see "a noise of targets" will be disappointed. War also figures prominently in many of

SHAKESPEARE THE SOLDIER?

The many references to warfare in Shakespeare's plays have led some scholars to speculate that Shakespeare may have been a soldier at some point in his life. At least one other Elizabethan playwright had military experience: Ben Jonson served as a soldier in the Netherlands before he became a dramatist. Some historians believe Shakespeare enlisted during the period known as the "lost years" (1585–1592) for which no historical record of the playwright exists. Others argue that his detailed descriptions of battle, like the many medical and legal references in his plays, are simply the products of his immense knowledge and rich imagination.

the other plays. It forms the background of *Julius Caesar* and *Antony and Cleopatra,* although the actual battles in these plays are largely kept off-stage. Even plays that do not focus on war sometimes contain vivid portraits of soldiers. Among these are the tragedy *Othello* and the comedy *All's Well That Ends Well.*

War in the plays is often a symbolic event. In a society that believed firmly in the God-given right of kings to rule, a conflict over the throne could be seen as a test of God's will. To an Elizabethan audience Henry V's triumph over a vastly superior French force at Agincourt would have been a clear sign that God was on the English side. Likewise a single encounter between two soldiers can be symbolic of an entire battle. When the leaders of two opposing factions—for example, Macbeth and Macduff—appear fighting each other in single combat, it is clear that the outcome of the battle hinges on their duel.

Many Elizabethans saw an army as a miniature version of the ideal state: a group united under one strong, respected leader. Problems within this military body, such as corruption, cowardice, or disobedience, were signs of disruption in the divine order. Two symbolic encounters in *Henry VI, Part 3,* show that the civil war between the houses of York and Lancaster has thrown society into chaos. A young man fighting on King Henry's behalf kills his father, who has been pressed into service by the king's enemy, the rebellious duke of York. Immediately afterward, a father enters dragging the body of his only son, whom he has killed in the same battle. These two unnatural deaths reveal the absurdity and tragic turmoil of a nation divided against itself.

HENRY V AND HIS HAPPY FEW. Perhaps no scene in all of Shakespeare's plays is as inspiring as King Henry V's speech to his troops before the battle of Agincourt in *Henry V.* Never before in dramatic literature had a battle cry become such eloquent and unforgettable poetry. Although his force is heavily outnumbered, the king's powerful speech rouses his "happy few" to victory.

The real-life battle of Agincourt in 1415 was a legendary event in England's history. Modern viewers, especially Americans, may be at a disadvantage when watching this scene because they probably do not know the tradition as well as Shakespeare's viewers did. For the most part the events of Shakespeare's version reflect the known historical facts presented in HOLINSHED'S CHRONICLES. For example, the English really were outnumbered five to one at Agincourt, about 25,000 Frenchmen against 5,000 to 6,000 Englishmen. It is also true that there were very few deaths among the English troops, while the French lost so many men that they had to dig large pits to bury them.

One important fact that Shakespeare omitted was the vital role played by the English archers, who occupied the narrow end of the field and brought down the French horses and foot soldiers as they charged. Perhaps the difficulty of putting bowmen on the stage discouraged the playwright, or maybe he preferred to focus on hand-to-hand combat, which was more conventionally* heroic. Two film versions of this play, Laurence Olivier's (1944) and Kenneth Branagh's (1989), added archers to

* *conventional* following established practice

159

the battle scenes, to great effect. (*See also* **Arms and Armor; Games, Pastimes, and Sports; History in Shakespeare's Plays: England.**)

WARS OF THE ROSES

The Wars of the Roses, a series of struggles over the English crown, were fought from 1455 to 1485 between the rival houses of Lancaster and York. According to legend the Lancastrians' symbol was a red rose, while the Yorkists' was a white rose. Shakespeare used the Wars of the Roses as the basis for four plays: *Henry VI, Part 1*; *Henry VI, Part 2*; *Henry VI, Part 3*; and *Richard III*.

The primary cause of the civil conflict was poor leadership by Henry VI. This weak king was unable to stop the discord in which his nobles and his queen, Margaret, were engaged. In 1453 he suffered a bout of insanity, and Richard, the duke of York, took over the government. When Henry regained his health in 1455, he excluded York from power, leading the duke to take up arms against the crown. The Yorkists won several important victories, and Henry agreed to make York his heir. Outraged that her own son would not be heir, Margaret continued the conflict. Her armies defeated and killed the duke of York, but his son Edward quickly overwhelmed her forces, and she fled to France. Her conqueror took the throne as King Edward IV in 1461.

As monarch, Edward soon began to quarrel with his chief supporters, who then went to France and joined with Margaret in an invasion of England that restored Henry to the throne. In due course Edward defeated the invaders. Margaret was captured, her son was killed, and Henry was murdered in prison. Edward ruled until he died in 1483, and his brother Richard took the throne over the objections of some of the nobles. The opposition united behind Henry Tudor, a Lancastrian who eventually defeated Richard in battle at Bosworth Field in 1485. With the nobles weakened by the wars, Henry, by then King Henry VII, was able to establish a strong monarchy. The rule of the Tudor family continued through the reign of his granddaughter Queen ELIZABETH I, who died in 1603. (*See also* **History in Shakespeare's Plays: England.**)

WEAPONS

See *Arms and Armor.*

WEATHER AND THE SEASONS

Nature plays a leading role in many of Shakespeare's plays. Changes in the weather, such as violent storms, frequently reflect the human events taking place on the stage. Similarly, the changing seasons often represent stages in a character's development. The cycles of nature can also parallel the path of human life, from birth to old age, and reinforce patterns of real or symbolic death and rebirth.

* *protagonist* central character in a dramatic
  or literary work

In the plays storms on land or at sea are often a sign of troubled times, for a protagonist* or for an entire nation. Because Elizabethans saw the monarch as a link between the heavenly sphere and the earthy one, violent skies could indicate a threat to a nation's ruler. A particularly hideous tempest occurs in *Macbeth* just after the title character has killed King Duncan. The earth trembles and the wind carries "strange screams of death" (II.iii.56). The unusual weather mirrors a disruption in the universe, thrown out of order by the ruler's death. A similar disorder in nature occurs when King Lear's ungrateful daughters cast him out of their homes. A great storm arises, in which the king is forced to wander. The cruel weather parallels Lear's inner disturbance as he realizes what his foolish behavior has cost him and his kingdom. The rain, wind, and thunder serve both as a punishment to Lear and as a sign of his growing madness.

Shakespeare used the cycle of the seasons to explore the basic patterns of life and growth in his romance *The Winter's Tale*. This drama is divided into two parts, separated by a 16-year interval. The first part of the play is set in the cold season. Prince Mamillius notes, "A sad tale's best for winter" (II.i.25), and the first three acts do indeed tell a tragic story. Two characters die, and two others appear to die. With the passage of time, however, death gives way to rebirth. The second half of the play, set in the spring, restores the two characters who were believed to be dead. The general atmosphere of joy and renewal is reinforced by a scene set at a sheep-shearing festival, a celebration based on pagan* rituals in honor of spring and rebirth.

* *pagan* referring to ancient religions that
  worshiped many gods, or more generally,
  to any non-Christian religion

One of the characters, Perdita, is identified with Proserpine, a figure from ancient Roman mythology. Proserpine was the daughter of Ceres, goddess of the grain, who was kidnapped by Pluto, lord of the underworld. Ceres' lamentations for her lost daughter caused the earth to wither. Eventually the gods arranged to have Proserpine spend half the year in the underworld and half on earth. For the Romans the myth of Proserpine explained the cycle of the seasons: when she is with Pluto winter comes and the earth is barren, but when she returns the earth becomes fertile once again. Like Proserpine, Perdita is symbolically reborn when she returns after 16 years to a father who thought she had died. Her arrival, like the return of spring, brings joy and renewal of spirit to all the characters in the play. (*See also* **Nature.**)

WINDSOR CASTLE

See *Court Life.*

WINTER'S TALE, THE

One of Shakespeare's tragicomedies, or romances, *The Winter's Tale* was written near the end of his career. Its title suggests the sort of folktale that might be told around a fire on a winter's evening. Because such stories often involve fairies and other supernatural creatures, the title suggests that the events in this play may not be entirely realistic. At the same time, it recalls the very real and homey atmosphere of the family gatherings in which such tales were told. The play's title also provides a clue to the nature of the plot, which celebrates both nature and art—the everyday world of the storyteller and the fantasy world of the story.

PLOT SYNOPSIS. King Leontes of Sicilia is enjoying a visit from his childhood friend, King Polixenes of Bohemia. When Polixenes says he must return home, both Leontes and his wife Hermione plead with him to stay longer. When Polixenes consents, however, Leontes begins to suspect that Hermione is romantically involved with him. He therefore orders Camillo, a nobleman, to murder the Bohemian king. Camillo warns Polixenes instead, and they both decide to flee to Bohemia. Their sudden departure convinces Leontes that his jealous suspicions were correct. He accuses the queen of adultery and of plotting with Polixenes and Camillo to murder him. He then casts Hermione into prison and sends two messengers to consult the oracle* of the god Apollo concerning her guilt.

While in prison the queen gives birth to a daughter. Paulina, a lady of the court, takes the baby to the king, hoping that the sight of the beautiful infant will soften his heart. But instead Leontes curses the child as a female bastard. He orders Antigonus, Paulina's husband, to take the baby to "some remote and desert place" (II.iii.176) and leave it to the mercy of the elements.

Leontes then puts Hermione on trial. She claims innocence and calls on the oracle as her witness. The messengers read the message brought from the oracle, which states that all of the accused are innocent and that Leontes "shall live without an heir, if that which is lost be not found" (III.ii.133–36). But the king is unmoved, declaring, "There is no truth at all [in the] oracle" (140). Just then a servant arrives to announce that the king's son and heir, the sickly Prince Mamillius, has died, overcome with fear and sorrow for his mother. At this the queen faints and is quickly carried away from the court. The king immediately regrets his folly, but his repentance comes too late. Paulina enters and announces that Hermione is dead.

Meanwhile Antigonus arrives in Bohemia with the baby. He reveals that Hermione has appeared to him in a dream and instructed him to name her daughter Perdita (meaning "lost") and to take her to Bohemia. He sets the child on the ground, along with a scroll explaining her identity and a bundle of rich clothes and jewels in case someone finds her. He then departs, according to a famous stage direction, "pursued by a bear" (III.iii.58). An old shepherd finds the baby and, hearing from his son that Antigonus has been killed by the bear, decides to raise the girl himself.

As Act IV opens, the Chorus, representing Time, informs the audience that 16 years have passed. Camillo is still at the Bohemian court but privately longs to see Sicilia again. Meanwhile Polixenes is concerned that his son, Prince Florizel, has fallen in love with a shepherdess. This shepherdess is Perdita, who has grown up with no knowledge of her birth. Her

__oracle__ person through whom a god is thought to speak

A MOVING SCENE

Although some critics find the statue scene too absurd to accept, audiences have often been struck by its peculiar power. According to tradition an audience in the early 1800s was literally moved by this scene. When Hermione's statue stepped down from the pedestal and began walking toward her husband, the entire audience rose to its feet and began walking toward her. Victor Hugo believed that the scene was so effective because the audience, as well as the characters, believed Hermione to be dead. It therefore appears that as "marble becomes flesh . . . at this unexpected resurrection, we feel an indescribable emotion of wonder and surprise."

In this scene from the 1981 Royal Shakespeare Company performance of *The Winter's Tale,* King Leontes is happily reunited with his wife, who he believed had died many years earlier.

family does not know her lover's identity. Polixenes and Camillo disguise themselves in order to attend a sheep-shearing festival and spy on the young lovers. After hearing Florizel declare his love for Perdita, the king reveals his presence. He threatens to disinherit Florizel and have Perdita and her whole family killed if she and the prince ever see each other again, then leaves in a rage.

Florizel refuses to abandon Perdita, so Camillo advises the young lovers to flee to Sicilia, where Leontes is sure to welcome them. Secretly he plans to tell the king of their flight in the hope of being sent to Sicilia himself. The prince disguises himself by exchanging clothes with Autolycus, a roguish peddler who has spent a profitable day at the fair selling "trumpery" (cheap or useless items) and stealing purses. Autolycus then overhears the shepherd and his son planning to tell Polixenes that Perdita is not their relative but a foundling. He decides to take them both to Sicilia and present them to Leontes, hoping the king will reward him for doing so.

The final act takes place at the Sicilian court, where Paulina has persuaded Leontes not to remarry until he finds another woman exactly like Hermione. The king is surprised by the arrival of Florizel and the girl he calls his "princess." Their greetings are cut short by the news that Polixenes has come to Sicilia demanding the return of his son, who has eloped with a shepherdess. Florizel confesses to this and begs Leontes to help them win his father's permission to marry. The court is then thrown into confusion and delight by the news of Perdita's true identity, brought by

the old shepherd. Paulina, to complete the happiness of the royal families, invites them to see a statue of Hermione that she keeps in her private chapel. As they all marvel at how lifelike it is, Hermione descends from the pedestal and embraces her husband. Paulina explains that the queen has been alive and in hiding all these years, hoping to see her daughter return to Sicilia. An overjoyed Leontes urges Paulina to share in their happiness by marrying Camillo.

TEXT AND SOURCES. Shakespeare based *The Winter's Tale* primarily on a romance* by Robert Greene called *Pandosto, or the Triumph of Time* (1588). The playwright closely followed Greene's plot, in many cases picking up its words almost exactly. He made a significant change, however, in the fate of the Sicilian king and queen. In the source the queen dies and her husband commits suicide. The joyous reunion at the end of the play is Shakespeare's own invention. One other change, for which Shakespeare has often been criticized, was his decision to reverse the locations of Bohemia and Sicilia. This required him to have Antigonus's ship land on the shores of Bohemia, which in reality did not have a seacoast. Many critics, including Shakespeare' friend Ben JONSON, considered this change ridiculous.

Several details of the plot come from other recognizable sources. The character of Autolycus, who was a minor and uninteresting figure in *Pandosto,* has been transformed into a colorful rogue whose tricks resemble those described in other stories by Greene. The story of a statue coming to life is probably based on the legend of Pygmalion and Galatea, one of the stories recounted in the *Metamorphoses* by the ancient Roman poet OVID. A speech by Autolycus (in Act IV, Scene iv) describing various types of torture appears to be drawn from a story in the *Decameron,* by Italian writer Giovanni Boccacio, which was also the primary source for Shakespeare's *Cymbeline.*

The Winter's Tale was probably written in early 1611. A contemporary account records a performance of the play at the GLOBE THEATER on May 15, 1611. Two facts suggest that the play was written later than 1610. First, it shows a much greater mastery of the romance genre* than Shakespeare's earlier romances. Critics therefore believe it was written after *Cymbeline,* which was completed in 1610. Also the scene at the sheep-shearing festival includes a dance of 12 men dressed as satyrs*, and the servant who introduces them says that some of them have previously danced before the king (IV.iv.337–38). This line is thought to be a reference to a dancing satyr in *The Masque of Oberon,* written by Jonson and performed at the court of JAMES I on January 1, 1611. Either the play was written after this date, or this line was added afterward as a reference to Jonson's MASQUE.

COMMENTARY. The dramatic 16-year time gap between Acts III and IV (a violation of classical* practice for which Shakespeare has been sharply criticized) divides the play neatly into two parts. The first, centering on Leontes' mad jealousy, is a tragedy, ending with the supposed death of Hermione and the real deaths of Mamillius and Antigonus. The second

* *romance* story of love and adventure, the forerunner of the modern novel

* *genre* literary form

* *satyr* mythical creature with the body of a man and the legs and horns of a goat

* *classical* in the tradition of ancient Greece and Rome

* *pastoral* relating to the countryside; often used to draw a contrast between the innocence and serenity of rural life and the corruption and extravagance of court life

* *allegory* literary device in which characters, events, and settings represent abstract qualities and in which the author intends a different meaning to be read beneath the surface

* *morality play* religious dramatic work that teaches a moral lesson through the use of symbolic characters

* *pagan* referring to ancient religions that worshiped many gods, or more generally, to any non-Christian religion

part, the love story of Florizel and Perdita, is a comedy in the pastoral* style. The playwright provides a familiar setting—the sheep-shearing festival in Act IV paints a vivid picture of Elizabethan country life. He also gives the audience humorous characters, and a traditional comedy ending with multiple marriages.

The story is highly unrealistic, even though Shakespeare deliberately altered some of the more outrageous plot twists in his source. For example, in *Pandosto* the infant Perdita is cast out to sea in an open boat that finds its way to Bohemia by sheer chance. Likewise, when the young lovers flee Bohemia, they wander at random, reaching Sicilia only by coincidence. In Shakespeare's version Perdita and Florizel reach Sicilia by a human plan (Camillo's) rather than a divine one. Similarly, in Shakespeare the death of young Prince Mamillius is not entirely due to grief over his mother's dishonor, since he has already been reported to be ill. Yet other elements of the play remain bizarre. Leontes' wild jealousy is never adequately explained, nor is his sudden change of heart when Mamillius dies.

Perhaps the most confusing plot element is Hermione's decision to spend 16 years in hiding. Some critics, notably Charlotte Lennox, have attacked the final scene as absurd. Others see it as simply an indication that the play is not intended to be realistic. They believe that having Hermione's statue come to life is a sly reference to the power of art to create the illusion of reality. Leontes notes how lifelike his wife's statue appears, remarking that "we are mock'd with art" (V.iii.68), and the audience watching the play is equally mocked by Shakespeare's artful drama. The statue scene can also be seen as an allegory* for Christianity, with its promise that the dead will be restored to life. In this respect it resembles a morality play*, providing a Christian moral for a play that is set in a pagan* world. Leontes sins in the first part of the play but is redeemed by his 16 years of suffering and by the wise counsel of Paulina (whose name suggests Saint Paul, the first major teacher of Christian doctrine).

Although the play acknowledges the power of supernatural forces, it also celebrates natural ones. There are many references to the cycles of the year, particularly during the sheep-shearing festival, a reflection of ancient pagan rituals that mark the changing seasons. Perdita distributes seasonal flowers to the various guests according to their ages, linking the cycle of the seasons to the larger cycle of birth, growth, and death. The ties between birth and death are noted in other scenes as well. When the old Shepherd discovers Perdita, he says to his son, "Thou met'st with things dying, I with things new-born" (III.iii.113–14). The cycles of time bring sorrow, but they also provide occasions for joy. These contrasting effects of time appear most vividly in the final scene, when the viewers of Hermione's statue observe wrinkles the queen did not have 16 years before. Time has not stood still but has been hard at work, curing Leontes' mad jealousy, bringing Florizel and Perdita together, and preparing everyone for the final reunion and resolution.

The Winter's Tale celebrates both nature and art, and also explores the links between them. Polixenes notes that while art may appear to change nature, the humans who create art are themselves the products of nature

* *protagonist* central character in a dramatic
or literary work

(IV.iv.89–97). The union between nature and art, therefore, is like the union of divine and human endeavors. The gods aid the protagonists* through the words of the oracle and the vision of Hermione that is granted to Antigonus. The happy resolution also depends on human deeds of courage and kindness, however. Ultimately, the most powerful forces in the play are love and forgiveness, qualities that unite human nature with the divine.

PERFORMANCE HISTORY. The Globe performance in 1611 is the only known public presentation of *The Winter's Tale* during the 1600s. Evidence suggests that the play was also performed several times at court, including a performance in 1612 to celebrate the engagement of King James's daughter, Princess Elizabeth. After 1640 the play apparently disappeared from the stage. A revival in 1741 was advertised as the play's first performance in a century.

Most productions during the 1700s were adaptations centering on the love story between Florizel and Perdita, with most of the first three acts removed. The two best-known versions were written by McNamara Morgan and by the legendary Shakespearean actor David Garrick, who played the greatly reduced role of Leontes in his own production. A minor revival of Shakespeare's full text in 1771 was not successful. In the early 1800s John Philip Kemble restored most of Shakespeare's text in a production that featured his sister, Sarah Siddons, as Hermione and himself as Leontes.

Most 19th-century stagings of *The Winter's Tale* featured spectacular sets and costumes. The most extreme example was Charles Kean's 1856 production, which changed the location of Polixenes' kingdom from Bohemia to the ancient realm of Bithynia. In his typical fashion Kean created a set that elaborately reproduced the architecture and clothing of the ancient world. His production also included eight-year-old actress Ellen Terry as Mamillius, her first speaking role. (Fifty years later Terry played the role of Hermione under the direction of Herbert Beerbohm Tree.) Mary Anderson directed another grand production in 1887, with 13 different sets. She herself played the roles of both Hermione and Perdita.

The play's popularity declined in the early 1900s, but there were several noteworthy productions. Harley Granville-Barker, in 1912, presented the play on a nearly bare stage with only six lines cut from Shakespeare's text. Wildly controversial, Granville-Barker's production was not a commercial success and closed after six weeks. Perhaps the most notable 20th-century staging was Peter Brook's 1951 production, starring John Gielgud as Leontes. Gielgud played the king as a naturally jealous man, making his suspicions of Hermione seem more convincing. To date, *The Winter's Tale* has been presented four times on film (three of them silent movies produced before 1915) and twice on television. (*See also* **Directors and Shakespeare; Disguises; Dreams; Ghosts and Apparitions; Groatsworth of Wit; Pastoralism; Plays: The Romances; Playwrights and Poets; Shakespearean Theater: 19th Century; Shakespearean Theater: 20th Century; Shakespeare's Works, Adaptations of.**)

WITCHES AND EVIL SPIRITS

Many Elizabethans believed in an invisible supernatural world that existed alongside, and interacted regularly with, the natural world. This other world teemed with spirits, both good and evil, whose actions affected the fortunes of human beings. Some humans were thought to have the power to communicate with or control these spirits. Those who were believed to interact with the supernatural world were called witches (generally female) or wizards (male).

The popular idea of a witch was an old woman who had the ability to summon evil spirits or even Satan himself. Witches were assumed to use their powers to harm human victims and to increase the influence of evil in the world. They were thought to cause crops to wither, make people sick, and kill animals. Some people believed that witches had fabulous powers, such as the ability to fly and to change their shapes at will. Many also thought that witches were assisted in their foul deeds by "familiars," demons that typically took the form of ordinary animals, such as cats.

In addition to evil or "black" witches, many Elizabethans believed in good or "white" witches, who used their powers to help their neighbors. Most villages had a "cunning woman" (or sometimes a man) who claimed the ability to heal the sick, create love charms, or ward off evil spirits. The church, however, frowned on all "witchcraft," even if it appeared harmless or perhaps helpful. Some theologians claimed that good spirits could not be contacted or controlled by humans, and therefore any spirit summoned by a witch must necessarily be evil. Others complained that the common people were quick to blame their misfortunes on witchcraft instead of accepting them as God's will and seeking grace through prayer.

In his play *The Witch*, Thomas Middleton listed some of the many types of evil spirits that were believed to inhabit the world. They included "Urchins, elves, hags, satires, pans, fauns, . . . Kit with the candle stick, tritons, centaures, dwarfs, imps, the spoorne, the mare, the man i'th'oak, the hell wayne, the fire drake, [and] the puckle." Spirits were blamed for mischief of all sorts, from merely causing milk to go sour to stealing human children and replacing them with ugly "changelings." Laws passed in 1542, 1563, and 1604 made the summoning of evil spirits and the use of magical spells to kill anyone crimes punishable by death. Under these laws between 500 and 1,000 "witches" were executed in England during the 1500s and 1600s.

The belief in witchcraft, though common, was not universal. One of the best-known skeptics was Reginald Scot, a student at Oxford University, who argued in *The Discoverie of Witchcraft* (1584) that notions of witches and spirits were pure superstition. The book was banned by King JAMES I, who published his own argument for the existence of witchcraft in *Daemonologie* (1597). In 1591 King James personally tried two women in Scotland for attempting to murder him through spells. The belief in witches and evil sprits was slow to fade, and women were still being executed for witchcraft in England as late as 1751.

Shakespeare's portrayal of the "weird sisters" in *Macbeth* (called "weyward" or "weyard" in the first printing of the play) reflects popular ideas about witches. These "secret, black, and midnight hags" chant evil spells,

Many Elizabethans believed that witches were responsible for disturbances in the weather. This woodcut from 1489 shows witches using their powers to brew a hailstorm.

See
color plate 1,
vol. 2.

protagonist central character in a dramatic
or literary work

have animal familiars, and stir a magical brew in a bubbling cauldron. They appear to have the power to foretell the future, but their "supernatural soliciting" has a negative effect on Macbeth, encouraging the overarching ambition that eventually leads him to kill King Duncan. It is unclear whether the witches have supernatural power or whether they merely provoke the existing evil within an ambitious protagonist*. In either case it is important to note that Macbeth's own actions are what lead to his tragedy, not the workings of supernatural forces. Interestingly, the source for the play, HOLINSHED'S CHRONICLES, describes the witches as morally neutral "fairies" rather than as evil spirits. Shakespeare may have altered his source to appeal to King James's known interest in witchcraft. (*See also* **Magic and Folklore; Supernatural Phenomena.**)

WOMEN

See *Craftworkers; Feminist Interpretations; Gender and Sexuality; Marriage and Family; Work.*

WORK

In the late 1500s England's economy was still based primarily on agriculture. Most people lived in the country and made their living by growing, processing, and selling farm products. Because they lived on the land they cultivated, their labor was not so much a job as a way of life. Even for those who resided in towns and cities, there was no rigid distinction between work and personal life. Most people lived in or near their workplaces, and many had close personal relationships with their employers or employees.

AGRICULTURE. Elizabethan England was an overwhelmingly rural society. The great majority of its population lived in villages with fewer than 500 residents, while less than 10 percent of the people inhabited the largest towns and cities. Most of these villagers were agricultural workers of one type or another, and they did all their farmwork by hand.

In the countryside men and women divided the duties of farming. Men spent their days in the fields, plowing, weeding, sowing seed, fertilizing, and harvesting. Women also helped in the fields during harvest time, and they assisted in winnowing the grain (separating the edible portion from the inedible portion) afterward. During the remainder of the year, they devoted themselves to household tasks such as cooking, cleaning, and sewing. Women were usually responsible for tending the family's livestock. Most families had at least one cow, and smaller animals such as pigs, goats, chickens, and geese were common.

By Shakespeare's day it was no longer typical for rural households to be self-sufficient, living solely off what they could produce themselves. Instead a typical family produced more food than it needed and sold its

Most workers in the cities and towns of Shakespeare's day were employed in crafts and trades. The baker, brewer, tailor, and blacksmith were familiar figures in any English town.

See color plate 5, vol. 1.

surplus in local market towns. Most farmers had little choice in this matter because the landlords who owned the fields they cultivated were increasingly likely to demand rent payments in cash rather than in the form of goods or labor as had been the case in the Middle Ages.

The parts of the countryside that were not farmed were mostly devoted to raising sheep. Wool was England's single most important product. In 1558 when Queen Elizabeth ascended the throne, there were nearly four times as many sheep as there were people in her kingdom. Unlike farming, which required the work of several people, tending a flock of sheep could be done by a single individual. Many landlords therefore found it profitable to convert their lands into pastures, displacing many of their tenant farmers. Shepherds appear as major characters in Shakespeare's *As You Like It* and *The Winter's Tale.*

Most wool processing was done by hand in private homes. After the sheep were sheared, the raw wool had to be washed and carded (combed) to free it of tangles so that it could be spun into thread. The woolen thread was then woven into cloth and fulled, or washed, to shrink the fibers and bind them together more tightly. Many farm wives engaged in spinning and weaving as a part-time activity to earn extra money. As the

cloth industry grew throughout the late 1500s, however, more and more people earned their living exclusively by manufacturing cloth.

CRAFTS AND TRADES.

Dotted among England's many villages were hundreds of small towns, with populations typically between 500 and 5,000. Workers in these towns were primarily involved in crafts and trades as butchers, bakers, tailors, weavers, blacksmiths, and carpenters. A group of such craftsmen—scornfully described by the fairy Puck as "rude mechanicals"—is featured in Shakespeare's *A Midsummer Night's Dream.*

Unlike modern manufacturing, Elizabethan crafts and trades did not involve mass production in a factory setting. Skilled craftsmen (nearly all craftworkers were male) manufactured goods by hand, helped by assistants known as apprentices and journeymen. A typical craftsman kept a shop on the ground floor of his home where goods were both made and sold. Typically the workshop was toward the rear, with the store in the front part. Windows facing the street were used to display finished products. Many shopkeepers who sold only goods made by others objected to this practice and sought, largely without success, to outlaw it.

Each craft was controlled by a GUILD—a professional association, also known as a company, that set standards for the trade and looked after the interests of its members. The guild decided who could practice a particular trade or craft, how much members could charge for their services, and with whom they could do business. In Shakespeare's day these organizations were still powerful, but their influence was gradually being weakened by the presence of merchants, retailers, and others involved with trade and commerce.

A person seeking membership in a guild had to serve a term as apprentice to a master craftsman. If a boy's father practiced a trade, he would almost certainly serve an apprenticeship under him and eventually take over the family business. An apprentice lived in his master's home and ate with the family. He received no regular wages, but his master sometimes gave him a little spending money. The master was expected not only to teach his apprentice a trade but also to give him moral instruction. Many masters charged their apprentices a fine whenever they misbehaved in any way, such as using foul language or wearing a dirty shirt on Sunday. An apprenticeship lasted seven years, regardless of how long it actually took to learn the trade. After serving this term an apprentice paid his dues to the guild and became a journeyman, with the right to offer his services for wages. Eventually he could set up his own shop and become a master, with apprentices and journeymen of his own to supervise.

Many townspeople who did not make goods still earned a living by selling them. Some shopkeepers sold items purchased from local manufacturers who did not have shops of their own. Others dealt in goods brought into the country by merchant traders. Some craft and trade workers resented the flow of imported products into England, which cut into their business. Foreign cloth in particular posed a threat to English manufacturers of woolen goods. To aid the wool industry, Queen Elizabeth's

A WOMAN'S WORK

Most Elizabethan women worked in the home. Housework included cooking and cleaning, mending and sewing, spinning and weaving, and caring for children. In the country, women were also responsible for tending livestock, collecting eggs, milking cows, and making cheese and butter from the milk. Women cared for the garden, and many were skilled in extracting medicines, flavorings, and fragrances from homegrown herbs. In towns, women might earn money by making clothing, doing laundry, or selling goods from street carts. Sometimes the wife of a craftsman helped her husband in his trade, and she might even run the business by herself if he died.

* ***Privy Council*** body of advisers serving an English monarch

Privy Council* enacted a set of sumptuary laws in 1559. Under these laws, which regulated people's dress according to their SOCIAL CLASS, no one below the rank of earl could wear woolen cloth made outside of England.

OTHER OCCUPATIONS. Among the most respected occupations in England were the professions, such as MEDICINE, LAW, EDUCATION, and the CHURCH. Most of these careers required university training. Professionals were regarded as gentlemen, equal in rank to landholders in the country or merchants in the city. Like craftsmen, most professionals worked from home, although many in the larger towns and cities had separate offices. The professions could be very profitable. A well-respected physician or lawyer could make a handsome living even in a small town, and the larger towns and cities provided still better opportunities. A small-town schoolteacher by contrast might well have difficulty making ends meet on his meager salary. Professionals, especially doctors, appear in several of Shakespeare's plays, including *Macbeth, Henry VIII,* and *The Merry Wives of Windsor.*

A remarkably large number of people were employed as domestic servants, perhaps as much as one-fourth of England's entire population. Among young people the percentage was considerably higher. Scholars estimate that about 80 percent of all men between the ages of 20 and 24 and 50 percent of the women in the same age range were servants. For many people domestic service was a step up to a better job and social position. Even the children of wealthy and influential parents sometimes became servants in upper-class households, where they perfected the manners of polite society and made connections with people who could help them in later life.

Like apprentices, servants lived with the families they worked for and were treated much like children of those families. Unlike apprenticeship, however, domestic service had no fixed term. The majority of young men and women in this field were servants from early adolescence until they married, a period of about ten years. Others remained servants all their lives. Male domestics were known as grooms and females as maids. Some servants were personal attendants who tended to the needs of a specific household member. Others served the family in general. One of the most notable servants in Shakespeare's plays is MALVOLIO, the haughty steward* of the lady Olivia in *Twelfth Night.*

* ***steward*** person who manages another person's household or estate

Those who had difficulty finding work might choose to join the military. England did not have a full-time army but instead hired soldiers as needed. Officers were members of the upper classes, sometimes younger sons from aristocratic families who needed a way to support themselves in a society where only the oldest son could expect to inherit the family's land. Footsoldiers came from the lower classes. Some of them volunteered to join the army because they had no better prospects, while others were drafted, or pressed, into military service.

During the reigns of ELIZABETH I and JAMES I, there were no military conflicts within England. Some soldiers were hired to fight on behalf of England's allies in Europe, however, particularly in the Netherlands, a

Protestant nation seeking protection from its Catholic rivals. Other soldiers participated in campaigns to conquer Ireland, which England had been attempting to do for 400 years without success. Soldiers returning from these overseas campaigns often had difficulty finding work in England. Some became criminals, while others used their military training to keep the peace as law enforcers. (*See also* **Agriculture; Banking and Commerce; Cities, Towns, and Villages; Clothing; Country Life; Craftworkers; Gender and Sexuality; Schools and Universities; Trade; Vagabonds, Beggars, and Rogues; Warfare.**)

WRITERS INSPIRED
BY SHAKESPEARE

See *Literature Inspired by Shakespeare.*

SUGGESTED RESOURCES

*Asterisk denotes books recommended for young readers.

DICTIONARIES AND COMPANIONS

Andrews, John F., ed. *William Shakespeare: His World, His Work, His Influence.* 3 vols. New York: Scribners, 1985.

Bartlett, John, ed. *A Complete Concordance or Verbal Index to Words, Phrases, and Passages in the Dramatic Works of Shakespeare: With a Supplement Concordance to the Poems.* New York: St. Martin's Press, 1969.

*Boyce, Charles. *Shakespeare A to Z: The Essential Reference to His Plays, His Poems, His Life and Times, and More.* New York: Dell Publishing, 1990.

Shakespeare: A Book of Quotations. Mineola, N.Y.: Dover Publications, 1998.

Campbell, Oscar James, ed. *The Reader's Encyclopedia of Shakespeare.* New York: MJF Books, 1966.

Clark, Sandra, ed. *The Penguin Shakespeare Dictionary.* New York: Penguin Books, 1999.

*Doyle, John, and Ray Lischner. *Shakespeare for Dummies.* Foster City, Calif.: IDG Books Worldwide, 1999.

Eagleson, Robert D., ed. *A Shakespeare Glossary.* New York: Oxford University Press, 1986.

*Epstein, Norrie. *The Friendly Shakespeare: A Thoroughly Painless Guide to the Best of the Bard.* New York: Viking, 1993.

*Fox, Levi. *The Shakespeare Handbook: The Essential Companion to Shakespeare's Works, Life, and Times.* Boston: G. K. Hall, 1987.

McDonald, Russ. *The Bedford Companion to Shakespeare: An Introduction with Documents.* Boston: Bedford Books, 1996.

Suggested Resources

*McQuain, Jeffrey, and Stanley Malless. *Coined by Shakespeare*. Springfield, Mass.: Merriam-Webster, 1998.

*Schoenbaum, S. *Shakespeare: The Globe & the World*. New York: Oxford University Press, 1979.

Shewmaker, Eugene F. *Shakespeare's Language: A Glossary of Unfamiliar Words in His Plays and Poems*. New York: Facts on File, 1999.

Wagner, John A. *Historical Dictionary of the Elizabethan World: Britain, Ireland, Europe, and America*. Phoenix, Ariz.: Oryx Press, 1999.

Wells, Stanley, ed. *Shakespeare: An Illustrated Dictionary*. Oxford, England: Oxford University Press, 1986.

Daily Life

*Ashby, Ruth. *Elizabethan England*. Cultures of the Past Series. New York: Benchmark Books, 1999.

Byrne, M. St. Clair. *Elizabethan Life in Town and Country*. London: Methuen, 1961.

*Davis, William Stearns. *Life in Elizabethan Days*. New York: Harper & Row, 1991.

*Dodd, A. H. *Elizabethan England*. New York: G. P. Putnam's Sons, 1973.

*Emerson, Kathy Lynn. *The Writer's Guide to Everyday Life in Renaissance England: From 1485–1649*. Cincinnati, Ohio: Writer's Digest Books, 1996.

Ferris, Julie. *Shakespeare's London: A Guide to Elizabethan London*. New York: Larousse Kingfisher Chambers, 2000.

Guy, John. *Tudor England*. New York: Oxford University Press, 1990.

In the Realm of Elizabeth. What Life Was Like Series. New York: Time-Life Books, 1999.

*Lace, William W. *Elizabethan England*. World History Series. San Diego: Lucent Books, 1995.

*McMurty, Jo. *Understanding Shakespeare's England: A Companion for the American Reader*. Hamden, Conn.: Archon Books, 1989.

Palmer, Alan, and Veronica Palmer. *Who's Who in Shakespeare's England*. New York: St. Martin's Press, 1981.

Papp, Joseph, and Elizabeth Kirkland. *Shakespeare Alive!* New York: Bantam Books, 1988.

Pritchard, Ron. *Shakespeare's England: Life in Elizabethan and Jacobean Times*. Old Greenwich, Conn.: Sutton Publishing, 2000.

*Singman, Jeffrey L. *Daily Life in Elizabethan England*. Daily Life Through History Series. Westport, Conn.: Greenwood Publishing Group, 1995.

Smith, Lacey Baldwin. *The Horizon Book of the Elizabethan World*. New York: American Heritage, 1967.

Tillyard, E.M.W. *The Elizabethan World Picture*. New York: Random House, 1959.

Shakespeare Studies: General

Barker, Deborah, and Ivo Kamps, eds. *Shakespeare and Gender: A History*. London: Verso, 1995.

Blake, N. F. *Shakespeare's Language: An Introduction*. New York: St. Martin's Press, 1983.

Bloom, Harold. *Shakespeare: The Invention of the Human*. New York: Riverhead Books, 1998.

Bradley, A. C. *Shakespearean Tragedy*. New York: Penguin, 1992.

*Charney, Maurice. *All of Shakespeare*. New York: Columbia University Press, 1993.

Dusinberre, Juliet. *Shakespeare and the Nature of Women*. London: Macmillan, 1975.

Eastman, Arthur M. *A Short History of Shakespearean Criticism*. New York: Random House, 1968.

Edelman, Charles, ed. *Shakespeare: Readers, Audiences, and Players*. Portland, Ore.: International Specialized Book Services, 1998.

Frey, Charles H. *Making Sense of Shakespeare*. Madison, N.J.: Fairleigh Dickinson University Press, 1999.

Gay, Penny. *As She Likes It: Shakespeare's Unruly Women*. London: Routledge, 1994.

Goddard, Harold C. *Meaning of Shakespeare*. Chicago: University of Chicago Press, 1960.

Halpern, Richard. *Shakespeare Among the Moderns*. Ithaca, N.Y.: Cornell University Press, 1996.

Harbage, Alfred. *As They Liked It: A Study of Shakespeare's Moral Artistry*. New York: Harper and Brothers, 1947.

Hartnoll, Phyllis, ed. *Shakespeare in Music*. London: Macmillan, 1964.

Howard, Jean, and Phyllis Rackin. *Engendering a Nation: A Feminist Account of Shakespeare's English Histories*. New York: Routledge, 1997.

Hussey, S. S. *The Literary Language of Shakespeare*. 2nd ed. New York: Longman Publishing Group, 1992.

Joseph, Sister Miriam. *Shakespeare's Use of the Arts of Language*. New York: Hafner Publishing, 1966.

Kermode, Frank. *Shakespeare's Language*. New York: Farrar, Straus and Giroux, 2000.

Knott, Jan. *Shakespeare Our Contemporary.* New York: W. W. Norton, 1974.

Muir, Kenneth. *The Sources of Shakespeare's Plays.* London: Methuen, 1977.

Robinson, Randal. *Unlocking Shakespeare's Language: Help for the Teacher and Student.* Washington, D.C.: National Council of Teachers of English, 1988.

Salomone, Ronald E., and James E. Davis, eds. *Teaching Shakespeare into the Twenty-first Century.* Athens: Ohio University Press, 1997.

Shakespeare, William. *All the World's a Stage: Poems and Songs from Shakespeare.* Golden, Colo.: Fulcrum Publishing, 1996.

Shapiro, James. *Shakespeare and the Jews.* New York: Columbia University Press, 1996.

Spurgeon, Caroline. *Shakespeare's Imagery and What It Tells Us.* Cambridge, England: Cambridge University Press, 1989.

Taylor, Gary. *Reinventing Shakespeare: A Cultural History from the Restoration to the Present.* New York: Oxford University Press, 1989.

Wells, Stanley, ed. *The Cambridge Companion to Shakespeare Studies.* Cambridge: Cambridge University Press, 1986.

———. *Shakespeare in the Theatre: An Anthology of Criticism.* New York: Oxford University Press, 2000.

SHAKESPEARE STUDIES: PLAYS

Andrews, John, ed. *Romeo and Juliet: Critical Essays.* New York: Garland, 1993.

Barber, C. L. *Shakespeare's Festive Comedy. [Twelfth Night]* Princeton: Princeton University Press, 1959.

Bloom, Harold, ed. *Interpretations: William Shakespeare's "The Taming of the Shrew."* New York: Chelsea House, 1988.

Calderwood, James L. *If It Were Done: Macbeth and Tragic Action.* Amherst: University of Massachusetts Press, 1986.

Campbell, Oscar James. *Comicall Satyre and Shakespeare's "Troilus and Cressida."* San Marino, Calif.: Huntington Library, 1938.

Carroll, William C. *The Great Feast of Language in "Love's Labor's Lost."* Princeton: Princeton University Press, 1959.

Danson, Lawrence. *The Harmonies of "The Merchant of Venice."* New Haven, Conn.: Yale University Press, 1978.

Foakes, R. A. *Hamlet Versus Lear.* Cambridge: Cambridge University Press, 1993.

Gross, John. *Shylock: Four Hundred Years in the Life of a Legend.* London: Chatto and Windus, 1992.

Hawkins, Harriet. *Likenesses of Truth in Elizabethan and Restoration Drama. [Measure for Measure.]* Oxford, England: Clarendon Press, 1972.

King, Walter N. *Hamlet's Search for Meaning.* Athens: University of Georgia Press, 1982.

Leggatt, Alexander. *Shakespeare's Comedy of Love. [Twelfth Night.]* London: Methuen, 1974.

Mack, Maynard. *King Lear in Our Time.* Berkeley: University of California Press, 1965.

Mangan, Michael. *A Preface to Shakespeare's Comedies, 1594–1603.* New York: Longman, 1996.

Rosenberg, Marvin. *The Masks of Hamlet.* Newark: University of Delaware Press, 1992.

———. *The Masks of King Lear.* Berkeley: University of California Press, 1972.

Salingar, Leo. *Shakespeare and the Traditions of Comedy.* Cambridge: Cambridge University Press, 1974.

Soellner, Rolf. *"Timon of Athens:" Shakespeare's Pessimistic Tragedy.* Columbus: Ohio University Press, 1979.

Williams, Gary J. *Our Moonlight Revels: "A Midsummer Night's Dream in the Theatre."* Iowa City: University of Iowa Press, 1997.

SHAKESPEARE STUDIES: SCREEN

Bulman, J. C., and H. R. Coursen. *Shakespeare on Television: An Anthology of Essays and Reviews.* Hanover: University of New Hampshire Press, 1988.

Davies, Anthony. *Filming Shakespeare's Plays: The Adaptations of Laurence Olivier, Orson Welles, Peter Brook, and Akira Kurosawa.* Cambridge: Cambridge University Press, 1990.

———. *Shakespeare and the Moving Image.* Cambridge: Cambridge University Press, 1994.

Rothwell, Kenneth S. *A History of Shakespeare on Screen: A Century of Film and Television.* Cambridge: Cambridge University Press, 1999.

Suggested Resources

———. *Shakespeare on Screen: An International Filmography and Videography.* New York: Neal-Schuman, 1990.

SHAKESPEARE'S SOURCES

Holinshed's Chronicles. Farmington, Hills, Mich.: Macmillan Library Reference, 1999.

*Plutarch's Lives. John S. White, ed. Cheshire, Conn.: Biblo & Tannen, 1995.

BIOGRAPHY

Bentley, Gerald E., Jr. *Shakespeare: A Biographical Handbook.* Belmont, Calif.: Greenwood Press, 1986.

Bruce, Anthony. *Shakespeare Country.* New York: Viking Penguin, 1999.

*Cahn, Victor. *Shakespeare the Playwright.* New York: Greenwood Press, 1991.

Carrier, Irene. *James VI and I: King of Great Britain.* Cambridge: Cambridge University Press, 1998.

*Dominic, Shellard. *William Shakespeare.* The British Library Writer's Lives Series. New York: Oxford University Press, 1998.

*Dwyer, Frank. *Henry VIII.* World Leaders Past and Present Series. New York: Chelsea House, 1988.

Fraser, Russell. *Young Shakespeare.* New York: Columbia University Press, 1988.

*Haines, Charles. *William Shakespeare and His Plays.* New York: Franklin Watts, 1986.

Halliday, F. E. *Shakespeare.* Literary Lives Series. New York: W. W. Norton & Co., 1998.

*Hanff, Helen. *Queen of England: The Story of Elizabeth.* Garden City, N.Y.: Doubleday, 1969.

Holden, Anthony. *William Shakespeare: The Man Behind the Genius.* Boston: Little, Brown, 2000.

Kay, W. David. *Ben Jonson: A Literary Life.* New York: St. Martin's Press, 1995.

Martin, Christopher. *Shakespeare.* Vero Beach, Fla.: Rourke Publishing Group, 1989.

Nicholl, Charles. *Elizabethan Writers.* London: National Portrait Gallery Publishing, 1997.

———. *The Reckoning: The Murder of Christopher Marlowe.* Chicago: University of Chicago Press, 1995.

*Rowse, A. L. *Shakespeare the Elizabethan.* New York: Putnam Books, 1977.

*———. *Shakespeare the Man.* New York: St. Martin's Press, 1988.

Sams, Eric. *The Real Shakespeare: Retrieving the Early Years 1564–94.* New Haven, Conn.: Yale University Press, 1995.

Schoenbaum, S. *Shakespeare's Lives.* New York: Oxford University Press, 1991.

*Stanley, Diane, and Peter Vennema. *Bard of Avon: The Story of William Shakespeare.* New York: Morrow Junior Books, 1992.

*———. *Good Queen Bess: The Story of Elizabeth I of England.* New York: Four Winds Press, 1990.

Weir, Alison. *The Life of Elizabeth I.* New York: Ballantine Books, 1999.

Wells, Stanley. *Shakespeare: A Life in Drama.* New York: W. W. Norton, 1995.

THEATER

Ashton, Geoffrey. *The Collector's Shakespeare: His Life and Work in Paintings, Prints, and Photographs.* New York: Crescent Books, 1990.

Bentley, Gerald Eades. *The Profession of Player in Shakespeare's Time, 1590–1642.* Princeton: Princeton University Press, 1984.

Brook, Peter. *The Empty Space.* London: MacGibbon and Kee, 1968.

*Brown, John Russell. *Shakespeare and His Theater.* New York: Lothrop, Lee and Shepard Books, 1982.

Dutton, Richard. *Mastering the Revels: The Regulation and Censorship of English Renaissance Drama.* Iowa City: University of Iowa Press, 1991.

Foakes, R. A. *Illustrations of the English Stage, 1580–1642.* Stanford: Stanford University Press, 1985.

Gurr, Andrew. *Playgoing in Shakespeare's London.* Cambridge: Cambridge University Press, 1987

———. *The Shakespearean Stage, 1574–1642.* 3rd ed. Cambridge: Cambridge University Press, 1992.

Harbage, Alfred. *Shakespeare's Audience.* New York: Columbia University Press, 1941.

Harrison, G. B. *Elizabethan Plays and Players.* Ann Arbor: University of Michigan Press, 1956.

———. *The Story of Elizabethan Drama.* New York: Octagon, 1973.

Hill, Erroll, and John Houseman. *Shakespeare in Sable: A History of Black Shakespearean Actors.* Amherst: University of Massachusetts Press, 1986.

*Hodges, C. Walter. *Shakespeare's Theatre.* New York: Coward, McCann and Geoghegan, 1964.

Ingram, William. *The Business of Playing: The Beginnings of Adult Professional Theater in Elizabethan London.* Ithaca, N.Y.: Cornell University Press, 1992.

*Langley, Andrew. *Shakespeare's Theater.* New York: Oxford University Press, 1999.

Mullin, Michael. *Design by Motley.* Newark: University of Delaware Press, 1996.

Mulryne, J. R., and Margaret Shewring, eds. *Shakespeare's Globe Rebuilt.* Cambridge: Cambridge University Press, 1990.

Papp, Joseph. *Shakespeare Alive!* Madison, Wis.: Demco, Inc., 1988.

Shapiro, Michael. *Gender in Play on the Shakespearean Stage: Boy Heroines and Female Pages.* Ann Arbor: University of Michigan Press, 1994.

Slater, Ann Pasternak. *Shakespeare the Director.* Brighton, England: Harvester Press, 1982.

Smith, Irwin. *Shakespeare's Blackfriars Playhouse.* New York: New York University Press, 1964.

*Stewart, Philippa. *Shakespeare and His Theatre.* London: Wayland Publishers, 1973.

*Yancey, Diane. *Life in the Elizabethan Theater.* The Way People Live Series. San Diego: Lucent Books, 1997.

ELIZABETHAN WRITERS

Adams, Robert M., ed. *Ben Jonson's Plays and Masques.* New York: W. W. Norton, 1979.

Bacon, Francis. *Essays.* New York: Viking Press, 1986.

Gassner, John, and William Green, eds. *Elizabethan Drama: Eight Plays.* New York: Applause Theater Book Publishing, 1990.

Kimbrough, Robert, ed. *Sir Philip Sidney: Selected Prose and Poetry.* Madison: University of Wisconsin Press, 1983.

Lodge, Thomas. *Rosalynd.* New York: Columbia University Press, 1998.

Marlowe, Christopher. *The Complete Plays.* New York: Viking Press, 1969.

Salzman, Paul, ed. *An Anthology of Elizabethan Prose Fiction.* New York: Oxford University Press, 1998.

Spenser, Edmund. *The Faerie Queene.* Reading, Mass.: Addison-Wesley, 1981.

ADAPTATIONS

*Lamb, Charles, and Mary Lamb. *Tales from Shakespeare.* New York: Random House, 1999.

Stoppard, Tom. *Rosencrantz and Guildenstern Are Dead.* New York: Faber and Faber, 1976.

FILMS AND VIDEOS

Forbidden Planet. 1956. Directed by Fred M. Wilcox and based on *The Tempest.*

Hamlet. 1948. Directed by and starring Laurence Olivier.

Hamlet. 1991. Directed by Franco Zeffirelli and starring Mel Gibson.

Henry V. Directed by and starring Laurence Olivier.

Henry V. 1989. Directed by and starring Kenneth Branagh.

Julius Caesar. 1953. Directed by Joseph L. Mankiewicz and starring James Mason and Marlon Brando.

King Lear. 1984. Directed by Michael Elliott and starring Laurence Olivier.

Kiss Me Kate. 1953. Directed by George Sidney and based on *The Taming of the Shrew.*

Looking for Richard. 1996. Directed by and starring Al Pacino. Based on *Richard III.*

Macbeth. 1948. Directed by and starring Orson Welles.

Midsummer Night's Dream. A. 1999. Directed by Michael Hoffman and starring Kevin Kline and Michelle Pfeiffer.

Much Ado About Nothing. 1993. Directed by and starring Kenneth Branagh.

Othello. 1995. Directed by Oliver Parker and starring Laurence Fishburne.

Ran. 1985. Directed by Akira Kurosawa and based on *King Lear.*

Richard III. Directed by and starring Laurence Olivier.

Richard III. 1995. Directed by Richard Loncraine and starring Ian McKellen.

Romeo and Juliet. 1968. Directed by Franco Zeffirelli and starring Leonard Whiting and Olivia Hussey.

Taming of the Shrew, The. 1966. Directed by Franco Zeffirelli and starring Richard Burton and Elizabeth Taylor.

Throne of Blood. 1957. Directed by Akira Kurosawa and based on *Macbeth.*

West Side Story. 1961. Directed by Robert Wise and Jerome Robbins and based on *Romeo and Juliet.*

William Shakespeare's Romeo + Juliet. 1996. Directed by Baz Luhrmann and starring Leonardo Di Caprio.

Suggested Resources

PERIODICALS
Shakespeare Newsletter
Shakespeare Quarterly
Shakespeare Studies
Shakespeare Survey

ON-LINE RESOURCES
*A Compendium of Common Knowledge. *Provides information about daily life in Elizabethan England.*
http://www.ren.dm.net/compendium

The Complete Works of William Shakespeare. *Contains a searchable guide to Shakespeare's works and links to other resources.*
http://tech-two.mit.edu/Shakespeare/works.html

Encyclopaedia Britannica's Shakespeare and the Globe: Then and Now. *Contains information about Shakespeare's life and work, the Globe, and the lives of important Elizabethans.*
http://shakespeare.eb.com

The Folger Shakespeare Library. *Contains on-line exhibitions dedicated to understanding Shakespeare and his world.*
http://www.folger.edu

Royal Shakespeare Company. *Contains information on the world's leading Shakespearean acting company.*
http://www.rsc.org.uk

Shakespeare Birthplace Trust. *Dedicated to promoting the appreciation of Shakespeare's works.*
http://www.shakespeare.org.uk

Shakespeare On-line. *Includes resources for the study of Shakespeare's works.*
http://www.shakespeare-online.com

Shakespeare Oxford Society. *Dedicated to proving that Edward de Vere, the earl of Oxford, wrote the works attributed to William Shakespeare.*
http://www.shakespeare-oxford.com

PHOTO CREDITS

VOLUME 1

COLOR PLATES

for Elizabethan Life

1: National Portrait Gallery, London/Bridgeman Art Library; 2: National Portrait Gallery, London/SuperStock; 3: Buddy Mays/Corbis; 4: Adrian Arbib/Corbis; 5: The Art Archive/Eileen Tweedy; 6: The Granger Collection, New York; 7: The Granger Collection, New York; 8: British Library, London/Bridgeman Art Library; 9: Ancient Art & Architecture Collection, Ltd.; 10: The Granger Collection, New York; 11: The Art Archive/Victoria and Albert Museum, London; 12: The Granger Collection, New York; 13: The Granger Collection, New York; 14: The Art Archive/Eileen Tweedy; 15: National Portrait Gallery, London/Bridgeman Art Library.

BLACK-AND-WHITE PHOTOGRAPHS

2: The Folger Shakespeare Library; 5: Bridgeman Art Library; 12: The Folger Shakespeare Library; 13: Donald Cooper/Photostage; 17: Donald Cooper/Photostage; 20: Bettmann/Corbis; 25: The Folger Shakespeare Library; 28: Louvre Museum, Paris/ET Archive, London/SuperStock; 31: Donald Cooper/Photostage; 34: The Granger Collection, New York; 35: Courtesy Board of Trustees, Victoria and Albert Museum, London/ET Archive, London/SuperStock; 39: The Folger Shakespeare Library; 44: The Folger Shakespeare Library; 45: The Folger Shakespeare Library; 48: The Folger Shakespeare Library; 50: The Folger Shakespeare Library; 54: The Folger Shakespeare Library; 56: The Folger Shakespeare Library; 59: The Granger Collection; 62: The Folger Shakespeare Library; 65: Donald Cooper/Photostage; 68: Bridgeman Art Library; 69: Donald Cooper/Photostage; 71: Mary Evans Picture Library; 73: The Granger Collection; 77: The Folger Shakespeare Library; 81: The Folger Shakespeare Library; 84: Donald Cooper/Photostage; 85: The Granger Collection; 90: Mansell Collection/Time, Inc.; 97: Mansell Collection/TimePix; 98: Donald Cooper/Photostage; 104: National Gallery of Art; 105: The Folger Shakespeare Library; 108: The Folger Shakespeare Library; 110: National Portrait Gallery, London/Bridgeman Art Library; 115: Art Resource; 120: The Folger Shakespeare Library; 124: The Folger Shakespeare Library; 127: The Folger Shakespeare Library; 133: Bettmann/Corbis; 140: The Folger Shakespeare Library; 144: The Folger Shakespeare Library; 147: The Folger Shakespeare Library; 150: The Folger Shakespeare Library; 153: The Folger Shakespeare Library; 155: The Granger Collection; 158: Springer/Corbis-Bettmann; 169: Donald Cooper/Photostage; 172: Donald Cooper/Photostage; 177: Birmingham Museums and Art Galleries/Bridgeman Art Library; 180: Carnegie Museum of Art; 182: Guildhall Art Gallery; 187: The Folger Shakespeare Library; 188: Philadelphia Museum of Art/Bridgeman Art Library.

VOLUME 2

COLOR PLATES

for The Plays

1: Victoria and Albert Museum, London/Art Resource, New York; 2: Photofest; 3: Photofest; 4: Donald Cooper/Photostage; 5: Washington, D.C., Theatre; 6: Utah Shakespeare Festival; 7: The Folger Shakespeare Library; 8: The Granger Collection, New York; 9: Donald Cooper/Photostage; 10: Martha Swope/TimePix; 11: Washington, D.C., Theatre; 12: Donald Cooper/Photostage; 13: Tate Gallery, London/Art Resource, New York; 14: Beth Bergman; 15: Martha Swope/TimePix.

Photo Credits

INDEX

A

Academy concept of education, 2:68

Act for Regulating the Theaters (1843), 1:3

Act of Uniformity, 1:111

Acting companies, Elizabethan, **1:1–2** *(illus.)*
  acting profession and, 1:4–5
  actors of, 1:7
  censorship of, 1:46–47
  costumes of, 1:70
  court life and, 1:74–75
  directors of, 1:92–93
  Elizabeth I and, 1:112
  finances and organization, 1:1–2, 4
  friends in, 1:136–37
  Heminges and, 1:163
  Henslowe and, 1:186–87
  at Hope theater, 2:7
  King's Men, 2:36–37
  master of the revels and, 2:91–92
  patron as company's "master," 3:89
  patronage of, 2:141, 142
  performances in inn yards, 2:17
  printing and publishing manuscripts of, 2:192
  prompt book for, 2:193

Acting companies, modern, **1:2–4,** 2:35–36
  actors in, 1:8–10
  directors of, 1:95–96
  Royal Shakespeare Company, 3:25–26 *(illus.)*
  of 20th century, 3:67–68

Acting profession, **1:4–6** *(illus.)*, 1:112–14 *(map)*

Actium, battle of, 1:192

Actor-managers, 1:93–95, 96, 3:57–58, 60–63

Actors, Shakespearean, **1:7–10**
  acting profession and, 1:5
  children's companies, 1:52
  collections from, in museums and archives, 2:121, 122
  costumes of, 1:69–72 *(illus.)*
  directors and, 1:91–96
  in 18th century, 3:56–58
  in Elizabethan acting companies, 1:2
  in films, 3:50–52
  friends and contemporaries, 1:136–37
  interpretations of characters, 1:51–52
  in jigs, 2:22
  in King's Men, 2:36–37
  in 19th century, 3:60–64
  reputations based on Shakespeare's characters, 3:72

in 17th century, 3:54, 55

as Shylock, 2:104–5

in 20th century, 3:67–68

See also specific plays and actors

Acts and Monuments (Foxe), 1:183

Acts, division of plays into, 1:101, 2:151

Adaptations. *See* Shakespeare's works, adaptations of

Adelman, Janet, 1:122

Admiral's Men, 1:6

Africans, stereotypes of, 3:4. *See also* Race and ethnicity

Agincourt, battle of (1415), 1:24, 174, 175, 2:3, 4 *(illus.)*, 3:159

Agriculture, **1:11–12** *(illus.)*
  country life and, 1:72–74 *(illus.)*
  gardens and gardening, 1:143–45 *(illus.)*
  laborers in, 3:88
  land laws and, 2:46
  poverty due to changes in, 3:152
  trade and, 3:130
  village life and, 1:58
  work in, 3:168–70

Alchemist, The (Jonson), 2:79, 3:34

Alchemy, 2:78, 79–80, 3:34

Aldermen, 2:59

Aldridge, Ira Frederick, 2:134, 3:63, 126

Aldwych Theatre, 3:68

Ale, 1:130

Alexander, Peter, 1:181

Alfar, Cristina León, 3:79

All for Love (Dryden), 1:19

All Hallow's Eve (Halloween), 1:126

Allegory, 3:101, 102–3

Alleyn, Edward, 1:5 *(illus.)*, 6, 70, 92, 186

All's Well That Ends Well, **1:12–15** *(illus.)*, 2:62, 164, 3:48

Alma-Tadema, Lawrence, 2:28, 3:62

American Shakespeare Festival Theater and Academy, 3:42

Americas, exploration of the, 1:116–18

Amphitryon (Plautus), 1:66

Analysis of Shakespeare's works. *See* Shakespeare's reputation; Shakespeare's works, changing views; *individual works*

Ancient influences and sources, 3:74–75

Anderson, Judith, 1:10

Anderson, Mary, 3:22, 166

Anglin, Margaret, 3:106

Animal imagery, 1:170

Anne of Denmark, Princess, 2:20

Annesley, Brian, 2:34

Annual fairs, 2:86

Antony and Cleopatra, **1:16–19** *(illus.)*, 1:192, 2:63, 167, 170, 3:37, 48, 113

Antony. *See Antony and Cleopatra*

Apocrypha, 2:60–61

Apologie for Poetrie (Sidney), 3:86

Apothecaries, 2:98

Apparel. *See* Costumes

Apparitions. *See* Ghosts and apparitions

Appian, 1:18

Apprenticeship, 1:5, 78, 2:98, 3:170

Aquinas, Thomas, 2:114–15, 149

Arcadia (Sidney), 1:32, 2:34, 162, 3:86

Archdeacons, 1:53

Archery, 1:141, 3:127, 159

Architecture, **1:19–22** *(illus.)*, 2:8–9, 58

Archives. *See* Museums and archives

Arden, Forest of, **1:22**, 1:30–32, 134, 2:126, 131, 140, 3:23, 38

Arden, Mary, 1:22

Arden of Feversham, 1:100

Arden, Robert, 3:43

Ariel, 1:118, 2:113, 166, 3:1, 116, 117, 120

Ariosto, Ludovico, 1:22, 32, 2:118, 162, 3:105

Aristarchus of Samos, 3:33

Aristocracy, **1:22–23**, 3:86–87
  in *All's Well That Ends Well*, 1:12–15
  clothing worn by, 1:60
  heraldry of, 1:187–88
  nobles incognito (in disguise), 1:99
  royalty and nobility, 3:26–28
  support of acting profession, 1:6

Aristotle, 1:63, 2:114, 115, 148, 167–68

Armin, Robert, 1:51, 2:37, 172–73

Arms and armor, **1:23–27** *(illus.)*, 1:187–88, 3:127, 128, 155, 157–58

Art inspired by Shakespeare, **1:27–30** *(illus.)*, 1:70

Artichokes, 1:143

Artificers, 3:88

Artillery, 1:25, 26

Arts, patronage of. *See* Patronage of the arts

As You Like It, **1:30–34** *(illus.)*, 2:154
  Forest of Arden in, 1:22, 2:126
  friendship in, 1:139
  Orlando in, 2:131–32
  as pastoral, 2:140
  plot of, 2:155
  ridicule of duels and feuds in, 1:107
  romantic elements in, 2:62, 163
  Rosalind in, 3:23
  setting of, 3:38
  seven ages of man in, 3:39

Ascham, Roger, 3:30

Ashcroft, Peggy, 1:10, 15, 2:120, 3:26, 72

Index

Index

Index

Index

sources for, 2:158–60, 3:75
Tower of London and, 3:129
warfare, 3:158–60
Wars of the Roses, 3:160
History of Felix and Philomela, The, 3:149
History of King Richard III (More), 2:159
History of the Kings of Britain (Monmouth), 2:33
History, prose literature on, 2:52
Histriomastix (Marston and Dekker), 3:154
Hogarth, William, 1:27
Holbrook, Hal, 2:105
Holidays. *See* Festivals and holidays
Holinshed, Raphael, 2:6, 3:9
Holinshed's *Chronicles,* **2:5–6,** 2:52
    social classes listed in, 3:86
    as source, 1:165, 170, 175, 178, 181, 183, 185, 2:1, 31, 33, 72, 158, 3:16, 36, 75
Holm, Ian, 2:36
Homer, 1:192, 2:162, 172, 3:142
Homosexuality, 1:37, **2:6,** 2:20, 103–4, 3:93
Honor, 1:106, 2:115–16
Hooker, Richard, 2:52
Hope Theater, 1:185, 186, **2:7**
Hopkins, Anthony, 2:135, 3:126
Hornbook, 1:108
Horses, riding, 1:141
    travel and, 3:138–39, 141
    warhorses, 3:158
Hose, 1:59, 60
Hoskins, Bob, 2:135
Hotspur, 1:164–66, 167, 2:2, 3. *See also Henry IV, Part 1*
House of Commons, 1:154
House of Lords, 1:154
Households and furnishings, 1:21, **2:7–9,** 2:188
Houseman, John, 2:28
Houses, architecture of, 1:20–22, 2:8–9
Howard, Jean, 3:81
Howell, Jane, 3:115
Hubris, 3:17
Hugo, Victor, 3:162
Huguenots, 1:90
Hulks, 3:83–84
Humanism, 2:49–50, 68, 3:9
Humor in Shakespeare's plays, **2:9–13** *(illus.),* 2:42
    in *Comedy of Errors,* 1:64–67 *(illus.)*
    comic elements in tragedies, 2:167
    fools, clowns, and jesters, 1:132–33 *(illus.)*
    Italian influences on, 2:50
    in *Love's Labor's Lost,* 2:66
    in *Merry Wives of Windsor,* 2:106
    in *Much Ado about Nothing,* 2:117
    prose used for, 2:194, 196, 197
    in *Twelfth Night,* 2:82–83, 3:144
Humors, theory of, 2:75–76, 79, 96, 3:2, 34
Hundred Years' War, 1:177
Hunsdon, George Carey, Lord, 2:37, 141
Hunt, Leigh, 2:27
Hunt, the, 1:140 *(illus.),* 141–42

Huon of Bordeaux, 2:109, 130
Huxley, Aldous, 2:55
Hygiene. *See* Personal hygiene
Hytner, Nicholas, 2:36

I

I Hate Hamlet (Rudnick), 1:159
Iago, 1:88, **2:13–14** *(illus.),* 2:133–34
Iambic pentameter, 2:41, 49, 87, 174–75. *See also* Language; Poetic techniques
Ides of March, **2:14–15**
Iliad (Homer), 1:192, 3:142
Illustrated editions, 1:27
Illustrations for Shakespearean texts, 1:27
Image clusters, 2:16, 42
Imagery, **2:15–16,** 2:174, 177–78
    animal, 1:170
    character created through, 1:50
    language and, 2:39, 42, 43
    in *Romeo and Juliet,* 3:21
    symbolism and allegory, 3:101–3 *(illus.)*
Improvisation, 1:5
India, translations of Shakespeare in, 3:136
Indoor games, 1:142–43
Indoor playhouses, 1:113–14, 2:153
Indulgences, granting of, 3:8
Industry, guilds controlling, 1:155–56 *(illus.)*
Infidelity, theme of, 1:146
Influential editions. *See* Shakespeare's works, influential editions
Inheritance, **2:16–17**
Inn yards, **2:17**
Inns, 3:141
Inns of Chancery, 2:44
Inns of Court, 2:44–45, 57
Insanity. *See* Madness
Inside jokes, 2:11–12
Instrumentals, 2:123
Interludes, **2:17–18**
International trade, 3:133
Interpretation of Shakespeare. *See* Feminist interpretations; Marxist interpretations; Psychology; Shakespeare's reputation; Shakespeare's works, changing views
Interregnum period, 3:61–62, 63
Iron working, 1:39
Irving, Henry, 1:3, 9, 95, **2:18–19,** 2:74, 104, 120, 3:60, 61–62, 72
Isle of Dogs (Nash and Jonson), 1:46–47
Italian sonnets, 3:92
Italy in Shakespeare's plays, **2:19–20,** 3:38
Ivan IV, Czar, 1:115–16
Ivanov (Chekhov), 2:55

J

Jackson, Barry, 1:3, 3:26, 66
Jacob, Irène, 2:136
Jacobean literature, 2:50
Jacobi, Derek, 1:162, 3:15, 114
Jaggard, William, 2:140, 189–90

James I, 1:112, **2:20–21**
    belief in witches, 3:167
    the Church and, 1:55
    court of, 1:75
    Gunpowder Plot against, 1:156–57
    homosexuality of, 2:6
    King's Men and, 1:1, 2:36, 37
    Macbeth and, 2:72
    masques during reign of, 2:90–91
    opposition to dueling, 1:107
    as patron of arts, 2:141
    peers under, 3:86–87
    on smoking, 1:131
Jamestown colony, 1:118
Jarman, Derek, 3:120
Jarvet, Yuri, 2:36
Jerkin, 1:59
Jesters. *See* Fools, clowns, and jesters
Jew of Malta, The (Marlowe), 2:104, 156
Jews, 1:38, **2:21–22,** 2:100, 101–5, 3:4, 9, 85. *See also* Shylock
Jig, **2:22,** 2:143
Joan of Arc, 1:177, 178
Joe Macbeth, 3:52
John, King. *See King John*
Johnson, Ben, 1:6
Johnson, Charles, 2:120, 3:58
Johnson, Samuel, 1:170, 2:34, 3:37, 57 *(illus.),* 71, 79–80, 82, 107, 149
Johnson, William, 2:105
Jokes, 2:11–12
Jones, Ernest, 3:72, 79
Jones, Inigo, 2:90
Jones, James Earl, 3:124
Jonson, Ben, 1:46–47, 184, 2:20, **2:23,** 2:51, 52, 79, 86, 141, 172, 3:34, 72, 142, 164
    benefit of clergy pleaded by, 1:83
    in Friday Street Club, 2:105
    mixed reaction to Shakespeare, 3:79
    poem in First Folio, 1:127, 2:23
    Shakespeare's reputation and, 3:71
    as soldier, 3:158
    verbal art of masque, 2:91
    War of the Theaters and, 3:154
Jory, Victor, 2:110
Journeymen, 1:78, 3:170
Jousting tournaments, 3:127
Joyce, James, 2:56
Judge, 2:44
Judicial commissioners, 1:82–83
Jugge, Richard, 2:189
Juliet. *See Romeo and Juliet*
Julius Caesar, **2:23–28** *(illus.),* 2:167, 3:47
    alchemy as symbol in, 2:79–80
    Brutus in, 1:43
    divine plan concept in, 1:35
    history in, 1:191–92
    honor in, 2:115
    ides of March in, 2:14–15
    prophetic dreams in, 1:104
    prose and verse in, 2:197
    settings for, 3:37

Index

Index

love madness in, 2:77
prose and verse in, 2:196, 198
Othello (film), 3:50, 51
Outdoor recreation, 1:140–41
Overseas travel, 3:141–42
Ovid, 1:190, 2:108, **2:137**, 2:181, 3:5, 74, 118, 125, 153, 164
Oxford, Edward de Vere, earl of, 1:37
Oxford University, 1:108, 3:30–31

P

Pace of Elizabethan plays, 3:55
Packhorses, 3:139
Pageants and morality plays, 2:49, **2:137–39** (illus.)
allegory and, 3:101
at fairs, 2:86
interludes and, 2:17
Macbeth and, 2:74
masques, 2:90–91 (illus.)
Othello as outgrowth of, 2:133–34
stock characters in, 2:99
Vice in, 2:14, 3:154
Painter, William, 1:14, 3:5
Palace of Pleasure (Painter), 1:14
Palladis Tamia (Meres), 3:93
Pamphleteers, 1:154–55, 2:52, **2:139** (illus.)
Pandosto, or the Triumph of Time (Greene), 3:164, 165
Pantaloon tradition, 2:10
Paper making, 1:80
Papp, Joseph, 1:4, 3:42, 151
Paradise Lost (Milton), 2:53
Parallel Lives. See Plutarch's *Lives*
Parker, Oliver, 2:136
Parliament, 1:89, 153–54
Parody, 2:65
Parson, Robert, 3:8
Pascoe, Richard, 3:124
Passionate Pilgrim, The, **2:140**, 2:189–90
Pasternak, Boris, 2:55
Pastimes. *See* Games, pastimes, and sports
Pastoralism, 1:22, 30, 33, 134–35, **2:140–41**, 3:45, 96, 165
Pastorals, 2:49
Patrick, Anna, 2:136
Patronage of the arts, 1:1, 6, 74–75, 137, 2:21, **2:141–42** (illus.)
Patronage, politics and, 1:154
Patterson, Tom, 3:41
Pavier, Thomas, 2:190
Peacham, Henry, 1:27, 70
Pecorone, Il (The Dunce), 2:103
Peele, George, 1:154, 2:50
Peerage, 1:23, 3:27–28, 86–87
Penalties. *See* Crime and punishment
Pentecost, 1:125
Pepys, Samuel, 2:73, **2:142**, 3:22, 78
Performances, **2:142–43**
in 17th century, 3:53–56
in 18th century, 3:59

in 19th century, 3:60–64
prose and verse in, 2:197–98
theater performances on television, 3:112–13
See also specific plays
Pericles, 1:151, 2:127–28, **2:143–44**, 2:164–65, 3:48, 69, 102
Period analogue costume style, 1:72
Periodicals, Shakespeare, **2:144–46**
Perkins Folio, 2:121
Personal hygiene, 2:8, 9, 83, **2:146**, 3:28–29
Personification, 2:178
Petition, 1:152
Petrarch, 2:183, 3:75, 92, 94
Petruchio, 2:29, **2:147–48** (illus.), 3:103–7
Petty school, 1:73, 107–8, 109, 3:29–30
Petty theft, 1:82
Petty treason, 1:81
Phelps, John, 1:3
Phelps, Samuel, 3:22, 61
Philaster, 2:173
Philia, 2:114–15
Philip II of Spain, 1:91, 116, 3:95–96
Philippi, Battle of, 1:43, 191–92
Phillips, Augustin, 2:37
Phillips, Caryl, 2:136
Phillips, Robin, 2:67
Philosophy, 2:52, **2:148–50**
fate and fortune, 1:119–20 (illus.)
of history plays, 2:160–62
morality and ethics, 2:114–16
"Phoenix and Turtle, The," **2:150**, 2:182, 3:47, 103
Physicians, 2:97–98, 3:34–35, 171
Pickford, Mary, 3:50, 106
Pictorial style, 3:61
Pierce Penniless (Nash), 2:139, 161
Pike, 1:25
Pillory, 1:82
Pinnaces, 3:84
Piper, John, 1:29
Pistols, 1:27, 3:158
Pit in playhouse, 2:152–53
Pius V, Pope, 1:111
Plague, 1:47, 57, 97, 189, 2:95–96, 3:34
Planché, J.R., 1:71
Plantagenet, Richard. *See Richard III*
Plate armor, 1:25
Plato, 2:68, 148
Platter, Thomas, 2:24
Plautus, Titus Maccius, 1:50, 66, 2:9–10, 154, 156, 3:74
Play structure, 2:73, **2:151**
Play within a play, 1:159, 2:108, 125, **2:151–52**, 2:169
Playhouse structure, 1:103, 2:143, **2:152–53**, 3:53
Plays: the comedies, **2:153–57** (illus.)
All's Well That Ends Well, 1:12–15
As You Like It, 1:30–34 (illus.), 3:23
Comedy of Errors, 1:64–67 (illus.)
early, 3:44–45

humor in, 2:9–13 (illus.)
later, 3:46
Love's Labor's Lost, 2:65–68 (illus.)
mature, 3:48
Merry Wives of Windsor, 2:106–7
Much Ado about Nothing, 2:117–20 (illus.)
prose technique in, 2:194, 195 (illus.), 196
romantic love in, 2:61–62
on television, 3:115
Twelfth Night, 3:144–48 (illus.)
Two Gentlemen of Verona, 3:148–51 (illus.)
Plays: the histories, 2:1, 50, 51, **2:157–62** (illus.)
early, 3:44, 45
Falstaff in, 1:119
Henry IV, Part 1, 1:163–67
Henry IV, Part 2, 1:167–71 (illus.)
Henry V, 1:171–76 (illus.)
Henry VI, Part 1, 1:176–79 (illus.)
Henry VI, Part 2, 1:179–81 (illus.)
Henry VI, Part 3, 1:181–84 (illus.)
Henry VIII, 1:184–86
Holinshed's *Chronicles* as source, 2:5–6
King John, 2:29–31 (illus.)
later, 3:46
loyalty in, 2:69
prose technique in, 2:194, 196–97
Richard II, 3:12–15 (illus.)
Richard III, 3:15–18 (illus.)
Royal Shakespeare Company staging of, 3:68
settings for, 1:46–48 (illus.), 3:36–37
on television, 3:111–12, 115
Tower of London in, 3:128, 129
women in, 1:122–23
Plays: the romances, **2:162–66** (illus.), 3:48–49
comedies as romantic, 2:154, 155, 156–57
Cymbeline, 1:83–85 (illus.)
Jonson's criticism of, 2:23
Pericles, 2:143–44
Sidney and, 3:86
Tempest, 3:116–21 (illus.)
Two Noble Kinsmen, 3:151
Winter's Tale, 3:161–66 (illus.)
Plays: the tragedies, 2:50, 51, **2:166–70** (illus.), 3:45
Antony and Cleopatra, 1:16–19 (illus.)
Hamlet, 1:157–62 (illus.), 2:130–31 (illus.)
Julius Caesar, 2:23–28 (illus.)
King Lear, 1:67–68 (illus.), 2:31–36 (illus.)
Macbeth, 2:70–74 (illus.)
mature, 3:47–48
Othello, 2:132–36 (illus.)
romantic love in, 2:62–63
Romeo and Juliet, 3:19–23 (illus.)
settings for, 1:46, 3:36
on television, 3:112, 115
Titus Andronicus, 3:125–26 (illus.)
Playwrights and poets, 2:49, 50–52, **2:170–73** (illus.)

Index

Index

Index

Iago as, 2:14, 133–34
influence on tragedies, 2:169
in morality plays, 2:138–39
Richard III as, 3:17
Shylock in tradition of, 2:104
as stock character, 2:99
villainous characters and, 1:49–50
Village life, 1:72–74
Virgil, 3:118
Viscounts, 1:23, 3:27
Vision through madness, 2:77–78
Visual effects, 1:92
Vogel, Paula, 2:136
Voltaire, 2:55, 3:134–35
Voss, Johann Heinrich, 3:136

W

Wages, 1:62
Wake, 1:48, 87
Walker, William, 1:136
Walking, 3:138
Walsingham, Sir Francis, 3:97
Walsingham, Thomas, 2:87
Wanamaker, Sam, 1:150
War games, 1:141
War of the Theaters, 2:152, **3:154–55**
Warburton, William, 3:58
Ward, John, 3:49
Wardle, Irving, 2:95
Warfare, **3:155–60** (illus.)
    arms and armor for, 1:23–27 (illus.)
    foreign relations and, 1:91
    military life, 2:112
    naval, 3:84, 95–96 (illus.)
    Spanish Armada and, 3:95–96 (illus.)
    tournaments and, 3:127
Warhorses, 3:158
Warkworth Castle, 1:45
Warner, David, 3:15
Warner, Deborah, 2:36
Warning signs, 2:82
Wars of the Roses, **3:160**
    castles during, 1:44, 45–46
    Henry VI, Part 1 on, 1:176–79 (illus.)
    Henry VI, Part 2 on, 1:179–81
    Henry VI, Part 3 on, 1:181–84 (illus.)
    Richard III and final events of, 3:15–18 (illus.)
    sources on, 3:75
    television production on, 3:112

Washington Shakespeare Company, 3:107
Watchword to England, A (Munday), 2:139
Water supply for London, 2:59
Water transport, 3:132, 139–40
Watteau, Antoine, 3:115
Wealth. See Poverty and wealth
Weaponry. See Arms and armor
Weather and the seasons, 1:124–26 (illus.), 2:126–28, **3:160–61**, 3:165
Weddings, 1:48
Welles, Orson, 1:167, 2:28, 74, 135, 3:50–51
West, Benjamin, 1:28
West Side Story, 3:52, 69
Westminster, 2:58
Wet nurses, 2:129
Wheel of fortune, 2:100, 168–69
Wheeled vehicles, 3:139, 140
Whetstone, George, 2:92
Whipping, 1:82
White Tower, 3:128
White, Willard, 2:136
Whitehall Palace, 1:57
Whitsunday, 1:125–26
Wieland, Christoph Martin, 3:135
Wilhelm Meister (Goethe), 2:54
Will. See Shakespeare's will
William Shakespeare's Romeo + Juliet, 3:52
William the Conqueror, 1:46, 3:128
Windsor Castle, 1:75
Wine, 1:130
Winter festivals, 1:124–25
Winter's Tale, The, 2:156–57, 165–66, 3:48, **3:161–66** (illus.), 3:161
Witches and evil spirits, 3:100–101, **3:167–68** (illus.)
    dangers after childbirth from fairies, 1:47
    ghosts and apparitions, 1:149
    in Henry VI, Part 1, 1:178
    in Henry VI, Part 2, 1:179
    in Macbeth, 2:70, 71, 72
    spirit conjuring, 2:80–81
Woman's Prize, or The Tamer Tamed, The (Fletcher), 3:106
Women
    boys in roles of, 1:5–6
    clothing for, 1:60
    in comedies, 2:156
    death during childbirth, 1:87
    disguised as men, 1:98–99
    education of, 1:108–9

friendship between, 1:139
healers (wise women), 2:98
herbal remedies concocted by, 1:188–89 (illus.)
place in family, 2:88
roles in Elizabethan society, 1:145
roles in plays for, 1:121–23
on stage, 1:2, 8, 9, 10, 93, 3:55, 57
work of, 1:73, 78, 3:168, 169, 170
    See also Feminist interpretations; Gender and sexuality; Marriage and family
Women's Part: Feminist Criticism of Shakespeare, The (Lenz, Greene, and Neely), 1:120, 121
Woodlands, 1:134–35
Woodward, Henry, 1:14
Wool industry, 1:12, 39, 40, 3:130–31, 169–70, 170–71
Woolf, Virginia, 1:95
Word abuse and misuse, 2:10–11
Wordplay, 2:42, 119, 174, 176–77, 3:150
Wordsworth, William, 3:94
Work, **3:168–72** (illus.)
    country life and, 1:72, 73–74
    craftworkers and, 1:76–80 (illus.)
    farm labor and products, 1:11–12
    guilds and, 1:155–56 (illus.)
    in medicine, 2:96–98
    unemployment with agricultural changes, 1:73
World Shakespeare Bibliography, 3:74
Wriothesley, Henry, 2:141, 180, 3:45
Writ, 2:45
Writers inspired by Shakespeare. See Literature inspired by Shakespeare
Writers. See Playwrights and poets
Wyatt, Sir Thomas, 2:48, 3:92

Y

Yeomen, 1:11, 23, 3:87–88
Yong, Bartholomew, 3:149
Yorkist tetralogy, 2:2, 3–5. See also Henry VI, Part 1; Henry VI, Part 2; Henry VI, Part 3; Richard III

Z

Zeffirelli, Franco, 1:162, 3:22, 51, 69, 106
Zelauto (Munday), 2:139
Zoffany, John, 1:28